Crabbgate

Crabbgate

A failed MI6 spying mission
and a bungled
governmental cover-up

by

John Bevan

This is a revised and greatly expanded edition of the book:
Commander Crabb – What Really Happened? published in 2014.

This second edition incorporates further significant revelations disclosed by the National Archives in October 2015, the results of further research plus amendments and corrections to the first edition.

British Library Cataloguing in Publication Data.
A catalogue record for this book is available from the British Library.

Printed by LaserTryk.dk A/S   www.lasertryk.dk

ISBN 978 0 9508242 8 4

This book is dedicated to the memory of
Commander Lionel Crabb OBE GM RNVR(S) Retd,
a gallant hero of the Royal Navy, who gave his life in service
to his country and whose outstanding reputation
has been suppressed for too long to save "distress or
embarrassment" to those who were responsible
for sending him to his death over 60 years ago.

CONTENTS

PART 1

INTRODUCTION

PREFACE

Commander Crabb's disappearance continues to be an enduring mystery for the public. It has only been intensified by the unusual decision to extend the security classification of the official records to 100 years (until 2057). The partially disclosed declassified documents state that the reasons for the extended period of the embargo are:

1) exceptionally sensitive ... disclosure of which would be contrary to the public interest on security grounds;

2) containing information supplied in confidence, disclosure of which would ... constitute a breach of faith and

3) disclosure ... could cause distress or embarrassment to living personnel ...

The extension has encouraged the growth and popularisation of conspiracy theories that are arguably even more damaging and embarrassing to the authorities and "living personnel" than the truth itself. The subject of Cdr Crabb's disappearance has even found its way onto the official curriculum of at least one school.

So the question is - can the continued secrecy be seriously justified? Is it not now in the public interest to lift the veil of secrecy? Was the Inquest which formally confirmed the death of Crabb conducted in accordance with the law? Was there a link between Crabb and the "Cambridge Five" spies? What part did Admiral Mountbatten play in the story of Crabbgate? These questions, among many others, are addressed in more detail in the Conclusions section of this book.

Perhaps it is time to re-examine the issues and put the above reasons for the continued embargo to the test.

There is a growing body of opinion that believes it would now be in the public interest for all the remaining classified information and documents to be released into the public domain. This is not least as a mark of respect to the memory of this gallant World War II hero who gave his life for his country; something that seems to have been overlooked as the bungled cover-up unrolled, and continues to roll on with gathering momentum. Not one person the author has ever met, without exception, either in the services or civilian, throughout the many years while researching for this book, has disagreed with this premise. Indeed, everybody the author has ever met who actually knew Cdr Crabb personally, consider it a travesty of justice that his story has not been told and his courageous deeds for his country have not only failed to be fully recognised, but continue to be actively suppressed.

The following account is based on the best information available at the time of writing. This includes documents released by the National Archives under the Freedom of Information Act in 2006 and 2015, published books, in particular *The Final Dive* by Don Hale (2007) and a detailed personal investigation. The author gratefully acknowledges these sources of the information used in this book. But it has to be admitted that much of the information is hearsay.

The author would welcome any feedback, correction and constructive criticism of this account (email: info@drjohnbevan.com).

FOREWORD
by Vice Admiral Sir Michael Moore KBE LVO

Most of my generation, certainly those who served in the Royal Navy, will remember hearing and reading about Commander Lionel (Buster) Crabb who disappeared whilst diving under some visiting Russian warships in Portsmouth in 1956. When questioned further they will recall a Government cover-up, and a headless body being washed up in Chichester Harbour. And most of them will have a view as to what happened, and are probably unaware that they will never know the truth as The Government placed an embargo on the episode which will last for many years to come.

Almost every month nowadays startling information on what happened in Government 30 years ago will be trumpeted by the press, but The Government has ruled that the embargoed Crabb papers are not to be released until 2057. So my generation will never know the true story and we are left to speculate. What on earth can be so secret and sensitive that is has a 100 year embargo placed on it?

Commander Crabb was without doubt an unusual character but what is without question is that he was extremely brave which the award of a George Medal and OBE for his wartime service as a diver dealing with underwater mines recognise, and I would hope that those who read this book will keep this at the back of their minds as they hear about the other side of his life.

Dr John Bevan has dug deep to produce this second excellent edition about Commander Crabb, his life, and what might have happened in 1956.

The only thing for sure is that we will never know what happened unless the Government can be convinced that it is in the public interest to come clean. I commend this book to you

Michael Moore
September 2018

FOREWORD
by Peter Marshall, freelance reporter during 'Crabbgate'

For journalists, the Commander Crabb story hit all the right buttons: there was spying, Russian ships, frogmen, MI5, MI6, CIA, a cover-up, "questions in the House" and conspiracy theories … and later a body in Chichester Harbour. Then there were the names: Khrushchev, Bulganin, Prime Minister Anthony Eden, Lord Mountbatten, various Admirals and politicians of both parties. It all provided wonderful material for Fleet Street's headline writers, for week after week.

And remarkably, it all happened on my doorstep in Portsmouth and media coverage dominated my waking hours for several months – as graphically illustrated here in Appendix 14 (which does not even include radio and TV reports).

To put my involvement into perspective, at the time I was a 23-years-old freelance reporter. By then, I had worked for five years on local evening newspapers in Bath and Portsmouth, interrupted by two years National Service in the Navy where I gained a commission and was therefore still serving as a Sub-Lieutenant RNVR. I had recently left the Portsmouth Evening News, where I was Deputy Naval Correspondent, to start my own news agency as local representative for most of the Fleet Street papers, the Press Association and the BBC.

Then came the day when I took a call from the News Editor of the Daily Mail asking me if I could help to locate a retired Navy diver called Commander Crabb because "a friend is writing his biography and hasn't heard from him for a couple of weeks and he was last known to be going to Portsmouth".

What followed is brilliantly documented here in "Crabbgate" – but for me the world moved on and the "Buster" Crabb event became no more than just six pages in my autobiography of fifty years in the news business. That is, until I heard recently about John Bevan.

A long-time BBC friend saw a notice that Dr. Bevan was giving a talk in Petersfield about his book on the Commander Crabb story and knowing of my involvement back in the 1950's, my friend invited me to join him at the local U3A meeting. It was fascinating to hear about the revelations which had emerged from dogged research into both the diving venture itself and then the botched attempts to cover up the story. Naturally, I had a question or two for the speaker – which led to an invitation to get together for a more detailed discussion of my very minor role. However, John Bevan was intrigued, not least because I was one of the few people involved in 1956 still alive!

I am therefore delighted to have been able to make some contribution to his follow-up book and I am flattered to have been invited to contribute this Foreword. I most sincerely compliment John on the depth and detail of his research and there can now be little new to discover when the official Government documents are finally released in 2056. I do agree with the author that the decomposed body eventually discovered in Sussex was probably that of Lionel Crabb, in a somewhat clumsy attempt to "close the file".

The phrase "poor trade craft", as it applies to so-called secret operations, crops up frequently throughout – which leads me to a final question: I am still intrigued to know why, when there was a planned operation under the Russian ships by serving Navy divers, the 'authorities' (whoever they were) did not call off the risky, solo and tragic adventure by an unfit "Buster" Crabb? Unless, of course, it was simply his unstoppable determination and strong personality.

So read on and be prepared to follow every detail of one of the most extraordinary episodes of the Cold War period – and make up your own mind! And then, if you are young enough, wait for 2057.

BACKGROUND

Lionel Kenneth Philip Crabb was born on 28 January 1909 to Hugh and Beatrice Crabb in South London. Their circumstances were poor. Hugh Crabb was posted as missing during WW1 and his son Lionel Crabb was taken in by his cousin's family, Frank and Kitty Jarvis.

From these early days onwards, Lionel Crabb's life never really ran along conventional lines. This chapter gives a brief timeline of Crabb's life and career leading up to his fatal dive.

After a short period in Brighton College he spent three years (1922-1924) on HMS *Conway*, a floating training school in the River Mersey, near Liverpool. His career between the wars included several years at sea with an apprenticeship as a cadet in the merchant navy (which he never completed) and a wide variety of short-term jobs ashore in the USA, Far East and England.

In London, he had a brief and fairly successful partnership as a salesman with the Frenchman Louis de Corlieu, the inventor of swim-fins or "flippers". In 1936 he went to China and worked as an undertaker while allegedly gun-running and spying against the communists.

He arrived back in England in the autumn of 1938 and looked up his old friend Maitland Pendock in London who got him a job in a new art gallery and antique store off Bond Street. It was called "Cameo Corner" and one of the partners was Anthony Blunt, who he got to know well. Through Blunt, Crabb was introduced to Guy Burgess and Donald Maclean both of whom were working successfully in British

Intelligence at the time. It is perhaps around this time that Crabb began to develop his left wing, anti-fascist sympathies.

When war broke out in 1939 he tried to join the navy full-time but was failed because he was too old at 30 years of age, he was colour-blind and had a weakness in his left eye. Crabb was quoted as saying *"The doctor seemed surprised I was still alive when he examined me"*. However, he eventually managed to join the merchant navy as a carpenter and *"somehow slipped into the Royal Navy"*. He became an Able Seaman and Gunner on a tanker about to leave from Thames Haven. After about a year at sea he transferred to the RN Patrol Service in Lowestoft. He found the duties were tedious, mainly sailing on old trawlers and fishing boats on coastal protection duties. This early period of Crabb's life is covered in detail in Don Hale's book, *"The Final Dive"*.

His service record shows he joined the Royal Navy Voluntary Reserve (RNVR) at the shore establishment HMS *King Alfred*, a requisitioned leisure centre in Hove, Sussex on 7 August 1941. The establishment was a centre for training new officers of the RNVR including instruction in *"officer-like qualities"*. The normal training course consisted of ten weeks but for some reason Crabb went through in just two weeks. The men emerged as Temporary Acting Probationary Sub-Lieutenants. He was then posted to the Coastal Forces Base at HMS *Wasp* at Dover as a Drainage and Passive Duties Officer. From there it appears he spent a short time in Swansea, South Wales. Here he found it far too quiet and his unorthodox training regime, involving mock explosions day and night, made him very unpopular with the local authorities. Some of his related hobbies included shooting, the art of knife-throwing and the use of a catapult.

A concerned friend suggested to Crabb he should apply for a voluntary job in a new, top secret training unit. The duties would be dangerous and involved dealing with unexploded bombs and mines. This appealed to Crabb and in 1942 he arrived at HMS *Volcano* in Cumbria, a new land-based training establishment specialising in explosives. Crabb was on the first course to be run there. While there he developed a life-long fascination with explosives. His applications of explosives later extended into playing tricks on trainees using tiny amounts of mercury fulminate (a highly explosive chemical) for booby-trap explosions.

His training progressed to HMS *Vernon* and HMS *Excellent* in Portsmouth where he was instructed in diving with standard dress, the old copper-helmeted diver equipment and the Davis Submerged Escape Apparatus (DSEA), an oxygen breathing set. It was the underwater breathing apparatus normally used in submarines for emergency escape but was also drawn into service for short, shallow dives. It was a simple breathing apparatus consisting of a small cylinder of oxygen, a breathing bag ("counterlung") and a canister of carbon dioxide absorbent. The DSEA course was carried out in Horsea Lake on Horsea Island, a shallow (25 feet deep) man-made lake designed for testing torpedoes. It is still used for military diver training to this day as the Defence Diving School.

A young conscript marine named William Stanley Stevens described his meetings with Crabb while they were both on parallel diver training courses at Horsea. Stevens said that Crabb was a *"dreadful, arrogant and awful person"* and quite unlike other officers. He described an incident where Crabb and his buddy diver broke a rule by untying themselves from their lifelines to shore and swam through an anti-torpedo net stretched across the lake. Crabb's buddy diver subsequently drowned on that dive.

On completion of the training, Crabb's superiors decided to transfer him to Gibraltar to join the Underwater Working Party (UWWP) led by Lt William 'Bill' Bailey. The UWWP was a small and heavily over-stretched team of divers tasked with searching

Cdr Crabb's "Truflite Throwing Knife".

Crabb doing some target practice with an army rifle.

ships' hulls for various types of limpet mines using the Davis Submerged Escape Apparatus (DSEA) oxygen set.

Crabb arrived in November 1942. Some six million tons of shipping had been lost in the Mediterranean during the previous year through the combined action of German U-boats, saboteurs and frogmen attacks. There had also been an increasing number of sabotage attacks on shipping actually anchored in the Bay of Gibraltar, five of them by Italian human torpedoes and "Gamma" swimmers before Crabb had arrived. Through their dangerous mine-clearing operations, Bailey's team saved hundreds of lives and tens of thousands of tons of shipping and essential war supplies for the North African campaign.

However, contrary to popular understanding, Crabb was never in charge of the Underwater Working Party throughout the hostilities with Italy and he was only part of the team for the last three of nine Italian attacks. He did however take over the team after Italy had capitulated and after Lt Bill Bailey had been obliged to leave due to a broken ankle. The film "Silent Enemy" released in 1958 purported to portray Crabb's activities in Gibraltar. However, while Crabb certainly carried out some heroic deeds for which he was deservedly awarded the George Medal and OBE, it completely misrepresents and exaggerates Crabb's contribution to the work of the UWWP in Gibraltar during the war. *The Daily Herald* reported on the film on 5 March 1958 with the headline "*Frogman Crabb film is nearly all fiction*". The true story of the work of the UWWP at Gibraltar is told in the book *Operation Tadpole* by this author.

Just one year after arriving in Gibraltar, Crabb, who was still only a temporary lieutenant, was awarded the George Medal in November 1943 for "*gallantry and undaunted devotion to duty*" during his hazardous diving operations in clearing mines from ships anchored in Gibraltar Bay. In December 1945 he received his OBE for further hazardous

Commander Crabb's medals.

Lt Crabb wearing the oxygen Davis Submarine Escape Apparatus. Its endurance underwater was limited to 15 to 20 minutes if the wearer was working hard.

Above: Lt Crabb in the summer of 1945 with the team including Italian
frogmen of the Gamma Group working to clear mines in Venice.

Lt Crabb astride an Italian
motorbike in Venice in 1945.

diving operations clearing German mines in Leghorn and Venice, Italy. In addition to these two medals for gallantry he qualified for three campaign medals: the 1939-45 Star, the

Star plus the Defence
ar Medal 1939-1945.
e covered extensively
nd other publications

war record would
a man who was just
(1.6m) and a feeble
wim about 90m (100
once jokingly confided
lost his fins he would
had a healthy dislike
technical matters.

when Lt Cdr Crabb
Royal Navy (or was
bb himself put it, in
rapher Marshall Pugh
:

a demobilization centre
dboard box which held
el suit. He hadn't the
slightest idea of what sort of job he should try, other than a job in diving.*

He was however, enrolled as a member of the Royal Naval Volunteer Supplementary Reserve as a Temporary Lt Cdr (SP). He found temporary accommodation in the Cavendish Hotel, in London. He had previously stayed there before the war and it was still owned by his eccentric friend, the legendary and controversial Rosa Lewis, otherwise known as *"the Duchess of Jermyn Street"*.

Crabb became engaged to Patricia Rose *"a society beauty"* in 1948, on the same day he actually received his George Medal. However, the engagement did not last long and they split

and went their separate ways (though they got re-engaged about seven years later). Pat Rose was herself an enigmatic character, having changed her name from Phoebe Pauline to Patricia and had been married three times (to Harry Goodstadt, Peter Sutehall and George Douglas Rose) by the time she met Crabb. Her second husband, Peter Sutehall had died in an aircraft crash in 1945 while in the RAF.

The first diving job opportunity that arose for Crabb came in October 1948. At the suggestion of Robert Foreman of the Caledonian Fishselling and Marine Stores Company, he sailed from Great Yarmouth on the *Helen Hern*, a motor drifter from Fraserburg. He had persuaded Foreman that he could settle such questions as why herring do not rise at certain times, how they behave when approaching the trawl net, why only 5% of a shoal is caught, and various other problems which had always baffled fishing experts.

He got off to a good start on only their second day out at sea when he was able to dive and free the drifter's propeller of a fishing net which had become entangled on it. He was delighted to discover the sea conditions were *"warm and visibility was excellent"*. He carried out a successful trial dive to 50 feet on the fishing net using a specially-built 35mm underwater camera. The project was a modest success and reveals to us that he was somehow able to obtain a very special camera and furthermore that he had an interest in underwater photography. Where could such a highly specialised camera have come from and where would he have received the instructions on how to use it?

Crabb was in touch with the very secret Admiralty Photographic and Instrumentation Research Laboratory (APIRL) then located at

21 The Boltons, South Kensington, London, where Lt Cdr G A 'Jimmy' Hodges GM RNVR[1] was involved in developing underwater photographic and filming equipment[1]. In 1949, APIRL relocated to the Admiralty Research Laboratory in Upper Lodge, Teddington (ARL U/L). They were renamed the Instrumentation Group (K-Group) and were headed by Walter Rosse Stamp.

Supporting evidence comes from a photograph of Cdr Crabb along with Jimmy Hodges and two other civilians on board the RV *Platessa*, a 90-foot motor fishing vessel (MFV) owned by the Centre for Environment, Fisheries & Aquaculture Science (CEFAS). It was probably taken around 1948. According to Richard Compton-Hall, Crabb's biographer in the Oxford Dictionary of National Biography, Crabb was *"seconded to the Ministry of Agriculture and Fisheries"* for this operation.

While visiting APIRL and later at the Admiralty Research Laboratory (ARL), Crabb had noticed they had accumulated a considerable amount of unique footage of divers operating underwater. He suggested they should put together a film demonstrating the capabilities of divers to help promote their usefulness, which of course was quite novel at the time. The idea caught on and he subsequently became a Technical Adviser to the Director of Boom Defence and Marine Salvage. Crabb wrote a script and the film *Report from the Sea Bed* was quickly produced. It was later released to the public under the new title *Wonders of the Deep*. This led to him landing a 3-year contract as a civilian

Experimental Officer at ARL in K-Group in the spring of 1949. He worked closely with Jimmy Hodges throughout this period. His duties were as a diver and underwater photographer and his role was concentrated on the operational aspects rather than the technical side. Developing underwater photographic and filming techniques thus became one of Crabb's principal interests.

He travelled daily to ARL in Teddington from London on the number 667 double-decker trolley bus. A colleague recalled that he always sat at the front, upstairs, chin resting on his sword stick and swearing about the poor bus service.

Crabb and Hodges went on to work together on a series of challenging underwater filming projects around the UK, in Malta and the Far East, many of them classified. On one hazardous project Crabb successfully filmed the cavitation from the propellers of a British cruiser as it sped past a mooring buoy to which he was clinging underwater. Cavitation is the production of noisy vapour bubbles off the tips of fast-turning propeller blades. His Diving Supervisor at the time was Lt Commander Bill Filer who had been most reluctant to allow the project to go ahead given the obvious risk of a fatal accident with the propeller.

On 3 August 1949 Crabb joined up with four other famous frogmen from WW2 to record a programme for the BBC Home Service. The programme was called *The Frogmen* and his companions were Lt B C G Place VC, Leading Seaman J Magennis VC, Ian Fraser VC and Lt Cdr D Cameron VC.

---

1. Jimmy Hodges had been Mentioned in Dispatches for his submarine operation in X23 on Sword Beach during the Normandy landings on D-Day, 6 June 1944. Lt Cdr Jimmy Hodges died on 16 April 1954 while filming with Dr Hans Hass in Bonaire, West Indies, as a result of going too deep while breathing oxygen. Cdr Crabb's ultimate fate two years later, almost to the day, was perhaps not entirely dissimilar.

Cdr Crabb (wearing woolly hat) with Lt Cdr Jimmy Hodges (extreme left in duffle coat)
on board RV *Platessa* during their diving project with CEFAS

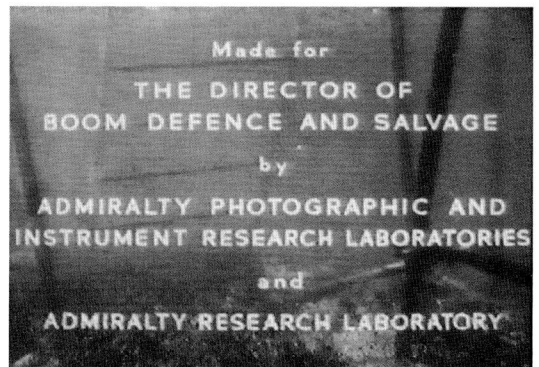

Report from the Sea Bed - A very early underwater film
produced by Hodges and Crabb by APIRL and ARL.

On their way from a public house in Marylebone to the BBC in Portland Place to record *The Frogmen*.
Left to right: Cdr L K P Crabb OBE GM, Lt B C G Place VC, Leading Seaman J Magennis VC, Tom
Waldron, Lt Cdr Ian Fraser VC, James Gleeson, Lt Cdr D Cameron VC.

The programme, which was broadcast on 18
August, was written by James Gleeson and
Produced by Tom Waldron both of whom
went on to write the book by the same name
published the following year.

Crabb ran into financial difficulties again
towards the end of the year. On 14 December
1949 he found it necessary to raise some cash
by pawning something in a pawnbrokers
in the Kings Road, Chelsea, for which he
raised £2.0.0. He was sharing a house, The
Gatehouse, 29a Ennismore Mews in South
Kensington at the time.

When HM Submarine *Truculent* sank after
a collision in the Thames estuary on 12 January
1950, both Crabb and Hodges offered their
services to assist in investigating the wreck.
The diving conditions were very difficult, with

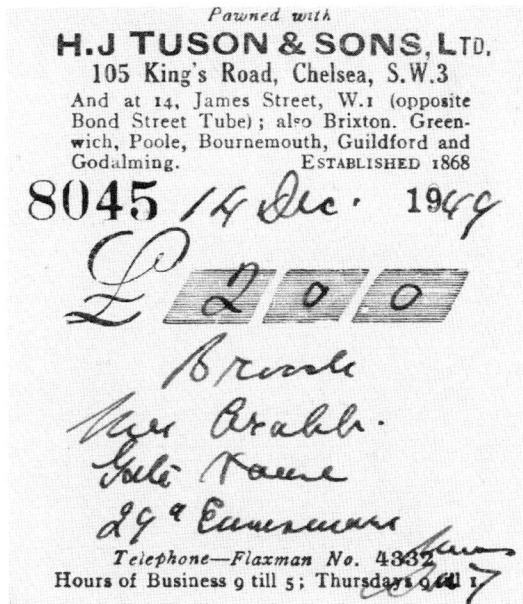

Crabb's receipt for the pawned item on
14 December 1949.

Crabb and Hodges during their diving operation
on the lost submarine HMS *Truculent*
in the Thames estuary

zero visibility and fast-running tidal streams, but they did succeed in providing a helpful damage report.

Commander Crabb obtained his new Passport on 19 April 1950 just in time for him to be able to visit Malta, arriving on 11 May. His task was to photograph an unexploded aerial bomb near a sunken liner in deep water.

Around this time he was again suffering from crippling lumbago (a severe pain in the muscles and joints in the lower back).

In April 1950, Crabb joined a Royal Navy expedition to Tobermory in Scotland to search for the wreck thought to be the *San Juan Baptista*, one of the casualties of the Spanish Armada of 1588. Rumour had it that it was carrying £3m in specie. The expedition was at the invitation of the Duke of Argyll and Lt Cdr Reay Parkinson was in overall charge of the operations.

The diving team was led by Commander Crabb's old friend, Lt Cdr John 'Jock' Crawford. Commander R F 'Bob' Harland paid a social visit from HMS *Lochinvar*, a shore establishment at South Queensferry on the Firth of Forth on the east coast of Scotland where he ran a small RN Clearance Diver school. The alleged treasure alluded them. Marshall Pugh noted that Commander Crabb was still *"crippled"* with lumbago but he nevertheless persevered with the project.

Commander Crabb's
Passport.

The following year, on 17 April 1951, HM Submarine *Affray* was declared missing in the English Channel. The Admiralty immediately searched a huge area of the sea bed using sonar to try and locate the lost submarine. Unfortunately, there were so many sonar targets scattered around from two world wars that it became a difficult challenge to identify the *Affray* amongst them all.

HMS *Reclaim*, the Royal Navy's deep diving and submarine rescue vessel, was part of the search fleet and Crabb was on board within 36 hours of the *Subsunk* report, having volunteered his diving services. One of the navy divers on board was Lt Cdr Bill Filer, an old friend of Commander Crabb's. As soon as it was realised that the *Affray* must have been lost in very deep water, beyond the depth capability of his air diving range, Crabb returned immediately to ARL and challenged his boss, Rosse Stamp to

build a remote viewing system employing closed-circuit television technology, suitable for seabed searches. ARL happened to be experimenting with the use of television at low light intensities at the time. Stamp agreed and a Top Secret working system codenamed *"Lacquer"* with a maximum operating depth of 200 feet was built in the remarkably short time of three weeks. In stark contrast with today's miniaturised cameras, they were quite pleased that their camera weighed less than one hundredweight (about 50 kg) in air.

After convincing the naval officer in charge of the search, Captain Bill Shelford, of the practicality of using the underwater TV camera, Crabb as Liaison Officer, accompanied by his line manager Rosse Stamp and Laboratory Mechanic Jock Phillips, mobilised the underwater TV camera system on board HMS *Reclaim*. On 12 June a likely sonar contact was discovered in 278 feet of water in

Rosse Stamp (*left*) and Jock Phillips (*right*) with their hastily-built underwater television camera onboard HMS *Reclaim*

the Hurd Deep. The camera was only rated to 200 feet but Crabb took the calculated risk and deployed it over the target, personally operating the winch which lowered it. The gamble paid off and the world's first underwater television camera successfully filmed the submarine's nameplate on the conning tower.

Shortly before his contract with ARL ended, towards the end of 1951, Crabb visited the Royal Naval Physiological Laboratory in Clayhall Road, Alverstoke. There he met Jack Eaton who was in charge of the experimental compression chambers at the laboratory. Probably not by coincidence, he also met up with the Experimental Diving Team from the Countermeasures Group of the Underwater Countermeasures & Weapons Establishment

(UCWE), led by Lt Cdr Gutteridge OBE. UCWE, in Havant, was an outpost of HMS *Vernon* (see Appendix 5). The work carried out at UCWE was closely related to Crabb's wartime operations in Gibraltar and he recognised a potential job opportunity there.

Probably after making a few enquiries, Crabb joined Gutteridge's diving team at UCWE on 12 October 1951 and he was simultaneously recalled into the RN with the substantive rank of Lieutenant Commander. He was given a 3-year contract, though as it turned out, he stayed a little longer than that. Crabb wasted no time in renewing his acquaintanceships with many of his naval colleagues. In early 1952 he was photographed with Lt Harry Wardle on the bridge of HMS

Back row:
Cdr Crabb, Jack Eaton (RNPL), unidentified, Lt Cdr Gutteridge OBE (UCWE)

Front row:
Petty Officer Ron McKinlay CGM, unidentified, Bill 'Sam' Muskett (All of the Experimental Diving Team).

The photograph was probably taken around 1950-1 while Crabb was a civilian Experimental Officer at ARL.

Lt Cdr Crabb with Lt Harry Wardle
on the bridge of HMS *Reclaim*.
(Author: I doubt very much that is tea in the cup!)

Lt Cdr Crabb pictured at an informal party
onboard HMS *Reclaim*, dressed as a
foreign navy admiral.

Reclaim, the navy's diving and submarine rescue ship. Wardle had been the First Lieutenant of the ship in 1951 and was by then the Senior Diving Officer at HMS *Vernon*. Crabb was pictured again on HMS *Reclaim* on a less formal occasion when he dressed himself up as an Admiral.

Now with the security of a steady job, on 15 March 1952 Lt Cdr Crabb, who was then 42 years old, married 37-year-old Margaret Elaine 'Willie' Player (née Williamson) at Thanet Registry Office in Kent. At the time, she had a seven-year-old son Michael Anthony Player

from a previous marriage. He was renamed Michael Anthony Crabb and sent off to St John's Church of England Primary School in nearby Whichers Gate Road. The newly married couple and son initially lived in a caravan in the grounds of UCWE's administration facilities at Leigh Park. This was a four-berth Berkeley "Ambassador" caravan with connections to mains electricity and water supply. Crabb's postal address was given as "c/o Leigh Park House, n. Havant". This was not a particularly comfortable arrangement. It must have been a little crowded for the three of them. So just

Margaret Crabb and her son Michael in their cottage in Rowlands Castle.

A Berkeley "Ambassador" 4-berth caravan of the type Crabb had at Leigh Park, Havant.

NAMES (in full)		Sex	PARENT or GUARDIAN	
SURNAME	CHRISTIAN	M or F	NAME	ADDRESS
Crabb.	Michael Anthony	M.	Lionel Kenneth Philip	90 Leigh Park Hse n. Havant.

Cdr Crabb's step son, Michael Crabb's entrance details at St John's School. Note the address referred to the caravan's location.

Cdr Crabb's cottage in Durrants Road, Rowlands Castle as seen today. It has had major refurbishment and several extensions built on to it since the 1950s.

25

under a year later, on 10 January 1953, they moved into Durrants Cottage, 45 Durrants Road, Rowlands Castle, a distance of about three miles from the operational site of UCWE in West Leigh House where Crabb worked.

Around this time (early 1952), Cdr Crabb's diving team at UCWE was made up of Lt Cdr Gutteridge, PO McKinlay, Able Seaman Bill Muskett and Able Seaman Robert Smith. Bill Muskett left the navy a little later for family reasons. Cdr Crabb wrote him a glowing reference letter on UCWE-headed paper (see image below).

On 30 June 1952, Lt Cdr Crabb was promoted to Commander over the head of Gutteridge his commanding officer, and put in charge of the UCWE Experimental Clearance Diving. This took Gutteridge by surprise and he was not entirely happy with the new arrangement. However, despite Crabb's promotion and by mutual agreement, Lt Cdr Gutteridge continued to be effectively in charge. Gutteridge described Cdr Crabb as not a natural manager and:

… quite remarkably untechnical. Electrical circuits were a lifelong mystery to him, mechanical complexity was a bore, tools were for others to use … who hated scientists and innovation with a passion … his assessment of experimental equipment and techniques bordered on the bizarre … he was an elderly, unfit, near alcoholic chap … prone to propping up bars, heavy smoker and given to post-prandial naps.

Gutteridge added:

… a diver of enormous experience with a singular ability to endure discomfort, but not given to long, hard slogs underwater. His lack of fear was unquestioned … quintessentially curmudgeonly but kindly bantam cock, complete with swordstick with a silver engraved crab on the knob … with his friends a most pleasant and lively individual … Small, dapper, given to velvet trousers, smoking jacket, spats, cane, monocle, extreme right wing and Royalist views and diffident, a staccato, rather

Commander Crabb's letter of reference for Bill Muskett.

Lt Commander Gutteridge (holding the spanner) and Commander Crabb
during diving trials at Horsea Lake, Portsmouth.

Cdr Crabb *(centre, front row)* wearing his three-striped Commander uniform at a gathering in HMS *Vernon*. To his left is Lt Cdr Jackie Warner on his right, Lt Cdr Gordon Gutteridge.

wry way of speaking … lazy, not prone to making physical effort.

The reference to *"extreme right wing and Royalist"* conflicts with another description by his neighbours at Rowlands Castle as *"left wing and almost communist"*. It appears that Crabb could display completely opposite affiliations depending on the company he was keeping.

Crabb's heavy drinking habit did not go unnoticed outside the navy. Ron Chamberlain, a manager at Siebe Gorman & Co Ltd (developers and manufacturers of diving equipment) reminisced about Cdr Crabb:

When he was in the Navy, he used to come to Siebe Gormans with the RN experimental team, *to use our pressure pot - so I got to know him pretty well. Boy could he drink, he used to go down to the Toby Jug at Tolworth, have three or four pints, then do a pot dive (where he couldn't get out, until the dive was over), the water level in the Pot certainly rised* [sic].

During his time at UCWE, Crabb's 'local' was an old coaching inn, the Staunton Arms where he was known as a popular customer. He and his team of divers would regularly occupy the 'snug' for their lunchtime discussions. Crabb's favourite tipple there was a very strong Merrydown cider (ABV 8.2%) brewed at Horam Manor in East Sussex. No doubt it was an atmospheric, old-style pub in those days,

The Mine
Recovery Suit
(MRS) was being
trialled at the
time.
On Cdr Crabb's
left is Taff Roberts
and top right
is Bill 'Sam'
Muskett.

The Staunton Arms in Rowlands Castle. It was an old coaching
inn and Cdr Crabb's local during his time at UCWE.

but sadly it has now been converted into a modern pub/restaurant. Crabb played darts at the pub and would regularly meet his friends Mrs Florence Benfield and her husband there. They were particularly helpful to him whenever he was away on any of his projects by looking after his black cat, presumably after his divorce. However, there was not a lot of good said about Crabb amongst the local retailers. He had a reputation for not paying his bills. Others said he was a *"left-winger and almost communist"*.

Amongst Cdr Crabb's varied duties while at UCWE was to help out with running diver training courses. Colin Perry recalled he was on an eight-week 'steamer's' (hard-hat diving) course based at Horsea Island, Portsmouth which started in September 1952. Crabb was the officer in charge of the course but he was not directly involved in giving instruction. He was based in the Officers' Mess at HMS *Vernon*. Perry recalled that he was a strict disciplinarian and a heavy drinker. At that time Crabb's team of divers had grown in number to twelve, all based at HMS *Vernon*. However, he was also able to requisition the use of other, newly-qualified divers based on HMS *Deepwater* for

testing out various new types of equipment. For reasons best known to himself, he required these conscripted divers to dive wearing swimming trunks only which would have been a very cold experience in local waters. The younger divers quickly learnt to keep out of his way whenever they saw him coming.

Crabb's team had the use of MFV *1567* around this time which was also based at HMS *Vernon*. Crabb's long-time, entrepreneurial friend, Maitland Pendock, had lost touch with him and was curious as to his latest situation. He sent Crabb a letter on 1 December 1952 from his new, up-market address with a friend called Wendy in South Kensington. In it he referred to a drinking club called "The Patio", or more precisely "El Patio" at 41 Glebe Place in Chelsea. It appears that this had been another of Crabb's favoured drinking haunts in the past along with the "Cross Keys" in Lawrence Street. He referred to their mutual friend, Rosa Lewis, who ran the Cavendish Hotel and who had just passed away in November. His main reason for contacting Crabb was actually to try and enlist his support to market a new "oilingpen" to the Royal Navy.

His letter read:

MFV *1567*

The first page of Maitland Pendock's letter to Crabb, dated 1st December 1952

Dear Crabbie,

I was in The Patio today & suddenly remembered this was one of your Foundations so got your address. The last letter – to HMS Vernon – was returned.

Reading of Rosa, had already brought you into memory & and think it is time I heard from you.

Am keeping busy with lots of new & exciting adventures, including SLIX again.

Am now staying with Wendy, so note new address please. Best time to phone – before 10 a.m. as old. Saw Hugh Payne the other night – looking gigantic with beer drinking I think. He is getting around – Antarctic (2), Australia Sweden & so on building plants.

Simon had a tricky appendix – perforated – 5 weeks ago – have you heard at all of him since last time I saw you.

Am anxious to show you a new gadget – an oilingpen – which somehow I think may have a use in H.M.R.N. Looks like a fountainpen * & acts like a syringe.

*Film people like it as it does not over-oil, thus no surplus to affect soundstrip.

Sells at 15/-. Precision made. Maybe I'll send you one. Sell a few 1000 @ 11/- & you'll have peacock for Christmas. The RAF are contemplating an order of 20,000.

And how is Mrs Crabb (I still don't know whether you have an (?) or not) You never asked me to the caravan, you so & so. Hope all is well with you both. Make a date soon.

Yours

Maitland.

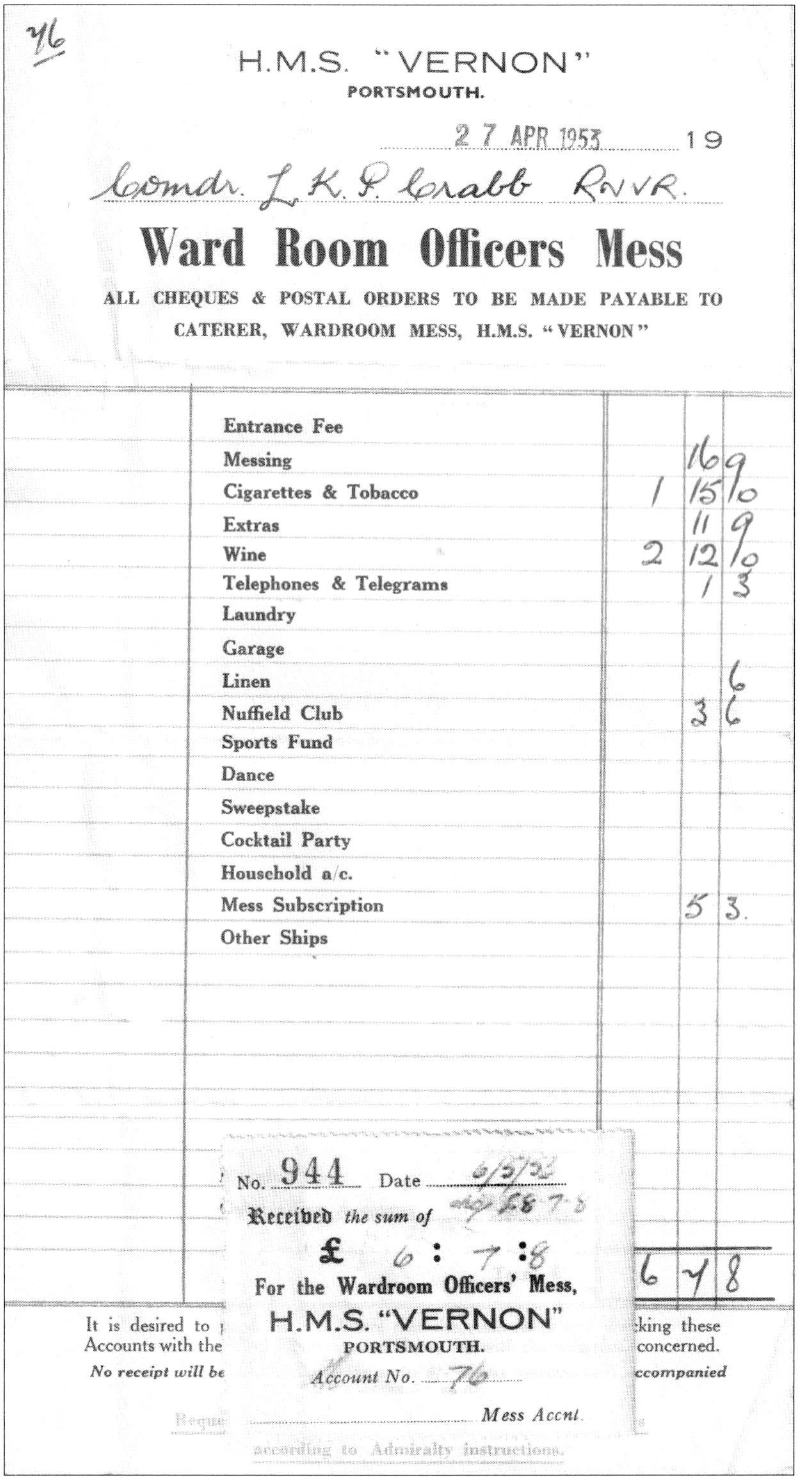

76

H.M.S. "VERNON"
PORTSMOUTH.

2 7 APR 1953   19

Comdr. L. K. P. Crabb RNVR.

Ward Room Officers Mess

ALL CHEQUES & POSTAL ORDERS TO BE MADE PAYABLE TO
CATERER, WARDROOM MESS, H.M.S. "VERNON"

Entrance Fee			
Messing		16	9
Cigarettes & Tobacco	1	15	0
Extras		11	9
Wine	2	12	0
Telephones & Telegrams		1	3
Laundry			
Garage			
Linen			6
Nuffield Club		3	6
Sports Fund			
Dance			
Sweepstake			
Cocktail Party			
Household a/c.			
Mess Subscription		5	3.
Other Ships			

No. 944   Date 6/5/5?
Received the sum of £8 7 8
£ 6 : 7 :8
For the Wardroom Officers' Mess,
H.M.S. "VERNON"
PORTSMOUTH.
Account No. 76

Mess Accnt.

6 7 8

It is desired to p...   ...king these
Accounts with the   ...concerned.
No receipt will be   ...ccompanied

Reque...

according to Admiralty instructions.

Crabb's Mess bill on 27 April 1953.

Whenever Crabb was busy or tied up with any project or course at HMS *Vernon*, he would stay at the Officers' Mess rather than commute from Rowlands Castle. Interestingly the greatest costs on his Mess bill were wine and cigarettes. This arrangement would not have been conducive to his marriage.

The Queen's coronation happened in 1953 and there was a Queen's Review of the Fleet off Portsmouth on 15 June. Over 300 ships were on show. Perry and his team carried out a close inspection of South Railway Jetty in preparation for the busy period around the time of the Review. They were restricted to the side of the jetty and the adjacent sea bed. All they found were small items if rubbish. Separate frogman teams inspected underneath the jetty.

Perry also recalled that Crabb went off to a meeting with the RN at Bath prior to the Review. He proposed to carry out a secret investigation of the Soviet cruiser *Sverdlov*. It was alleged that when HMS *Vanguard*, which was the navy's premier battleship and of similar size and power, had escorted the *Sverdlov* to Portsmouth, the Soviet cruiser could steam ten knots faster than *Vanguard*. Much to Crabb's disappointment, his proposal was turned down. When he returned to *Vernon*, just two days before the Review he was still red with rage.

Crabb's attitude to discipline within his own team was very relaxed. This added to his popularity with his men, but it was not received well by the higher echelons at HMS *Vernon*. The Commander of HMS *Vernon* was especially unhappy with the informality of Crabb's style of leadership. He was moved to making a written complaint to Crabb on one occasion:

I have just had cause to pick up one of your party. He was wearing a red scarf, top half of an oilskin two piece suit, Lochinvar cap ribbon & seaboot tops turned down.

If I meet him again half as badly dressed he will be spending some time drilling round the parade ground.

The rest of the party was passable but not smart.

Early in the summer of 1954 Crabb visited Malta. In his spare time, he hired a small Star Class yacht from the Royal Malta Sailing Club. He was assisted on two sailing trips by a nineteen-year-old midshipman named John Grattan. Grattan went on to enjoy an illustrious diving career in the Royal Navy and himself achieved the rank of Lieutenant Commander. Interestingly, after leaving the navy, he also went on to carry out salvage operations on the Spanish wreck at Tobermory. Grattan described Crabb at the time of their brief sailing partnerships as *"not chatty nor jokey, more dour than anything else"*.

Commander Crabb returned to Tobermory in August 1954, this time as the leader of the Royal Navy expedition to search again for the wreck of the much-disputed Spanish treasure ship *San Juan Baptista* (aka *Duque de Florencia*). He had originally been granted two months special leave by the Admiralty but the operation strung out to nearly six months. They operated from an old, 400-ton, coastal steamer, the *Ardchattan* which the Duke of Argyll had purchased especially for the project. Interestingly, to help them search for the wreck they had with them *"the latest type of TV cameras"*. This is consistent with Commander Crabb's close involvement with the development of underwater television during his employment at UCWE.

It provided a welcome reunion between Commander Crabb and an old diving partner from his Gibraltar days, Stoker Sydney

Midshipman John Grattan in the
Star Class yacht at Malta in 1954.

Cdr Crabb at Tobermory Pier in August 1954.

Stoker Sydney Knowles pictured in Tobermory.

Knowles (he had joined the Royal Navy in 1939 as an engine room stoker, later training as a diver). Other familiar divers on the project included Bill 'Sam' Muskett and Terry Yetton. Gus Britton, an ex-submariner and also part of the naval crew at Tobermory, stated that Crabb *"was a poor swimmer and once said to me: 'If I lose my flippers. I'll drown … Certainly the time spent in the Mish Nish hotel at Tobermory didn't help towards his general fitness"*. Crabb seemed to have an aversion to physical fitness. He once confided in Marshall Pugh:

I don't believe in training for training's sake. There are certain reserves of mind that you can call upon when it's necessary, when you have something important to do. The reserves don't come from the body. They come from some sort of spiritual stimulation. I've never found those muscley, overtrained physical fitness specimens much good.

Marshall Pugh,
author of Commander Crabb's biography.

Sketch by Lt A Sagar, HMS *Vernon*.

Lt Mark Terrell who took over as the lead diver of the UCWE Diving Trials Team.

When he returned to HMS *Vernon* in December, Lt A Sagar interviewed him about the expedition for the *Royal Navy Diving Magazine* and took the opportunity to pen his profile.

Cdr Crabb was retired from the position at UCWE and the Royal Navy on 8 April 1955. He was replaced by Lt Mark Terrell (much to the relief of Lt Cdr Gutteridge). Gutteridge therefore resumed the responsibility for and management of the diving team.

While Crabb was kept on in the RNVR, his return to civilian life was a major upheaval for him. It was a move he had been dreading. His marriage had failed, he no longer had a secure income, he had no savings and he had

no job prospects. His future looked pretty bleak and he was prone to depression. He sought his solace in drink.

Crabb's marriage had not lasted very long. Margaret Crabb had suddenly left him in April 1953, taking with her, her young son Michael with her. Their marriage had lasted only a year. It was an acrimonious separation for Margaret Crabb and her health suffered as a result. Her subsequent correspondence with Crabb clearly cited Crabb's *"abnormal"* sexual behaviour and his draining of her funds and income to support his life-style as her reasons for leaving him. Crabb tried relentlessly to persuade her to come back, even to the point of harassment. She was obliged to go into hiding to avoid his representations. They communicated by letter via one of Margaret Crabb's friends, W Brown of 33 Sutherland Crescent, Hayes, near Bromley in Kent.

However, Margaret Crabb began proceedings for divorce and obtained a decree. Crabb did not defend the proceedings and the Decree was made Absolute on 29 November 1954 (Serial No 8674) and Margaret reverted to her earlier name of Player. On 1 April 1955 she obtained an Order from the Court for Crabb to pay her £45 per month in maintenance during their joint lives.

Various other reasons have been given for the divorce. Locals in Rowlands Castle believed it was because he was away so much on his various projects. On one occasion Margaret Player, who was reluctant to declare the real reasons for her divorce, explained to friends that she decided to divorce Crabb because he was still holding a torch for his previous fiancée, Patricia. He kept asking her to use similar make-up and to dress like her and the final straw came when he asked her to dye her hair blonde like Pat Rose's.

Stories of the break-up being due to Cdr Crabb's alleged fetish for rubber bed sheets were unfounded according to Margaret Player. Lt Cdr Gutteridge commented on Crabb's interest in rubber:

His oddity was rubber. He liked shiny blue rubber bed sheets and a wide variety of mostly domestic items … he also wore a cut-down, pink, ladies' mackintosh underneath his uniform and Margaret once said, 'He rustled like a Christmas Tree.'

Crabb's interest in such materials would be supported by correspondence he had with Dannimac Ltd, in Manchester, manufacturers of rainproof and waterproof clothing. In June 1953, Mr D J Sharpe of Dannimac Ltd wrote back to Crabb to say:

We thank you for your letter dated 30 May but are extremely sorry that we do not sell our material by the piece, only in made up garments.

The divorce was stated to be *"on grounds of cruelty"* in the proceedings. They had previously agreed together that this was the simplest and most convenient way to annul the marriage. Divorces were quite rare in those days and there were only three options to choose from: cruelty, desertion or incurable insanity. It appears that "Cruelty" was the agreed option in order to facilitate a swift settlement.

Unfortunately, Margaret Player was not consistent in her explanations for the divorce. After his death, in her statements given to the police on 10 and 11 June 1957, she had said on the second day: *"It was because of my husband's abnormal sexual behaviour that I divorced him."* Another inconsistency referred to circumcision, which was later raised as an identification factor at the Inquest when his body had been found. On the first day of the Inquest she had said: *"It was also known to me that my husband had been circumcised at some time during his life …"* and then on the second day: *"I cannot be sure whether my husband had been circumcised or not as our sexual relations were not normal and our marriage was of short duration."*

After the divorce, Crabb occasionally sent Margaret Player a cheque or some cash as part of their maintenance settlement, though it appears he did not keep up with her full entitlement. They kept in touch through occasional correspondence and amongst her friends Margaret Player continued to refer affectionately to Commander Crabb as *"my Kenny"*. However, she was also not consistent in her description

Margaret Player inspects a Royal Naval human torpedo exhibit sometime after her divorce from Cdr Crabb.

Above:
The Brompton Oratory in London where Cdr Crabb chatted to the priests and said his prayers

Left:
Number 2A Hans Road is above the Opticians, opposite Harrods. Cdr Crabb rented a one-room apartment at this address.

of her former husband. When interviewed by a reporter from the *Herald* newspaper, published on 29 April 1957, she was quoted as saying *"People think of me as the woman who divorced a hero. He was no hero to me."*

From 1951 to 1956, Cdr Crabb had maintained a one-room apartment *"off and on"* on the first floor of 2A Hans Road, Knightsbridge, London, SW3, just across the road from Harrods. This of course includes the period of his marriage. However, after his contract with UCWE ended in April 1955, he moved in on a 'permanent' basis and opened an account at the National Provincial Bank, Brompton Road Branch. He only appeared once in the Register of Electors at that address, on 10 October 1955. The manageress was Amy Thomas who looked after nineteen service flatlets at 2A Hans Road.

While there, he was an occasional visitor to the Brompton Oratory in Brompton Road, a large neoclassical Roman Catholic church. Marshall Pugh wrote that he *spent a quiet hour with 'God's Butlers', which was his affectionate phrase for the priests … he would light a candle and offer a prayer for his future … "*. It is perhaps an unfortunate coincidence that the Brompton Oratory was later discovered to be one of the favoured locations for 'dead letter drops' by Soviet agents (behind a marble pillar on the right, inside the front door). The Soviet embassy was just a short walk away, across Hyde Park.

Meanwhile at HMS *Vernon*, Portsmouth, Lt Cdr Bill Filer was appointed the Officer in Charge of the Acceptance Trials Team for *"self-contained diving equipment and other equipment used by CDs"*.

The team was drawn from the Clearance Diving (CD) Instructors Staff at the Admiralty Experimental Diving Unit in HMS *Vernon*

in 1954. Later, Filer was sent to Scotland to take command of HMS *Diver* and Lt Cdr Joe Brooks took over command of the Acceptance Trials Team.

The period from when Cdr Crabb left the navy to his disappearance a year later is best covered by Marshall Pugh in his book *Commander Crabb* which was published in 1956 by Macmillan's & Co Ltd. The two worked closely together during that time writing the biography. Pugh was a freelance journalist and writer with an office in Odham's Press. MI6 (the foreign intelligence service of the government of the United Kingdom) noted that the member of Macmillan's publishing company dealing directly with Pugh's book was Alan Maclean, none other than Donald Maclean's brother (who was exposed some

Lt Cdr Bill Filer, the Officer in Charge of the Acceptance Trials Team

time later as one of the notorious "Cambridge five" Soviet spies).

Crabb tried his best to put on a brave face and maintained his contacts with his naval colleagues. He visited HMS *Vernon* and the diving school on HMS *Deepwater* from time to time. But he found it difficult to obtain work in civvy street. He initially approached one of his old diving friends, Lt Ian Fraser VC, who had retired from the navy and established a commercial diving company in Liverpool called Universal Divers Ltd. Unfortunately, the business was still quite early in its development and Fraser did not have a suitable opening for him. Crabb once told his old naval colleague Lt Cdr Harry Wardle that at one low point he got a job as a model for a jock strap manufacturer. When Knowles, the former navy stoker and diver, paid him a visit on one of his regular trips to London as a lorry driver, he found Crabb on the street carrying a sandwich board. He was in a depressed state and became tearful when they discussed his menial situation.

Then a stroke of luck came out of the blue with the offer of a good-paying diving job on a secret MI6 operation (Appendix 12).

The Admiralty had placed an embargo on the use of naval divers for the operation, but they provided MI6 with a list of names of possible non-serving divers. Cdr Crabb had been selected from this list and he in turn persuaded Sydney Knowles to dive with him. He was to be paid £60 plus expenses for the operation (this conflicts with Knowles who has stated Cdr Crabb received £2,000 while he received £1,000). The windfall would allow Crabb to pay off his debts and enjoy a brief period of relative affluence.

With the prospect of a nice little earner in the offing, Crabb bought himself a new two-piece, "Delta" diving dry-suit from C E Heinke & Co Ltd in Bermondsey, London on 11 October 1955. It is understandable why he preferred this design of suit because it would fit his short body better than the standard issue RN dry suit. Unusually, he had requested a suit with a neck seal as opposed to the standard, hood-attached version. He did not like the hood being attached to the suit. He preferred to wear a woolly balaclava covered by a bathing cap. He once told a colleague *"I like the feeling of seawater in my ears, and I don't have to worry about my ear drums."* As an aside, the Works Manager at Heinke at the time was a Mr Harold Short. His daughter said that her father met Crabb briefly and came to the conclusion *"he would not trust him"*.

The reference to worrying about his eardrums was because the hood-attached version occasionally caused a condition called 'reversed ears'. This was when the rubber latex hood accidentally made a seal against the side of the head during a descent. This prevented the increasing pressure outside the ear from reaching the eardrum. Meanwhile the increasing pressure developing inside the naso-pharynx caused the eardrums to distend painfully outwards. This is the opposite direction the ear drums are normally pushed when diving without a hood.

Prior to the diving operation, it was alleged that Cdr Crabb had borrowed an old Italian oxygen set from the Experimental Diving Team and he tested the equipment by diving in Horsea Lake at Horsea Island, Portsmouth. Knowles had a different version saying that he and Crabb had retained the Italian oxygen sets from their WW2 operations in Gibraltar and Italy. It has been said that Crabb preferred this set to any other. However, corroborating evidence of his use of the Italian breathing equipment has not been found.

The occasion which was of such special interest to MI6 was when Britain and the USSR carried out a reciprocal good-will visit of their respective navies. Between 12 and 17 October 1955, six Soviet and six British warships carried out simultaneous visits to Portsmouth and Leningrad (now called St Petersburg) respectively. The British squadron consisted of HMS *Triumph*, Colossus-class, light fleet aircraft carrier; HMS *Decoy* and HMS *Diana*, Daring-class; HMS *Apollo*, Abdiel-class minelayer; HMS *Chevron* and HMS *Chieftain*, destroyers. The Soviet squadron consisted of the flagship *Sverdlov*, with *Alexander Suvarov*, cruisers, and *Sovershenny, Smotryashchie, Sposebiry* and *Smetlivy*, destroyers. The two squadrons passed each other in the Kattegat, between Denmark and Sweden on their way to their respective destinations. They would have exchanged salutes, but they were in such thick fog they could hardly see each other.

Crabb had previously tried to get permission to investigate the *Sverdlov* at the time of the first Queen's Coronation Review of the Fleet back in 1953. However, much to his consternation, his proposal had been turned down. So he was quite elated that he could at last achieve his ambition.

The mission, which was the first time Cdr Crabb had worked for MI6, was successful and they discovered that the *Sverdlov* had a retractable bow thruster. This was an important discovery and it helped to explain the ship's exceptional manoeuvrability.

It is important to note here that both sides got up to the same tricks.

So while MI6 was busily managing their survey under the *Sverdlov* at Portsmouth (with Crabb and Knowles), the KGB were equally busy running their diver investigations under the Royal Navy cruisers in Leningrad. Nicholas Elliott of MI6 stated that *"a British cruiser had visited Leningrad and frogmen had popped up all over the place without protest on our part."* Sir Edward Bridges made the same observation and noted:

... when the ships had requested that a stern buoy be laid for one of the destroyers the Russians had sent three times as many divers as were necessary to moor the buoy. It seemed beyond reasonable doubt that some of these divers had taken the opportunity for underwater examination of British ships.

Unfortunately, such job-opportunities were very rare and following the short MI6 engagement Crabb was left once more with the problem of a regular income. He eventually managed to pin down a steady job when he went to work for his old friend Harold Victor Maitland Pendock in London (Appendix 3) around Christmas 1955. Pendock, who was what may be termed a bit of a 'wheeler dealer', had established a new business as an antique furniture dealer. Crabb started work as the office manager and became involved in furnishing coffee bars. One of these was the "Two Bare Feet" at 57 Westbourne Grove, Bayswater, owned by Dominick Brown & Co Ltd. Pendock, it seems, was his closest friend and they had known each other since before the war. Pendock also circulated in the art world and rubbed shoulders with the likes of Anthony Blunt. He mixed fortunes running a series of business ventures and been declared bankrupt in 1949. He was alleged to have been a soviet spy and later died under mysterious circumstances in Ireland.

Patricia Rose/Dill pictured sometime
after her relationship with Cdr Crabb.

The Nag's Head public house in Kinnerton Street,
Knightsbridge where Cdr Crabb frequently drank.

Sometime around December 1955, Cdr Crabb re-established his relationship with Patricia Rose, his former fiancée who herself had recently been divorced. They got 'engaged' once more, though at the time she was mysteriously living under the name of Mrs Patricia Dill with her husband-to-be Victor Robert Colquhoun Dill at 19 Ovington Gardens, just a short walk down the Old Brompton Road from Hans Road. (Patricia Dill wrote under her name of Pat Rose in 1979: *"… at the time of his disappearance I was engaged to be married to him"*). The 'Dills' did actually get married later, in June 1957. Victor Dill was a notorious character having been jailed for nine months in March 1954 for his part in a racehorse substitution scam.

Pat Rose and Cdr Crabb were frequent visitors at the Nag's Head public house in Kinnerton Street, Knightsbridge where they had first met. This was one of Cdr Crabb's favourite pubs and he knew the landlord, Len Cole, well. According to Cole they called in the pub on an almost daily basis.

Though Crabb appeared to have a semblance of a steady job with his long-time friend Maitland Pendock, it seems he was still having problems making ends meet. Undoubtedly his heavy drinking and associated socialising made heavy demands on his limited funds.

To sum up, by March 1956, Commander Crabb was slipping deeper and deeper into debt, he was depressed and he was drinking heavily. On the positive side, he did have his biography being prepared for publication by Marshall Pugh.

It is against this backdrop that Cdr Crabb enthusiastically accepted another offer, this time of £100 from MI6 to carry out a dive under a Soviet ship due to visit Portsmouth Harbour.

PART 2
THE DIVING OPERATIONS

What were the objectives of the underwater investigations?

The Admiralty notified the intelligence organisations in December 1954 that the underwater noise characteristics of Soviet warships was their <u>top priority</u> requirement.

The information was needed *"for the effective offensive use of certain types of mine and torpedo"*. More precisely, Britain was at that time developing 'intelligent' mines and torpedoes which could recognise and target specific ships by their acoustic signatures. A further suggestion was that the noise characteristics were needed for the North Atlantic Sound Surveillance System (SOSUS). This is a chain of seabed listening posts in the Atlantic and Pacific originally intended for use during the Cold War to listen for the movements of Soviet submarines.

There are slightly differing versions of the objectives of the investigations involving Commander Crabb.

According to Peter Wright of MI5 (author of *Spycatcher*) MI6 wanted to measure the propeller because of confusion in the Admiralty as to why she was able to travel so much faster than had been originally estimated by Naval Intelligence. Nicholas Elliott, who employed Cdr Crabb for the mission, stated:

The navy were anxious to find out, as a matter of high intelligence priority, about certain equipment under the stern of the ship.

John Henry, Technical Liaison Officer in Section R3 at the London Station who was responsible for liaison with the navy, said

the navy had been pressing him for months for details of the *Ordzhonikidze's* propellers. Chapman Pincher, an investigative journalist (author of *Treachery* and a friend of Peter Wright's) also said Cdr Crabb was to investigate the propellers and the rudder as well. This included measuring the pitch of the propeller blades. In fact, simply knowing the number of propeller blades was a most important requirement because this was a fundamental contributor to the acoustic signature.

In particular, he claimed that Cdr Crabb was to check to see if the ship was fitted with a device called *"Agouti"* (also known as a *"nightshirt"* propeller silencer). It is a system to reduce cavitation noise from the propellers. It consists of minute holes along the leading edge of the propeller. Compressed air is pumped through these holes to ventilate the vapour layer and minimise the noisy implosion of the cavitation bubbles. Another, less reliable claim suggested Cdr Crabb was to look for anti-sonar equipment and any mine-laying hatches.

The most credible version comes from Sir Edward Bridges, the Head of the Civil Service, who was commissioned by the Prime Minister to investigate the Cdr Crabb affair. He stated that Cdr Crabb's *"operating instructions were to restrict himself to an examination of the rudder and screws of the Russian cruiser."* He further explained that:

Since December, 1954, one of the outstanding intelligence requirements notified to MI6 by the Admiralty has been information about the underwater noise characteristics of Russian warships. Indeed, this comes first in the list of Admiralty requirements since information is necessary for the effective use of certain types of mine and torpedo.

A golden opportunity to meet this critical intelligence requirement presented itself in April 1956. This was when Nikita Khrushchev and Marshal Bulganin paid a diplomatic visit to Britain at the invitation of the Prime Minister, Sir Anthony Eden. This was at the height of the Cold War. They were brought to Britain in the Soviet cruiser *Ordzhonikidze* which was accompanied by two destroyers, the *Sovershenny* and the *Smotryashchy*.

The visit presented a rare opportunity to gather the intelligence information they needed and particularly from the high-value target, the cruiser *Ordzhonikidze*.

Both MI6 and Naval Intelligence Division (NID) were eligible departments to gather the

Above: Cavitation: the production of 'noisy' vapour bubbles at the tips of a propeller turning at high speed.

Right: The Agouti system being cleaned with the vessel in drydock. Water can be seen issuing from the holes through which air is pumped when in operation.

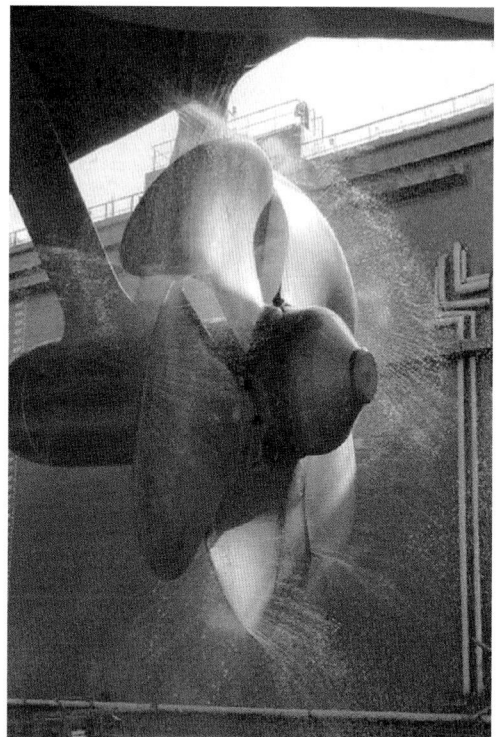

Conservative government Prime Minister, Sir Anthony Eden.

Premier of the Soviet Union, Nikolai Alexandrovich Bulganin.

First Secretary of the Communist Party, Nikita Sergeyevich Khrushchev.

information (Appendix 12). NID however were reluctant to do the job themselves and agreed to let MI6 undertake the task. The MI6 operation was run by Nicholas Elliott, their London Station Chief, from his offices in Queen Anne's Gate. He was put in charge of all home-based operations. He had just arrived back from Vienna where he had served as the Head of Station since 1953. He was assisted by his Technical Officer John Henry.

Peter Wright, then in MI5 (the United Kingdom's domestic counter-intelligence and security agency) stated the Cdr Crabb project *"was a typical piece of MI6 adventurism, ill-conceived and badly executed"*. He added that Cdr Crabb was *"overweight and overage"*. John Henry had stated, *"I told Nicholas not to use Buster; he was heading for a heart attack as it was."* In hindsight, on 14 May 1956, Sir Edward Bridges judged the operation as *"a thoroughly bad and unplanned one"*.

When someone asked why Cdr Crabb had been employed, the answer was given, *"that he was especially qualified in tests of the kind in question"*. And when asked why the test could not be carried out by HMS *Vernon*, the reply was that *"Vernon was not concerned with this type of test"*. This suggests that Cdr Crabb might have needed to take some sort of instrumentation or equipment with him on his dive, perhaps a camera capable of use in low visibility water.

Nicholas Elliott, MI6 London Station Chief.

However, there is no evidence that he did take any special equipment on his dives.

The Prime Minister had initially sanctioned the following intelligence gathering operations against the Soviet ships:

1   Photographic reconnaissance, noise listening and electronic intercept by aircraft (Operation Claret)
2   Magnetic signatures by means of a D.S. loop (a Degaussing System) at the entrance to Portsmouth Harbour.
3   'Y' coverage (a magnetic characteristic of a ship)
4   Photographic operations while in Portsmouth Harbour.

Another investigation proposed to Viscount Cilcennin, the First Lord of the Admiralty, was codenamed *"Catamaran"*. This was to measure the thickness of the armour plate on the hull of the cruiser.

But the Prime Minister ruled out any action that involved the remotest risk of detection and anything that involved attaching gadgets to the ships, including instruments which would even just touch the ships. The situation was summarised by Admiral Sir Charles Lambe, the Second Sea Lord, in a note to the First Lord on 6 June 1956:

... the only two operations proposed which involved service personnel were (1) that involving armour plate and a catamaran and (2) CLARET. Application for clearance for these two operations was therefore made to the 1st Lord. (1) was turned down by 1st Lord and (2) by the Prime Minister and both commented to the effect that nothing of the sort was to be carried out on that occasion. This comment was interpreted as applying to those operations (of the first type) for which the Admiralty was responsible. No such operation was conducted.

Viscount 'Jim' Cilcennin, the First Lord of the Admiralty, 1951-1956.

So both operations, Claret and Catamaran were officially cancelled.

The issue of the erroneously perceived official clearance for Cdr Crabb's operation became one of the major scandals within the government. No official clearance was actually given to MI6 by the Foreign Office, though MI6 was under the impression it had been. The misunderstanding arose between Michael Williams, the Foreign Office Adviser (FOA) inside MI6, and Sir John Bruce-Lockhart, Controller Western Europe (CWE), for which Williams was later *"severely censured"* and consequently *"moved"*. The complex scenario, a classic case of poor communications, was succinctly summed up by Ben Macintyre in his book *A Spy amongst Friends*:

Michael Williams, a Foreign Office official [FOA] recently posted to oversee MI6, was handed a list of possible operations for the Soviet

Michael S Williams, the Foreign Office Adviser in MI6 who was at the centre of the misunderstanding over the official approval of the Cdr Crabb diving operation.

visit. *'The dicey operations* [are] *at the beginning of the file and the safer ones at the back,' he was told* [by CWE]. *Williams was distracted by the death of his father that morning. A short while later he handed the file back without comment; Williams assumed someone senior to him must have already given the go-ahead; the Admiralty assumed that MI6 was responsible, since it was carrying out the mission; and MI6 assumed the Admiralty was in the driving seat, since it had asked for the information in the first place. And the Prime Minister assumed that no spies were doing anything, because that was exactly what he had ordered them to do.*

Further clues as to the reasons for the survey came from a letter to the Prime Minister, dated 27 March 1981, which the author assumes to be from Lt Cdr Joe Brooks (the whole letter is transcribed at Appendix 13).

I was in charge of the Naval operational team who successfully surveyed the undersides of the Russian ships at the time to ensure that all was either 'safe' or 'unsafe'. The security services, apart from alerting us as to the need for this underwater survey operation, engaged Crabbe [sic] *on a separate mission which failed disastrously.*

The reasons for ascribing this letter to Lt Cdr Joe Brooks (apart from personal knowledge) include the presence of the initials "JB" at the top left of the letter and a reference to having established his own successful commercial diving company (which would have been "Mobell Marine Ltd"). The separate, naval diving operation is discussed below. The detailed objectives and achievements of the underwater investigations of the Crabb/MI6 and RN/Naval Intelligence dives appear to have been slightly different and the latter have not yet been identified or disclosed.

Thus armed with the knowledge of the basic objectives of the diving operations, before we look in detail at Cdr Crabb's failed mission, it is perhaps timely to review a sampling of the many conspiracy theories that have been developed in consequence of the curtain of secrecy that has been drawn across the Crabb affair. They helpfully give us a sense of perspective of the forces at play behind the scene.

Various 'conspiracy' theories concerning Commander Crabb's disappearance

On the morning of Thursday, 19 April 1956, Cdr Crabb dived from a launch tied up alongside a row of pontoons in the Boat Pound, adjacent to the South Railway Jetty and just around the corner from the three Soviet warships. He failed to return from the dive. The Admiralty and MI6 attempted to cover up the disastrous venture but botched it up. The bungled cover-up became an even bigger disaster than the original intelligence operation – hence "Crabbgate" (see later).

Since that time, the continued secrecy over the events has led to an ever-increasing series of sometimes bizarre theories as to what actually happened, not only during Cdr Crabb's fatal dive but over the two mysterious appearances of a body eventually recovered in Chichester Harbour, 7 and 14 months later. One of the fascinating attributes of conspiracy theories is that they illustrate the type and range of cloak-and-dagger activities that may conceivably have gone on. An embarrassing collection of skeletons is unveiled in the cupboard.

Even the Admiralty and MI6 were struggling to come to grips with Crabb's mysterious disappearance. Sir Edward Bridges recorded the official opinion at the time:

... the possible explanations for CRABB's loss seemed to be the following:-

1. That he had been observed by the Russians and taken aboard alive;

2. That he had been destroyed by Russian counter measures and that his body was either, (a) aboard the Russian ship, or (b) still in the water;

3 That he had been the victim of a natural mishap and that his body was still in the water

Possibility 1 was thought to be the least likely as it is extremely difficult to get a live swimmer aboard ship without considerable fuss and although our two observers in the boats moored by the pontoons were unsighted, they had heard nothing untoward. There was also the Naval signal tower nearby which overlooked the cruiser.

Possibility 2a was felt to be almost equally unlikely for similar reasons but by no means impossible.

Possibility 2b seemed much the more likely

The press were a little more imaginative in their interpretation of events. The following examples are representative of the diversity of their theories. When reviewing these theories, it should be borne in mind that as Lt Cdr Gutteridge pointed out, the Soviet vessels were under continuous and intense scrutiny throughout their stay: *"There were a good dozen pairs of ears and eyes paying constant attention to the Russian ships."* There were intelligence experts closely scrutinizing every square inch of the three vessels, 24 hours a day, seven days a week.

Theory 1: He was murdered by a Soviet frogman

In November 2007 an ex-Russian frogman named Eduard Koltsov appeared on a Russian TV documentary claiming to have killed Cdr Crabb. He claimed that he caught Cdr Crabb attaching a mine to the side of the cruiser at the location of its ammunition store (or electrical generators room). He attacked him and cut his throat with his diving knife (see Appendix 11).

Retired Soviet frogman Eduard Koltsov and the knife with which he claimed he slit Crabb's throat.

Theory 2: He was shot by a Soviet marksman when he surfaced between the vessels

Don Hale in his book *The Final Dive* described how a Russian Naval Intelligence Officer contacted an Israeli journalist named Igal Sarna in Tel Aviv and told him that one of the crew of the *Ordzhonikidze* saw Cdr Crabb surface and shot him and then his body sank.

Theory 3: He was caught by Soviet frogmen and abducted to Russia

One of the most popular theories is that Cdr Crabb somehow ended up alive and well in Russia. Bernard Hutton first promoted the theory that Cdr Crabb had gone to Russia in his books *Frogman Spy* and *The Fake Defector.* This has also been the theory promulgated by Mike Welham in his books. Once in Russia, Cdr Crabb subsequently joined the Soviet navy under the name of Commander Lev Lvovich Korablov and served at the Frogman Squadron of the Naval Training Command at Kronstadt.

The explanation of how he got to Russia varies but one theory was that Cdr Crabb had been caught near the Soviet cruiser by Soviet frogmen and dragged into an underwater airlock. A naval officer and Petty officer claimed to have seen the struggle on the surface. Cdr Crabb was then imprisoned on the ship and taken back to Russia. He was brainwashed and persuaded to work for the Russian navy.

The *Daily Mail* carried the following item on 30 June 1956:

CRABB 'HELD IN MOSCOW'
Lieut [sic] *Commander Lionel Crabb ace frogman who disappeared during the Soviet leaders' visit to Britain, is Prisoner No. 147 in a Moscow jail, according to a report yesterday in a West German newspaper, Bild Zeitung. A senior Russian naval officer is said to have given the news to a French politician.*

The closest thing to an official Russian government statement on the matter was given in the Russian newspaper *Izvestia* which represents the government views. The article strenuously denied Crabb was in Russia or that he was an officer in the Russian navy.

They accused the British press of a *"disgusting spectacle and fruitless labour … rattling skeletons in the cupboard"*. They further agreed that Cdr Crabb *"perished … while engaged in underwater espionage against the Soviet cruiser Ordzhonikidze"*.

Theory 4: He deliberately boarded the Soviet cruiser to defect

There are two versions of this theory. The first is that Cdr Crabb had become a communist sympathiser and deliberately gave himself up to the Russians on the Soviet cruiser, perhaps entering via an underwater air-lock. He thus defected to Russia and voluntarily offered his services to the Soviets.

This theory was suggested by Sydney Knowles in his book *A Diver in the Dark*.

He had been concerned about Cdr Crabb's association with known Soviet sympathisers, including Sir Anthony Blunt.

The second version is that Cdr Crabb deliberately allowed himself to be captured, as part of a MI6 plot, and taken to Russia where he worked for the Soviet navy. It was then intended that he escaped back to Britain bringing valuable intelligence on Soviet underwater capabilities with him. But for some reason the escape never took place.

Theory 5: Cdr Crabb died aboard the Russian cruiser

A former naval officer has suggested that Cdr Crabb died of respiratory problems after having been taken on board the *Ordzhonikidze*. He was subsequently buried at sea with full military honours.

Sir Anthony Blunt

A picture purporting to show Cdr Crabb as a serving officer in the Soviet navy.

Theory 6: The body found in Chichester harbour had been dumped from a Soviet submarine

J Bernard Hutton described in his book *The Fake Defector* how the Russians prepared a body, allowed it to decompose for over a year and then released it from a Soviet submarine off the entrance to Chichester harbour on 6 June 1957, on its way to Egypt. The purpose was to deflect suspicion that Cdr Crabb was still alive and secretly working for the Russians.

Theory 7: He was killed by an SBS diver

Sydney Knowles proposed this theory in his book *A Diver in the Dark* in 2009. He stated that an SBS diver had been sent to kill Cdr Crabb during the mission to eliminate him as a liability

to the government. He further theorised that the assassination went wrong. The two frogmen killed each other and the two bodies which were fished up in Chichester harbour were those of Cdr Crabb and the SBS diver.

Theory 8: He was killed by the Israeli secret service Mossad

Cdr Crabb had worked in Haifa, Palestine, between 1945 and 1947. A militant Zionist group Irgun was attacking British police launches and Commander Crabb was detailed to establish another Underwater Working Party similar to the one he had worked with in Gibraltar and Italy during WW2. Mossad agents, in an act of revenge, had tampered with Cdr Crabb's breathing set which resulted in his death.

A photo taken in Haifa during Cdr Crabb's operations there, along with his diving team.

Theory 9: Soviet spies had tampered with Cdr Crabb's breathing set

A similar theory was proposed by Don Hale in his book *The Final Dive* whereby Soviet spies had tampered with Cdr Crabb's breathing set.

Theory 10: Cdr Crabb died on the steps of King's Stairs

A naval officer has stated that Cdr Crabb returned from his dive to King's Stairs (from where he said he had set off) in an exhausted condition and died in his arms.

Theory 11: Cdr Crabb was electrocuted by steel netting under the Russian ships

Theory 12: Cdr Crabb died because of an accidental malfunction of his breathing apparatus

There are several possible modes of failure of any closed-circuit oxygen breathing apparatus with life-threatening consequences. One such mode of failure was if the Protosorb chemical filling was not correctly packed when the canister was freshly charged, 'channelling' could occur. This is when a proportion of the expired gas would pass directly through the canister without passing through the Protosorb granules and thus fail to have the carbon dioxide removed completely. This could lead to a dangerous carbon dioxide build-up in the breathing circuit which can poison the diver.

Another mode of failure with the single breathing hose arrangement was a "soda-lime cocktail" caused by water entering the Protosorb canister. A highly caustic foam is produced which expands up the breathing hose into the mouth. The result is painful chemical burns and renders the breathing apparatus unusable, with possible fatal results.

Theory 13: Cdr Crabb was struck by a berthing oil tanker

Not so much a conspiracy theory, but an alternative theory.

A small oil tanker or "oiler" boat (No C653) routinely came and berthed alongside the "oil wall" at the end of South Railway Jetty, along which Cdr Crabb made his dive on the morning of 19 April. The vessel normally carried a cargo of 80 tons of lubricating oil to be pumped ashore. The tide was ebbing strongly at the time and the vessel's captain had to make three attempts to come alongside. He was not helped by the fact that there were no jetty men ashore to assist by taking his lines. During one of these attempts, the Chief Engineer Ken Kirkbride down in the engine room, heard a dull *"thud"* as if the propeller had struck something solid. He was so concerned about possible damage to the propeller that he went along to the Piermaster's office at King's Stairs to request a diver survey.

He was surprised to see an office crowded with agitated officials including Chief Constable West and *"MI5 men"* in civilian clothes. He and the rest of the crew were sworn to secrecy and required to sign the Official Secrets Act before being sent on their way again. They were ordered to log they had been to Portland and not to Portsmouth.

The oiler C653 which tied up near the stern of the *Ordzhonikidze*.

The theory was subsequently developed that the "thud" had been caused by Cdr Crabb being accidentally struck by the oiler's propeller. However, Crabb would not have been present when the tide was running strongly.

This is by no means an exhaustive list of the conspiracy theories. However, they serve to illustrate the thriving range and extent of creative thinking behind their generation, all resulting directly from the government's inexplicable secrecy. The continued cloak of secrecy imposed by the government guarantees that they will continue to enjoy popular debate.

So could any of the above theories be true? One incontrovertible fact is that most, if not all, cannot be true. The protagonists might be accused of being overly creative or perhaps less than honest.

The following sections attempt to provide as near a factual account as possible. The reader may then be in a better position to form his/her own opinion and to judge how reasonable the author's conclusions may be in comparison with the conspiracy theories. In the meantime, the continued secrecy will undoubtedly fuel our speculation.

The Commander Crabb/MI6 diving operation

To avoid tedious repetition, the word 'allegedly' should be assumed to be used in most of the sentences below. The times of day quoted are all British Summer Time where appropriate. While the title "Secret Intelligence Service" (SIS) is the official title, the older title "Military Intelligence, Section 6" (MI6) is used throughout.

On 22 February 1956 a meeting was held at the Admiralty to discuss the rare opportunity for intelligence procurement presented by Russian naval visits to Western European ports. Shortly after this meeting, MI6 received a copy of the brief supplied by the Admiralty showing exactly what it was they wanted which frogmen could acquire on their behalf.

In mid-March 1956, another meeting was held at the Admiralty about intelligence operations to be carried out against the Russian warships scheduled to visit Portsmouth, and specifically addressed the use of frogmen. NID were not willing at this stage to allow official naval frogmen to carry out the operation, though the Admiralty stated their readiness to give unofficial facilities. This left MI6 with no alternative but to undertake the task themselves and to employ Cdr Crabb whom the Admiralty had already recommended for the operation. Cdr Edward 'Ted' Davies, who headed the MI6 Naval Liaison Unit, attended the meeting. He had been employed in MI6 since during the war. Davies sent Bernard Smith off to approach Cdr Crabb about the dive just as he had done for the *Sverdlov* operation in October the previous year.

Also in March 1956 Cdr Crabb was invited to a meeting at Cowdray Park near Midhurst, West Sussex, attended by the First Sea Lord (1954–1959), Admiral of the Fleet, The Earl Mountbatten of Burma. The latter was himself not only a keen polo player but also a very keen diver. It has been suggested that he had taken a personal interest in Cdr Crabb's exploits as early as during his Gibraltar days and had been responsible for Cdr Crabb's onward progress to Italy.

The Mountbatten connection was also raised in the *Daily Mail*:

There is no doubt whatever that he was frequently on secret missions. He worked at the Spithead Review when the Sverdlov was there, and did a special mission in the Canal Zone. The results of this he took straight to Lord Louis Mountbatten. Crabb walked off the plane, got in a car and saw Lord Louis after a polo match at Cowdray Park.

The Mountbatten connection becomes a little murkier with assertions that he himself had come under the influence of the KGB. Peter Wright wrote in his book *Spycatcher* that a defected senior KGB officer:

[Yuri] *Nossenko soon gave a priceless lead in the hunt for the British Naval spies. He claimed that the Gribinov recruitment had been obtained through homosexual blackmail, and that the agent had provided the KGB with "all NATO" secrets from a "Lord of the Navy."*

Neither was Mountbatten's military reputation entirely unblemished. Field Marshal Lord Alanbrooke wrote of him:

… seldom has a Supreme Commander been more deficient in the main attributes of a Supreme Commander than Dickie Mountbatten … and with the possible exception of Montgomery he was the most talented self-publicist among the senior British Commanders.

Cowdray House at Cowdray Park as it looks today and where it is alleged Commander Crabb had a meeting with Admiral Mountbatten.

Immediately following the Royal Navy dive under the Soviet ships for Naval Intelligence (see below), Mountbatten interviewed Lt Cdr Joe Brooks on two occasions. So there is a strong case for Mountbatten's close association with the spying missions.

Returning to Crabb's involvement, Sir Edward Bridges confirmed that Cdr Crabb was approached around mid-March to see if he would be willing to carry out the diving operation. He recorded:

Mr Smith got in touch with Commander Crabb at about this time [mid-March] to see if he was willing to carry out an operation against the Soviet cruiser bringing B and K to Portsmouth.

Nicholas Elliott of MI6 has stated, *"… he [Cdr Crabb] begged to be allowed to do the job for patriotic as well as personal motives. There was no discussion of finance."* Elliott was Head of the London Station. Davies worked for Elliott as Head of Naval Liaison in Section R3 in Vauxhall Bridge Road, London and he was responsible for several MI6 operations in

Admiral Mountbatten inspects a Royal Navy Clearance Diver.

Portsmouth during the Soviet visit. As Case Officer for Cdr Crabb's operation, he assigned Bernard Smith to directly supervise Crabb. Cdr Crabb had worked for both Davies and Smith on the *Sverdlov* operation in October the previous year. Bernard Smith, a tall, fair-haired 36 year-old, was a *"Temporary Foreign Office Official"* who had been employed by MI6 since 1950.

Smith decided that the most discreet method by which he could approach Cdr Crabb would be by purchasing two tables from him, at Elmbourne Ltd in 124 Seymour Place, London, where Crabb worked with Maitland Pendock. He first placed the order by telephone and then went around to collect them personally. Cdr Crabb issued him with an invoice for £4.18.6 for the two tables, which included a 10% discount. Smith gave Cdr Crabb his cheque made out to Elmbourne Ltd.

Cdr Crabb later discovered that Smith had entered the wrong date on the cheque (1955 instead of 1956) and that it needed to be corrected by Smith. He told Pendock that he would be seeing Smith in Portsmouth shortly and he would get it corrected there. He added that he expected to be back in London by Friday (20 April).

Smith explained that his reasoning for approaching Cdr Crabb in this way was so that if they were seen together by any friends he would have a cover story for explaining their relationship. This was later criticised as poor *"trade craft"*.

Cdr Crabb subsequently accepted the commission to undertake a dive under the Soviet cruiser. While no fee was discussed at the early stages, a fee of £100 was later agreed. This is roughly equivalent to a little over £2,000 in today's purchasing power. The Admiralty had a 'slush fund' for such discreet payments, the "£1000 Fund". W R Lewin (the Head of Naval Law Branch at the Admiralty) minuted on 3 July 1956: *"The sum of £100 had been promised to Commander Crabb as payment for the work in the course of which he is presumed to have been drowned"*. Smith telephoned Cdr Crabb and asked him to hold himself free to carry out the operation on 17 and 18 April.

Monday, 16 April 1956

The date of the planned operation was fast approaching.

Crabb appears to have spent his last days in London doing a circuit of old friends. Mike Borrow related a story that on the morning of the 16th April, Cdr Crabb called in to see him at his office on the second floor, 91 Regent Street, London where they chatted over a cup of coffee. At that time Borrow was working as the Sales Manager of P Frankenstein & Sons Ltd, a division of Beaufort (Air-Sea) Equipment Ltd, which produced Safety, Escape and Survival gear for submarine and high altitude applications. As lunchtime approached, they walked round to Chez Marcel's drinking club, opposite the New Theatre at 38a St Martin's Lane. This was a candle-lit, upstairs club that had become popular for some time with bomb and mine disposal personnel when in London. Borrow said that they never discussed Cdr Crabb's diving projects and he had assumed that Crabb was then simply selling furniture and fittings to new coffee bars on a commission basis (see Appendix 3).

Perhaps the reason he happened to call in on Mike Borrow in Regent Street was because that morning he had been into the nearby BBC studios to discuss a programme he had recorded earlier for children about underwater history.

Mike Borrow of P Frankenstein & Sons Ltd who Commander Crabb met socially before leaving for Portsmouth.

Later that day the arrangements in Portsmouth were confirmed. Smith telephoned Cdr Crabb and told him to meet him at midday the following day in the Bag O' Nails pub in Buckingham Palace Road. He would then drive them both to Portsmouth where they would meet Cdr Ted Davies of MI6 in The Keppel's Head Hotel at 17.00 hours.

Cdr Crabb wrote a brief note to his mother in Oxfordshire:

I am going on a job ... but it is a simple mission ... you are not to worry ... I'll be back in about two days' time. Please tear this letter up.

In an amazing breach of security, he reportedly told his friends he was *"going down to take a dekko at the Russian bottoms."*

On the same day, MI5 contacted the Police in Portsmouth to let them know that Cdr Ted Davies would be calling in to see them the next day and he would require their assistance.

Tuesday, 17 April 1956

MI6 approached Naval Intelligence Division (NID) to ask for the name of an officer to assist Cdr Crabb on the diving operation. NID obliged but on the understanding that:

a) he would be approached privately and unofficially by MI6.

b) his role would be limited to giving advice and playing a passive part.

c) that on no account whatsoever was he to be asked to dive.

Lieut. Commander Franklin's name and home address was given.

It is surprising that such important details had been left until the last moment before being settled. NID insisted that MI6 made the approach to Lt Cdr George Albert 'Frankie' Franklin who was the senior Clearance Diver at the Diving School based on HMS *Deepwater*, permanently berthed at HMS *Vernon*. NID did however assist by providing security passes for Smith, Franklin and Crabb to enter the Dockyard.

Cdr Ted Davies arrived in Portsmouth early in the morning. He established a joint office with NID Liaison Officer Cdr Forbes in the Signal Tower in the Dockyard and, with the assistance of MI5, a separate one with the Chief Constable West and Detective Superintendent Lamport at the Central Police Station in St Michael's Vicarage. Lamport was assigned as the liaison officer with the Davies/Smith/Crabb team and a scrambler telephone was installed in their office at the police station.

The same morning, Cdr Crabb said goodbye to Miss Amy Thomas, the manageress of the apartments at 2a Hans Road saying he would be back in a few days. He made his way to the Bag O' Nails pub and there met up with Smith at mid-day as arranged. After a liquid lunch, they went around the corner to Ebury Street where Smith had parked his (service) car *"with the gear"*. The *"gear"* presumably included Cdr Crabb's diving drysuit and fins. The frogman's oxygen breathing equipment was to be collected in Portsmouth. They drove to Portsmouth and arrived at about 16.30 hours.

They were not scheduled to meet up with Davies at the Keppel's Head Hotel on The Hard until 17.00 hours, so Cdr Crabb suggested they called in to HMS *Vernon* and look up some of his old friends there. They had a cup of tea (?) in the Officers' Mess. Crabb introduced *"my friend Smith"* to his colleagues and explained *"he was now in the furniture business"*. After about half an hour, Cdr Crabb and Smith left for the Keppel's Head and met up with Davies at around 17.30 hours.

They discussed the arrangements for the diving operation including the part that Lt Cdr Franklin of the Diving School in HMS *Vernon* was to play in assisting Crabb with his equipment and to get dressed into his diving suit. Following the discussion at the Keppel's Head, Davies went and checked in to the Gloucester Hotel, in St George's Road.

After their meeting with Davies, Crabb and Smith went to meet Chief Constable Arthur Charles West OBE KPM at the Portsmouth City Police Headquarters in Byculla House, Southsea, a mock Tudor mansion on the corner of Kent Road and Queens Road. It was also the headquarters for the South West Traffic Area. West was in charge of all the security arrangements for the Soviet visitors outside the naval Dockyard.

The Bag O' Nails public house in Buckingham Palace Road where Cdr Crabb and Bernard Smith met up before driving to Portsmouth.

The liaison between MI6 (Cdr Ted Davies and Smith) with Portsmouth City Police had been facilitated by MI5 and this was the limit of MI5's involvement in the operation.

From Byculla House, Crabb and Smith went to the City Central Police Station in St Michael's Vicarage in St Michael's Road, Southsea, the home of Portsmouth "A" Division. This was where Smith's boss, Cdr Ted Davies had set up a temporary office.

Having established their main contacts in Portsmouth, Crabb and Smith drove to the Sally Port Hotel in Old Portsmouth and checked in. They checked in with *"light luggage"*. The owner, Mr Edward Richman checked them in to single rooms 17 and 20 on the top floor, with Cdr Crabb taking the latter, the larger of the two. The key fob for room 20 which Crabb had used was retained as a memento by the owner before selling on the hotel some years later. Smith booked his room for two nights while Cdr Crabb said he would be staying for one or perhaps two nights. They both signed the hotel register with their true names and correct addresses with Smith giving his address as *"Attached Foreign Office"*. This inscription was to lead to an embarrassing issue later in the proceedings as a lapse in *"trade craft"*.

From there, Cdr Crabb telephoned his employer Pendock and then Lt Cdr Franklin. Franklin had previously agreed to assist Cdr Crabb and he had already been nominated by MI6 as the most suitable candidate for the task. Franklin agreed to meet Cdr Crabb at the "Country House" pub in Commercial

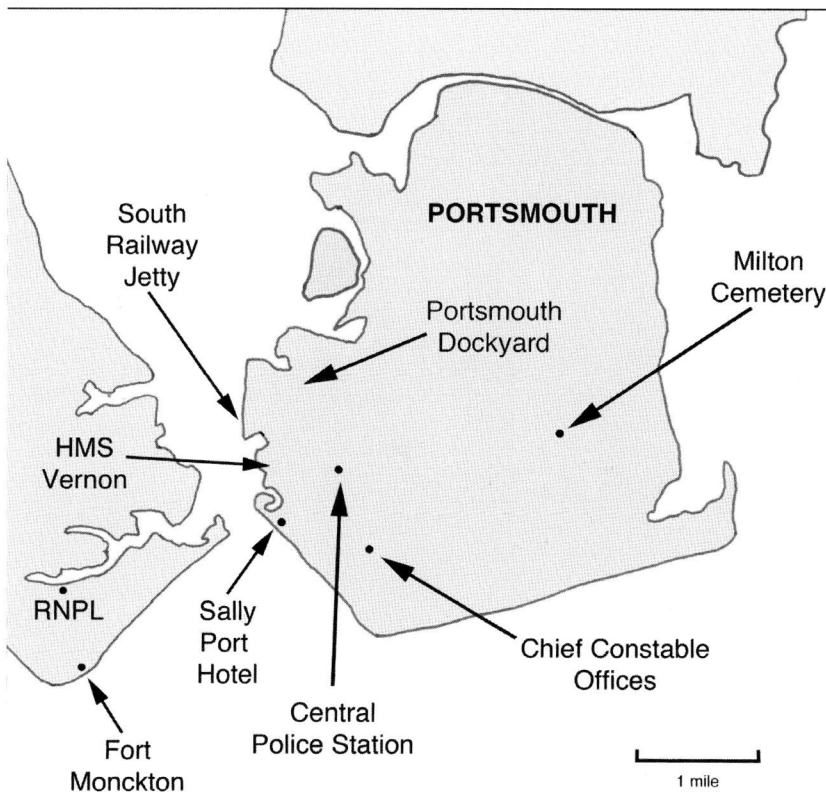

Map of the principal locations around Portsmouth.

Chief Constable Arthur Charles West
OBE KPM of the
Portsmouth City Police.

Portsmouth City Central Police Station in St Michael's Vicarage
in St Michael's Road, Southsea.

Portsmouth City Police Headquarters in Byculla House, Southsea.

Road, Portsmouth to discuss the operation. A police driver took them to the pub. This was PC 131, Police Constable John Victor Edwards, a former Regimental Sergeant Major in the army who was the senior driver and driving instructor at Portsmouth Central Police Station and who was provided with a Riley RMB fast patrol car.

At the pub they met up with Lt Cdr Franklin. It was near the Pitt Street swimming baths where Cdr Crabb had often joined his naval colleagues for training sessions before retiring to *"Martha's bar"*.

Over drinks, Cdr Crabb discussed with Franklin the assistance he needed with his dive the following day. In a later statement to the Admiralty, Franklin said he was asked whether (the author's underlining):

… I would be prepared to assist him entirely unofficially and in a strictly private capacity in connection with a dive he was undertaking a day or two later, the nature of which was not

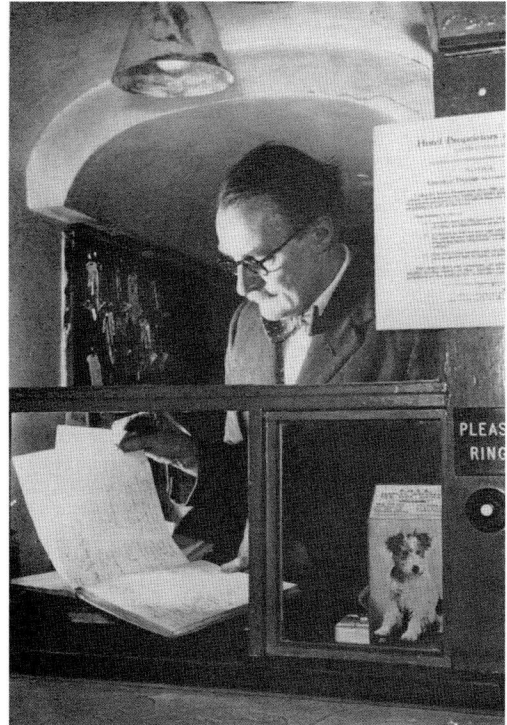

Above left: The Sally Port Hotel in the High Street, Portsmouth. Cdr Crabb's room was number 20, in the attic, top left in the photograph.

Above right: Mr Edward Richman, owner of the Sally Port Hotel inspecting the Visitor's Register.

Right: The key fob for room 20 at the Sally Port Hotel which Cdr Crabb used. It is presently on display at the Diving Museum in Gosport.

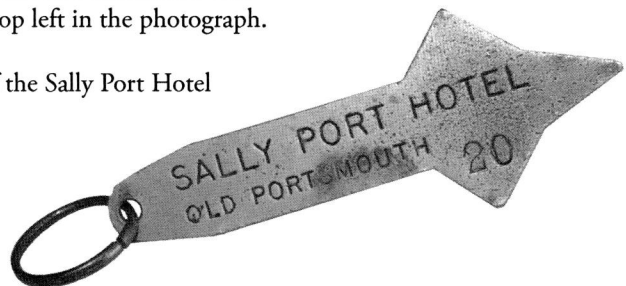

disclosed to me, and I was told by Commander Crabb that on no account was I to inform any responsible Naval Authority; I agreed on <u>my own responsibility.</u>

Franklin's statement was heavily influenced by W A Lewin, Assistant Head of Naval Law at the Admiralty. It was clearly the intention that Franklin emphasised his participation as being entirely unofficial and outside his naval duties. The Admiralty initially needed to demonstrate very clearly that they were not involved in the Cdr Crabb/MI6 operation. However, they were not entirely uninvolved. A note to the Prime Minister dated 8 June 1956 stated:

It is clear that the frogman operation was never regarded in the Admiralty as a naval responsibility and the Admiralty's concern with it was limited from the outset to providing "unofficial facilities" such as access to the dockyard.

The *"unofficial facilities"* would have also included the use of HMS *Maidstone's* launches and the use of a Royal Navy oxygen breathing set (see below and Appendix 8). *Maidstone* was also used as a Shallow Water Diver training school. The diving instructor was PO Riley and the team was headed by A Lewis. Senior MI6 officers, including Cdr Ted Davies had been assured at a meeting in the Admiralty in Mid-March that *"… the Admiralty were ready to give their unofficial facilities."*

During the debate in Parliament on 14 May 1956 on The Case of Commander Crabb, Mr John Dugdale MP stated:

Commander Crabb asked to borrow equipment from HMS Vernon and he was refused. It was said there: 'We shall not lend you the equipment'. Obviously, he wanted accommodation of the most convenient character, and, naturally, he would have stayed in an Admiralty establishment … but the Admiralty did not want him to do so and the

Commander-in-Chief, Portsmouth, did not want him to. So he had to resort to this extraordinary business of staying in an hotel, and signing the register, while his companion signed it with the wrong name."

This confirms that knowledge of Cdr Crabb's planned diving operation existed in the Admiralty at least up to the level of the C-in-C, Portsmouth, Admiral of the Fleet Sir George E Creasy. The statement contains at least one error in that Cdr Crabb's MI6 *"companion"* did indeed sign the register with his correct name, Bernard Smith (as well as giving his address as *"Foreign Office"*). The reference to the refusal to lend Cdr Crabb any naval equipment adds to the mystery as to what breathing equipment he ultimately used. There is strong evidence that he did actually use the contemporary RN frogman's oxygen rebreather equipment and it almost certainly came from HMS *Deepwater*/ HMS *Vernon* (see below).

Wednesday, 18 April 1956

Cdr Crabb and Smith breakfasted together at the Sally Port Hotel.

On schedule, at around 10.45 hours in the morning, the Soviet cruiser *Ordzhonikidze* accompanied by two destroyers, the *Sovershenny* and the *Smotryashchy* arrived at the Outer Spit Buoy, just outside Portsmouth Harbour at the start of their ten-day visit. One at a time, they proceeded slowly into the harbour, passing through the narrow entrance shortly before 11.00 hours. The tide was slack; low water was at 11.10 hours. On the bridge of the *Ordzhonikidze* stood Captain Adrian Paul Northey RN, liaison officer on behalf of the Admiralty.

The *Ordzhonikidze* was the first to tie up at the South Railway Jetty, starboard side on, with

Police Constable John Victor Edwards, PC 131, who drove Cdr Crabb around Portsmouth.

Police Constable John Edwards with his Riley RMB fast patrol car.

Lt Cdr George Albert 'Frankie' Franklin (pictured while a Lieutenant) the Senior Diving Instructor on HMS *Deepwater*.

The Country House pub where Cdr Crabb met up with Lt Cdr Franklin.

her bow pointing to the north. It was followed at ten-minute intervals, first by the *Sovershenny* and then the *Smotryashchy* which tied up alongside the cruiser. The *Ordzhonikidze* was 210 metres long and (importantly) had a draft of 6.9 metres (23 feet). It occupied the entire length of the South Railway Jetty. Just ahead and to the north of the Soviet vessels, the Royal Navy aircraft carrier, HMS *Bulwark* was berthed, at Pitch House jetty.

Amid extremely tight security, at precisely 11.50 hours, Bulganin and Khrushchev disembarked and a 19-gun salute was fired from HMS *Bulwark*. They were driven the short distance out of the Dockyard, past the Keppel's Head Hotel to Portsmouth Harbour Railway Station where they boarded their special train for London, departing promptly at 12.15 hours. Following their departure security arrangements in the Dockyard were significantly relaxed.

Cdr Crabb had originally intended to carry out his dive that morning. But because of the intense security precautions while Khruschev and Bulganin were still on board the *Ordzhonikidze*, Crabb had decided he could

not have carried out the dive without serious risk of being detected. The heightened security was in place to cover the transfer arrangements for Khruschev and Bulganin from the ship to the railway station, on their way to London to meet the Prime Minister. A Royal Navy helicopter had circled above the Soviet warships. Police numbers in the Dockyard had been considerably strengthened. Outside the Dockyard, police had lined the short route to the railway station.

Despite the high security, Cdr Davies, Smith, Cdr Crabb and Lt Cdr Franklin did manage to reconnoitre the area and layout of boats in the Boat Pound and Soviet ships from a distance. They would very likely have been able to gain access to the Harbour Railway Station to accomplish this, though the station was closed to the public. From there, they would also have been able to watch as the Soviet vessels entered the harbour and tied up at the South Railway Jetty.

With some time to kill until the next slack water in the evening, Cdr Crabb spent the morning strolling around the park and *"having the odd drink"*. At least one of his

Bulganin and Khrushchev arrive outside Portsmouth Harbour Railway Station to board their special train to London.
Another 'unofficial' but rare photo.

Above:
The cruiser *Ordzhonikidze* just off Southsea on its way into Portsmouth harbour.

Right:
The cruiser *Ordzhonikidze* edges its way into Portsmouth harbour. Very much an 'unofficial' photo but useful because it shows the small group at the Harbour Railway station/Gosport ferry. Was Crabb one of the onlookers in this picture and was the black car the police car he was using?

Below right:
The cruiser *Ordzhonikidze* with the two destroyers, the *Sovershenny* and *Smotryashchie* alongside. Note the presence of the oiler tied up at the south end of the jetty.

The Coal Exchange pub where Cdr Crabb had a drink and viewed the Soviet ships from the window (arrowed).

The view from where Cdr Crabb sat at the window in the Coal Exchange.

drinks was in the Coal Exchange pub in Old Portsmouth (today called the Spice Islands). When interviewed by the press, the wife of the Landlord, Mrs Greta Fennell, stated *"He sat by himself ... like a man with a mission on his mind."* He was in the tiny upstairs bar at the window which gave him a clear view northwards, up the harbour and of the Soviet warships. He never mentioned meeting any acquaintances to Smith during this period. Smith himself "spent the morning at an SIS Training Establishment nearby". This was Fort Monckton in Gosport, on the other side of Portsmouth Harbour (see Appendix 9).

Cdr Crabb scribbled a short note to his publishers, probably referring to the unexpected change of plan, which he mailed later that day:

The hastily written note sent by Cdr Crabb to his publishers while at Portsmouth.

> *From L K P Crabb*
> *Thank you for a very delightful lunch and break.*
> *Marshall tells me that the photo is to come back.*
> *Lots of trouble here. Chaos Complete.*
> *L K P Crabb*

The *"trouble"* and *"chaos"* were undoubtedly the burdensome restrictions on movement inside and around the Dockyard enforced by the high security arrangements while the two Soviet leaders were still on board the *Ordzhonikidze*.

He also wrote a short note to an old friend who had sent him a letter reminding him he still owed him £20[2]. This was Sir Francis Cyril Rose, 46 years old, a well-known artist and homosexual who was then living in Paris and who many years previously had presented Crabb with his treasured sword stick (Appendix 2). The note simply said:

I'll be in clover the first of the month. I've sold my invention.

The cryptic reference to an *"invention"* presumably was a cover story for the £100 payment for his diving operation from MI6. He was late posting the note because it did not leave Portsmouth until the following day and was postmarked 19 April.

The Diving School based on board HMS *Deepwater* at HMS *Vernon* shore establishment remained operational throughout this period. A Shallow Water Diving course (involving the use of oxygen rebreathers) was underway with three

---

2   On 16 June 1956 it was reported that an American visited Sir Francis in Paris and paid the debt off with a cheque and then went on his way to the USA. It would have been in the interest of MI6 to pay off Cdr Crabb's debts but the apparent involvement of an American is curious. Perhaps it was Bernard Smith. Like many of Crabb's friends and associates, Sir Francis was a complex character. Cecil Beaton was quoted as saying, "[Francis Rose] *is a man who causes such extraordinary violence around him. His life story is a long succession of suicides, killings, fatal accidents. In his wake he brings chaos."*

trainees under the instruction of Petty Officer F W Brady and Officer-in-Charge Lt 'Barry' Barrington. The course had commenced on 9 April and concluded on 27 April. This should not have had any impact on the activities in the Dockyard as the training facilities at Horsea Island and HMS *Vernon* were all that were needed. A report suggested that Crabb visited the Admiralty Experimental Diving Unit (AEDU, Appendix 6) at HMS *Vernon* sometime on Wednesday, 18 April, where he met Mary Barnett, the Clerical Officer. They were old friends and it was alleged that Barnett assisted with the arrangements for providing Crabb with his oxygen breathing set.

The attempt to carry out the dive was scheduled to be around high water slack tide at 18.35 hours. Accordingly, Cdr Crabb and Smith collected Lt Cdr Franklin from his apartment at 36 Southsea Terrace and drove to the Dockyard. Two launches from HMS *Maidstone* were tied up abreast at a row of marina-style pontoons comprising a boat pound immediately inside the Dockyard main gates. The participation of *Maidstone's* launches has not yet been officially admitted by the authorities.

Commander Crabb had previously noticed that the launch needed a canvas awning rigged to conceal him while on board. This should have been predicted much earlier but it had been

Mary Barnett, the Clerical Officer at AEDU in HMS *Vernon*.

Graph to show the relationship between the times of Cdr Crabb's dives and tides.

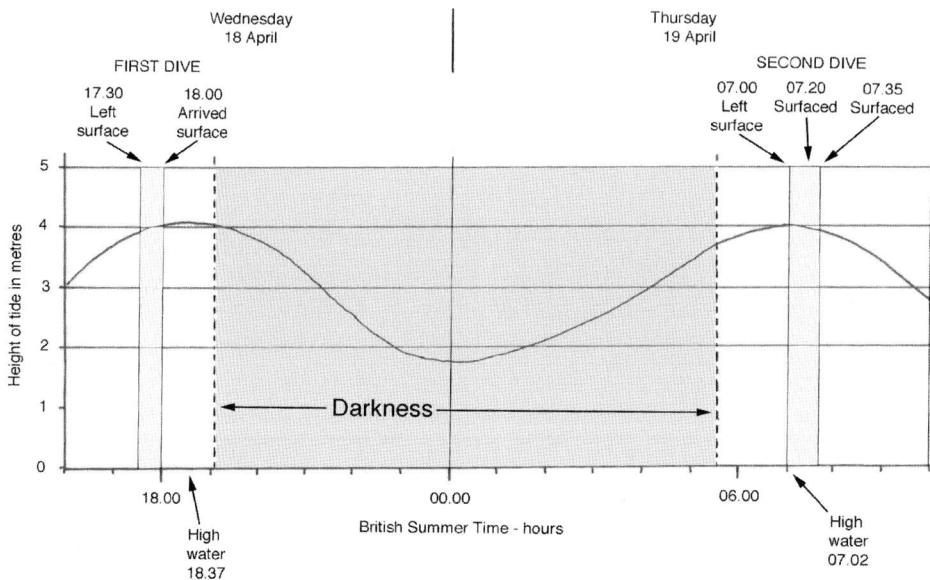

HMS *Maidstone* tied up at the South Railway Jetty shortly after the Soviet vessels had left. Note HMS *Bulwark* just ahead of her and one of *Maidstone's* launches appears to be alongside the jetty wall.

overlooked. In the event, Davies paid two Dockyard mateys to rig the awnings for a fee of £1 each. This exercise was to be criticised later by MI6 as another example of poor trade craft.

The disclosures from the National Archives in October 2015 included a crude sketch produced by MI6 indicating the path taken by Cdr Crabb, Smith and Franklin to the boat from which Commander Crabb dived and from there to the Soviet cruiser. The sketch is very poor from the point of view of geography and scale. The aerial photograph of the Boat Pound illustrates the actual layout of the pontoons around the time of the incident. The presumed location of the dive launch is arrowed. At the time of Commander Crabb's dive,

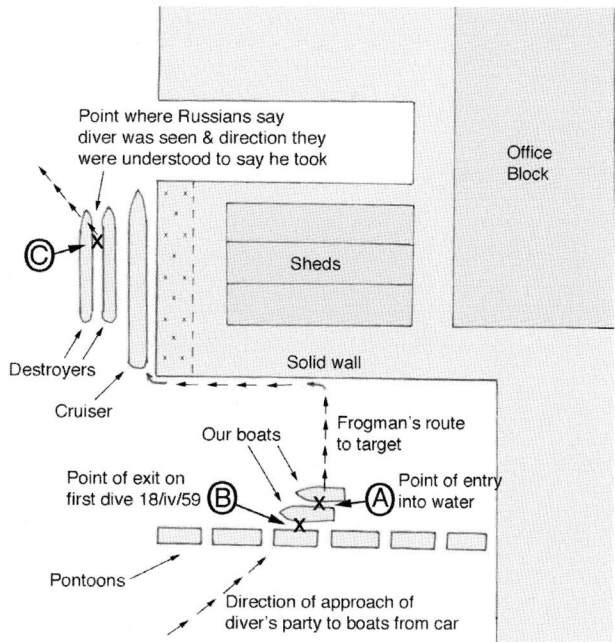

Redrawn sketch presumed to have been produced by MI6 to indicate the route followed by Commander Crabb from HMS *Maidstone's* launch to the Soviet cruiser.

there would also have been a disused railway viaduct drawn by a curving line on the aerial photograph. It was removed completely four years after Crabb's dive, in 1960.

One of the notes on the MI6 sketch states *"Direction of approach of diver's party to boats from car"*. Taken together with the arrows this is a strange piece of information. As can be seen from the aerial photograph, the expected approach would have been to enter at the Dockyard entrance, turn left to access the pontoons and right to head for the dive boat. It can only be assumed that whoever drew the sketch had only a very cursory knowledge of the area and drew it from a faded memory.

The time had come for Crabb to commence his dive. First, Franklin lowered a weighted shot line over the side, between the two launches. This was to assist Cdr Crabb's water entry and exit. He then assisted Cdr Crabb to dress into his Heinke Delta two-piece dry suit, Admiralty fins and oxygen breathing equipment in the launch. Franklin later confided to friends that Cdr Crabb was seriously unfit at the time. He even got out of breath while just dressing into his kit. This was contrary to what he said in an official statement. Cdr Crabb climbed over the side and disappeared underwater between the two boats at 17.30 hours. He followed the shot line to the sea bed some five metres below

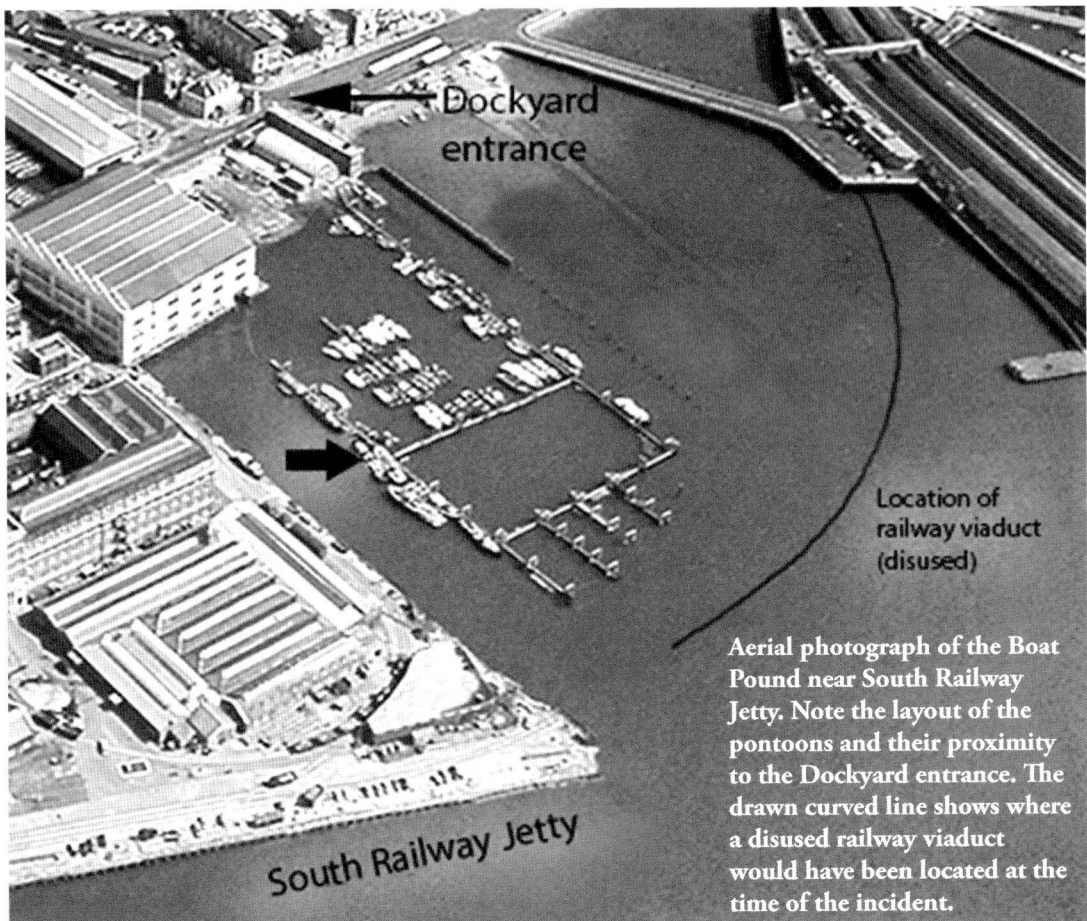

Aerial photograph of the Boat Pound near South Railway Jetty. Note the layout of the pontoons and their proximity to the Dockyard entrance. The drawn curved line shows where a disused railway viaduct would have been located at the time of the incident.

and headed due north about 25 metres until he bumped into the south wall of the South Railway Jetty. Turning to his left, he then swam about 100 metres along the side of the jetty until he reached the pilings.

This swim would have been carried out in total darkness and zero visibility so he would have been feeling his way, hand over hand, along the wall. Navigating the next 20 metres through the complex network of pilings would have been a particularly challenging exercise, especially so because of the presence of debris on the sea bed.

Things did not go according to plan.

At 18.00 hours approximately, Cdr Crabb reappeared at the surface between the inner launch and the pontoon. Franklin assisted him back on board. The dive had been abortive. Cdr Crabb had not got any further than the end of the jetty before having to turn back. He complained that he did not have sufficient lead weights and needed to add some before attempting another dive. Sir Edward Bridges recorded:

He had cut his hand and said that he had experienced a certain amount of trouble in getting his bearings, having got caught up in the piling of the jetty. He was however confident that he would be all right the next time. Before diving, there had been some doubt about his fitness as he had not done any diving for about six months. [Namely on his *Sverdlov* operation] *However Franklin was agreeably surprised to note that he had used comparatively little oxygen and appeared to be in good trim.*

Franklin's statement that Crabb *"appeared to be in good trim"* conflicts with his later private assertions. Perhaps this was simply an attempt to avoid embarrassment amongst the officials.

In the author's view, apart from the difficulties of navigating through the piled structure in zero visibility, the pilings themselves would not have presented a significant problem. However, there was a considerable amount of debris amongst the pilings which presented a serious snagging hazard, particularly in zero visibility. Crabb

The piling structure of South Railway jetty as seen today.

had undoubtedly cut his hand while trying to feel his way through the rusting and sharp-edged debris. The Admiralty were well aware of this and in a note following the incident addressing the problem of searching for Cdr Crabb's body, declared that:

> ... *an inspection of the space under the jetty* [by divers] *would be a dangerous operation because of obstructions, wire ropes, old anchors etc.*

These would have certainly been a problem for a diver operating in poor visibility conditions.

Assuming Cdr Crabb intended to use the same oxygen breathing set the following day, someone had to supply fresh cylinders or refill the used cylinders using a hand-pump that evening as well as placing a fresh charge of Protosorb in the cannister. That could have been done conveniently back on HMS *Deepwater* at HMS *Vernon* through Franklin's connections or aboard HMS *Maidstone* in the Dockyard.

At around 18.00 hours that same evening, John Towse, a young civilian technician working at the Admiralty Experimental Works in Gosport, happened to be crossing the harbour on the Gosport ferry on his way to night school in Portsmouth. It was dusk and he noticed activity on the sterns of the cruiser and two destroyers where groups of sailors assembled and shone powerful torches down and pointed down into the water. The local newspaper corroborated the incident:

> *Miniature searchlights blazed out over Portsmouth Harbour Wednesday from the sterns of the Soviet vessels ... they lit up the waters immediately to the rear of the three warships .... search-lights blazed from the sterns of the three ships as they lay at the South Railway Jetty ... The lights did not range about but were concentrated at the rear of the three vessels.*

John Towse who saw the Soviet sailors using powerful torches at the sterns of the vessels.

The *Sunday Dispatch* carried a similar report:

> *The night the Russian cruiser arrived floodlights over the stern covered the water where a frogman would be if he were trying to inspect the cruiser's screws that are said to drive her at a phenomenal speed. By day, Russian divers were seen round the ship.*

This strongly suggests that the Russians had detected suspicious activity near the stern of the cruiser. It is quite possible that Cdr Crabb's under-weighting problem had caused him to momentarily rise too close to the surface in amongst the piling. However, no positive sighting was reported by the Russians.

Back at HMS *Vernon*, after having made arrangements for meeting up with Franklin early the following morning, Cdr Crabb and Smith parted company at about 19.00 hours. Smith returned to the MI6 Training Establishment

Lt Crawford pictured in 1950 at Tobermory.

Senior Commissioned Boatswain Edward William 'Lofty' Gordon. He probably provided Cdr Crabb with his oxygen breathing set from the Diving Store at HMS *Vernon*

at Fort Monckton. Leaving Crabb to his own devices and to socialise with friends was later criticized as another lapse in trade craft.

Sometime that evening, Cdr Crabb telephoned his employer back in London, Maitland Pendock as arranged and declared *"Well, I'm not as old as I thought."*

That same evening, Cdr Crabb is said to have caught a train to Havant. He called in at the Bear Hotel and met up with his old friend Lt Cdr John 'Jock' Crawford and his wife Daphne. Crawford had been the first to be trained up as a Clearance Diver (CD) at HMS *Lochinvar*, South Queensferry, Scotland by Lt Gordon Gutteridge and Cdr Bob Harland before he moved to *Vernon* and established the

CD school there. At this time, he was attached to the Harwich Staff of NID. They were joined by Senior Commissioned Boatswain Edward William 'Lofty' Gordon, another diver of 'the old school'. He was fair-haired and spoke with a cultured Scottish accent. He stood six feet four inches tall and weighed in at 14.5-stone. He had been one of the first divers to go over to France after D-Day with the P-Parties to help clear the ports of German mines. At the time of Crabb's dive he was then reportedly in charge of the diving equipment store at HMS *Vernon* and lived in Drayton at the north end of Portsmouth. He was coming up for retirement, after which he took up the job as a postman in Havant. Crawford and Gordon are most likely

The Bear Hotel in Havant as it is today. Crabb had drinks with Lt Cdr Jock Crawford and Senior Commissioned Boatswain Lofty Gordon there on the evening of 18 April 1956.

responsible for providing Crabb with the oxygen breathing equipment he used on his dive.

Lofty Gordon was later interviewed by a *Daily Mail* reporter on 8 May and he said:

I just happened to bump into Buster in Portsmouth … For two or three hours we went around one or two pubs. We were with a lieutenant-commander and his wife … I did not think that a man committed to a hazardous operation should have stayed out as late as he did with me and my friends and gone on drink by drink with us.

The reference to meeting in Portsmouth conflicts with the version of meeting in Havant. The latter appears more likely to have been the case, though the session could have continued later in Portsmouth.

Cdr Crabb returned to Portsmouth Harbour Station and some reports say he called in at the Keppel's Head Hotel, just outside the station and one of his favourite drinking haunts before returning to the Sally

The Keppel's Head Hotel where Cdr Crabb was reported to have had a late drinking session with naval friends on the evening of 18 April 1956.

Port Hotel. He was reported to have been subdued but exceptionally generous to the barmaids. Various reports claimed that he "attended a late drinking party the evening before he disappeared" and he "slugged back five double whiskies …". From there it was a ten-minute walk back to the Sally Port Hotel.

Smith got back to the Sally Port hotel at 23.45 hours but saw nothing of Cdr Crabb. They had planned to meet at 05.30 the following morning, ready for Crabb's next dive.

Thursday, 19 April 1956

Crabb did not appear for his meeting with Smith at 05.30 hours so Smith had to wake him at 05.45 hours. Without having any breakfast, Cdr Crabb (presumably with his hangover) and Smith left the hotel and drove by car to collect Franklin from his home at Southsea Terrace. They had a cup of tea and then, according to Sir Edward Bridges, went:

… straight to the dockyard which they reached at about 06.30 hours.

Cdr Crabb could certainly have gained access to the Dockyard without any trouble since he had been issued with a suitable pass as arranged by MI6. Lt Gutteridge has stated:

The serving British Naval Officer who winkled Crabb and his SIS "minder" into Portsmouth dockyard and who dressed Crabb for his one and only and last dive [sic] *was/is a friend of mine.*

There is no mention in the disclosed literature of Cdr Crabb picking up any freshly charged oxygen cylinders. It may therefore be the case that when the breathing equipment was originally collected, it included spare fully-charged oxygen cylinders to replace those that were used up, as well as fresh charges of Protosorb. It is most likely that Franklin made all the necessary arrangements on behalf of Crabb.

High water at Portsmouth was at 07.02 hours and it was a neap tide (a small range of rise and fall). The initial intention would certainly have been for Cdr Crabb to have been in the water slightly before that time in order to catch slack water. So he was running a little late. Shortly before 07.00 hours Cdr Crabb, having been assisted by Franklin, left the surface and sank down the shot line having put on additional lead weights. His fresh oxygen supply and carbon dioxide absorbent were estimated to be capable of lasting about two hours maximum. He was expected to return in less than one hour. But the circumstances did not bode well for him.

Cdr Crabb was a physically unfit, 47-year-old, heavy smoking near alcoholic. He had not eaten any breakfast and he had been drinking the night (and day) before. So he would have been dehydrated, have a low blood sugar level, a residual high blood alcohol level and he would not have had very much sleep. The thermal protection he was wearing (see below) was not particularly effective for the cold water conditions, and in particular, he was wearing only a woolly balaclava and bathing cap on his head. He was using pure oxygen which was known to be toxic at depth. The fit young divers of the Royal Navy were restricted to a depth of 7 metres (23 feet) while swimming for this reason. Physical effort, such as active swimming and lack of fitness reduced the diver's tolerance to oxygen poisoning. Cdr Crabb was therefore diving to the limits of oxygen tolerance even for fit young men.

Furthermore, there was a possible danger of carbon dioxide poisoning if he was wearing a single hose rebreather such as the Pattern 5562 SWBA (see below). This operated on a 'pendulum breathing' principle. The term refers to the backwards and forwards rebreathing of the gas contained in the 'dead space' of the hose with each breathing cycle. It necessitated the diver having to avoid breathing with shallow breaths.

Both conditions, oxygen or carbon dioxide poisoning, would have led to unconsciousness followed usually by drowning or asphyxia. In addition, this particular breathing apparatus was also capable of giving the diver a life-threatening 'soda-lime cocktail' as described earlier.

Despite all these challenging and danger factors, Cdr Crabb characteristically committed himself to the underwater operation without reservation or concern for his own life.

According to Lt Cdr Franklin, he was wearing:
- cotton vest
- bathing trunks, maroon
- rayon combinations, service issue, fawn/khaki
- stockinet combinations
- socks
- little woolly balaclava with bathing cap on top
- Heinke two-piece diving suit
- rubber flippers
- breathing apparatus, 90 minutes comfortable endurance, 2 hours max.

A photograph of Cdr Crabb wearing virtually an identical set of equipment had been taken just a few years earlier. It shows him wearing a rubber bathing cap over a woolly cap or balaclava and a Heinke two-piece dry suit, Admiralty fins and a Clearance Diver's Breathing Apparatus (SWBA). Interestingly it shows him wearing a civilian-type half mask

and the breathing tube and mouthpiece is separate (i.e. not integral with the face mask as was the normal RN arrangement).

At about 07.20 hours, Cdr Crabb returned to the launch having failed to achieve his objective. He was out of breath, cold and complained that the visibility was bad. Franklin checked the equipment and Crabb re-entered the water. The tide was turning and soon the slack water period would end. It has to be assumed that Crabb had experienced serious difficulties during his short dive, otherwise he would not have returned to the launch.

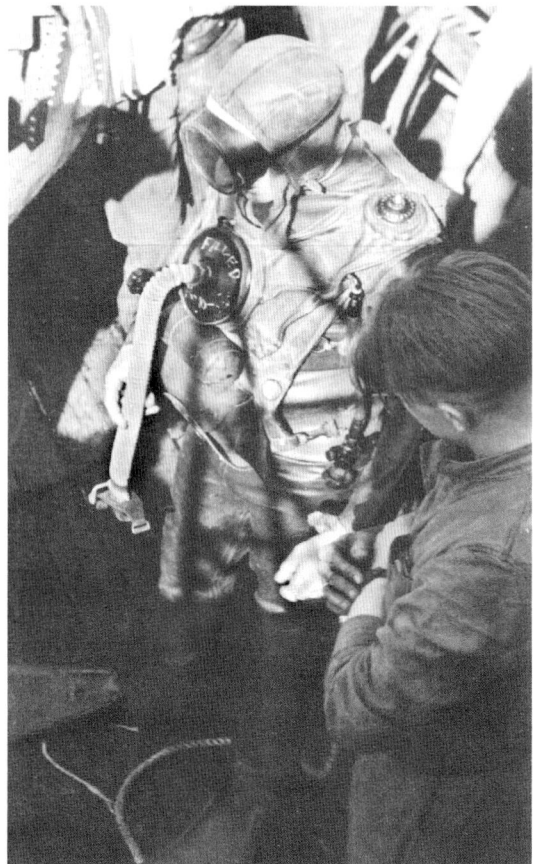

Commander Crabb wearing a similar set of equipment during a previous diving operation. Unfortunately, a poor picture but a very important one.

When he recommended the dive he was therefore, in addition to having already used up part of his oxygen supply and carbon dioxide absorbent, now also in a cold and tired condition, inevitably accompanied by a significant level of stress. Being unfit, relatively old, out of breath and cold means that his resistance to oxygen and carbon dioxide poisoning would have been reduced even further. A seriously dangerous situation was developing.

Crabb dived close to high water, so the sea surface was about 4 metres above chart datum. The sea bed under the *Ordzhonikidze* was dredged to 10 metres (33 feet) below chart datum, giving a total water depth of 14 metres (46 feet). The cruiser's draught was 6.9 metres (23 feet) which, by coincidence happened to be at the limit for safe diving

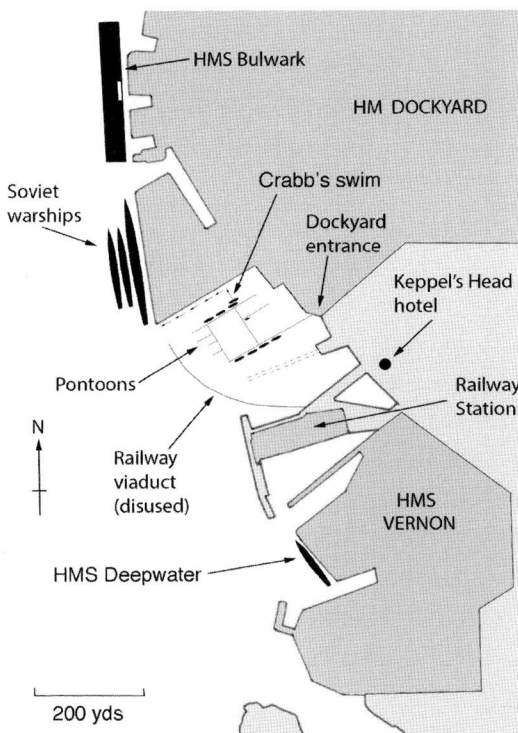

Diagrammatic representation of principal locations involved in Commander Crabb's dive.

using oxygen apparatus while swimming. If Crabb succumbed to oxygen poisoning, he would first have experienced involuntary muscle spasms followed by unconsciousness and convulsions, similar to a full epileptic fit.

The News Chronicle reported they knew of:

Three reliable witnesses who were on the early morning ferry between Portsmouth and Gosport on April 19 ... saw a man in a frogman's outfit. He was swimming on the surface near the Russian ships. Then he went underwater again.

The ferry would have approached fairly close to the sterns of the Russian warships, perhaps just 100 metres away from the stern of the *Ordzhonikidze*. However, no verification of this sighting has been found.

According to British sources, at around 07.30 to 08.00 hours, three Soviet sailors stationed some 20 metres (65 feet) up on the *Sovershenny* observed a diver, face-up on the surface for one or two minutes, between the bows of the two destroyers. One report suggested he appeared to be in difficulties. The diver then resubmerged under the *Smotryashchy*, the outermost of the two destroyers.

A Soviet note from the USSR Embassy in London to the Foreign Office gave a similar story and added that the diver *"then dived again near the side of the Smotryashchy."*

A report in Russia differs slightly in the detail. The Russian author Gennady E Sokolov quoted the sailor who first observed Cdr Crabb on the surface, namely Chief Boatswain Victor Gorokhov, in his book *The Spy N1* published in 2012 (the translation is by this book's author with the assistance of Google translate):

On the morning of April 19, 1956, boatswain Gorokhov was standing at the bow of the ship, where there was a designated place for smoking.

He stood at the edge and was looking down into the water between two ships – the destroyer Sovershenny and the cruiser Ordzhonikidze, moored side by side at Portsmouth. Suddenly a grey shadow appeared in the water. On the surface people gathered at the bows of the destroyers. The diver stared up at Gorokhov. They were only a few meters apart. A black rubber diving suit covered virtually the whole body of the diver. The boatswain could make out only the eyes behind glass mask. They were extremely abnormal eyes, as if they were popping out. Boatswain Gorokhov described what he had seen to Rear-Admiral Kotov. The diver frantically waved his hands above the water, as if trying to grab on to the hull of the destroyer. But the Sovershenny's hull was absolutely smooth, being welded and without rivets. There was nothing to grasp. Boatswain Gorokhov watched for a few seconds, as if in a daze. If only I had a rope — lamented boatswain Gorokhov, I would, of course, have thrown it to him in the water. But there was neither a rope nor life belt near him. And fifteen seconds later the diver disappeared. According to the boatswain, the diver was calling for help. Judging by the diver's eyes and movements of his hands, he was in trouble.

It may be safely assumed that this was indeed Cdr Crabb. To have surfaced means that he was certainly in serious trouble. Furthermore, since his objective was to investigate the propellers and rudder of the *Ordzhonikidze*, and *"not to attempt any reconnaissance of the destroyers,"* it would seem that he had also become disorientated and had lost his bearings. The evidence of whether Cdr Crabb surfaced between the two destroyers or between the cruiser and a destroyer is clearly conflicting. However, since the Soviet note expressly stipulated that the diver dived near

the side of the *Smotryashchy*, the outermost of the two destroyers, then he must have surfaced between the two destroyers.

To have resubmerged after suffering from any of the possible causes of his distress, oxygen poisoning, carbon dioxide poisoning, soda lime cocktail, hypothermia, exhaustion, heart failure etc., would have been almost certainly a non-survivable event. The inescapable conclusion appears to be that the Soviet sailors actually witnessed Cdr Crabb in his death throes.

Nobody ever saw Cdr Crabb alive again.

Cdr Crabb had estimated the job should only take him about one hour and his oxygen supply was estimated to last two hours maximum. So by 09.00 hours, some two hours since Cdr Crabb had first entered the water, Franklin and Smith were becoming very concerned that something had gone wrong. At 09.15 hours Franklin searched for Cdr Crabb along the pontoons and Smith went off and searched the pilings under the jetty.

… during their search, they neither heard or saw any sign of abnormal activities from the Russians.

Sir Edward Bridges recorded:

No one was about in the dockyard and no signs of life were evident on the ships until 08.00 when they came alive for "colours".

When they had given up hope of finding Cdr Crabb, Smith telephoned Davies at the Central Police Station at about 09.50 hours. Davies immediately drove over to meet Smith and Franklin at the boats. He arrived at 10.00 hours and took charge. They packed up all their gear but left the shot rope attached to the side of the boat. After a short discussion the group went over to the Naval Intelligence Division (NID) office in the dockyard and explained the situation to Commander Forbes, the NID Liaison Officer. Smith and

Franklin returned for one more fruitless search of the pilings under the jetty.

Davies instructed Smith to drive Franklin back to HMS *Vernon*. However, as it turned out, Lt Eric Edward Gash, the senior diving instructor from the diving school on Horsea Island, drove Franklin back to HMS *Vernon* in his Rover car. Once there, Franklin related his activities to his Commanding Officer, Captain John Grant, Captain of HMS *Vernon*. Captain Grant collected Rear Admiral Poland who was on the Naval Staff (DTSD) at the time and together with Lt Cdr Franklin immediately drove over from HMS *Vernon* to the Dockyard to see the Chief of Staff to the C-in-C Portsmouth, Rear Admiral Philip Burnett. They were immediately taken in to see Admiral of the Fleet Sir George E Creasy, the C-in-C who, it is said, went 'ballistic'.

Shortly after 10.00 hours, Davies telephoned his report to MI6 in London. The C-in-C's staff provided a motor launch in which Davies and Smith made a further and more widespread search as discreetly as they could, including going outside the harbour which also proved fruitless.

Sometime after mid-day Smith collected his and Cdr Crabb's effects from the Sally Port Hotel, paid the bill and drove back to London. Sir Edward Bridges recorded that amongst Cdr Crabb's belongings were:

... his wallet which contained correspondence showing him to be in pretty low water financially. In addition there were the following items of interest to SIS:-

*   a) a dockyard pass obtained for him by SIS*
*   b) his operational brief*
*   c) Smith's personal cheque for the tables from CRABB's firm.*

... At the time he was lost, CRABB was not wearing or carrying any item of clothing

Lt Edward Eric Gash, the Senior Diving Instructor at the Diving School at Horsea Island, who drove Lt Franklin back from the Dockyard to HMS *Vernon* to explain the loss of Cdr Crabb.

or equipment by which he could be identified. Most of his diving gear was of a type which is obtainable from normal civilian suppliers. Some items were Admiralty stores but it is believed that these also can be obtained commercially.

This is not entirely correct because the breathing set that Crabb was wearing was the contemporary RN Clearance Diving oxygen rebreather, Pattern 5562 (as explained below). MI6 had informed MI5 of the incident who told Detective Superintendent Lamport at 11.30 hours who then called Davies to the Central Police Station for a briefing. Davies first checked with Cumming at MI5 headquarters in Leconfield House, Curzon Street, London, on the telephone and then gave Lamport the full story.

Hugh Winterborne and John Henry of MI6 were swiftly despatched to Portsmouth to tie up loose ends. They had conferences with Davies, Lamport, Smith and Forbes. Then Winterborne, Henry and Forbes all returned to London in the evening. Everyone must have been in a state of shock, especially since absolutely no preparations had been made for such a tragic eventuality. There was no 'plan B' to fall back on (lapse in trade craft).

Friday, 20 April

Cdr Crabb had arranged to meet Lt Cdr Crawford on this day, presumably to return the breathing set to stores, but of course he failed to turn up. Maitland Pendock had also expected to see Cdr Crabb back in London later in the day. Concerns for Crabb's safety were beginning to grow amongst his circle of friends.

Saturday, 21 April

This was the probable day of the Royal Navy diving operation. See "The Royal Navy/Naval Intelligence Division diving operation" below. Apart from admitting to having carried it out, none of the details of the RN/NID diving operation have yet been disclosed by the government. Nevertheless, the RN operation was totally successful and the Soviets were unaware it had taken place. How this can possibly be still considered a sensitive issue is mystifying.

However, the Soviets were of course aware of Crabb's dive but not yet aware of his demise. Rear Admiral V F Kotov, the commander of the Soviet naval squadron mentioned casually to Rear Admiral Burnett, the Royal Navy Chief of Staff to the Commander-in-Chief, Portsmouth, at a dinner, that a frogman had been sighted from the cruiser two days previously, on 19 April.

Sir Edward Bridges reported that on 21 April:

Admiral Kotov who had spent the day informally with Admiral Burnett (Chief of Staff to the Chief-in-Command (C-in-C), Portsmouth) said, over the coffee after dinner, that three of his sailors had seen a frogman about 8 o'clock in the morning of the 19th, but he was not proposing to make a fuss about it or to lodge a complaint.

Rear Admiral Koltov, commander of the Soviet squadron in Portsmouth Harbour.

Rear Admiral Burnett, the Royal Navy Chief of Staff.

Rear Admiral Kotov later mentioned that the three sailors who had seen the diver surfacing were on the destroyer *Sovershenny* and that the diver wore *"a mask with a quadrangular cut for the eyes"*. This does not ring true since Crabb would have been wearing a mask with a circular faceplate. Perhaps this was a mischievous attempt to point an accusing finger at the RN through the use of a Sladen suit as used by the navy for mine clearance operations.

Monday, 23 April

Russian divers were observed operating under the stern of the *Ordzhonikidze*. They operated from one of their ship's own launches which was tied up between the *Ordzhonikidze's* stern and the jetty wall.

It was perfectly understandable that the Russians would have had concerns over the possibility of the attachment of monitoring devices on the underside of their vessel. They had seen a frogman surface nearby as well as RN diving activities at the stern of HMS *Bulwark*, berthed just ahead of them. A visual check around the rudder and propellers would have been an entirely appropriate security measure. Clearly they found nothing untoward as no accusations were ever made.

Tuesday, 24 April

An MI6 report recorded:

At about this stage two major factors dominated our minds. The first was that it was of the utmost importance to keep CRABB's activities quiet until after the Russian visit was over. The second was that the best hope of preventing early publicity and embarrassment to HMG would be for the Admiralty to assume responsibility for the action and admit sponsorship.

Apart from a later nominal complaint from the Soviet embassy about the observed frogman, that should have been the end of the matter. But events were about to take a turn for the worse. A scandal followed. It is ironic that it is not so much associated with Cdr Crabb's top secret spying mission but with the botched cover-up by the Admiralty, Naval Intelligence Division and MI6.

The handling of Crabb's estate was not a complicated matter. There was very little to administer. His ex-wife Margaret Player confided he was *"not good with money"*. Following his disappearance, an Admiralty note dated 14 May 1956 stated:

Crabb is believed to have been in debt to the tune of many hundreds of pounds, probably £2 - £3,000; These include arrears in alimony (about £500), divorce case costs (£120). There are no known assets, except for a share of royalties from his biography by a friend Pugh … We believe he died intestate … There is a statutory provision for the Admiralty to notify the Registrar General of deaths of naval officers and men … if this procedure is to be followed, a certain amount of

Crabb's betting slip during the Grand National on 7 April 1951. Neither of the bets won.

"wangling" will be involved … If the body turns up … there will be an inquest – in the place where the body is found.

Apart from living beyond his means, Crabb also had a bit of a gambling problem. Betting on horse racing had been a favourite pastime.

A little later, on 16 July 1956 it was reported that Cdr Crabb left £1,205.9.9 gross, £374.19.11 net. Letters of administration were granted to his mother, Mrs Beatrice Crabb on 10 July 1956, the only person entitled to the estate. The disappearance of the earlier debt would appear to be attributed to the royalties from Pugh's very successful book *Commander Crabb* following its publication which tragically Commander Crabb was never able to enjoy.

Tuesday, 15 May 1956

Margaret Crabb, Cdr Crabb's former wife claimed for unpaid maintenance payments through her solicitors.

Thursday, 17 May 1956

Cdr Crabb's swordstick and a pair of fins were delivered to Maitland Pendock at his home in Swiss Cottage.

Friday, 1 June 1956

The Admiralty issued a Death Certificate in response to a request from the lawyers acting for Cdr Crabb's mother, Beatrice Crabb, for a Certificate of Presumption of Death, in order that they could apply for a Grant of Letters of Administration since Cdr Crabb had not made a Will.

Certificate of Death
This is to certify that Commander L. K. P. Crabb, O.B.E., G.M., Royal Naval Volunteer Reserve is

presumed by the Admiralty for official purposes to have died on the nineteenth day of April 1956.
(signed) NIGEL J. ABERCROMBIE
Under Secretary

The Admiralty solicitor W R Lewin (the Head of Naval Law Branch at the Admiralty) informed Beatrice Crabb's solicitors that:

… all the effects recovered from Portsmouth were returned to your client, Mrs. Beatrice Crabb, and that nothing is known of the whereabouts of the wallet.

It appears that not everything had been returned from Portsmouth as seen from the item below.

Tuesday, 10 July 1956

A note in the National Archives reads as follows:

Enclosure to Messrs Tamplin Joseph and Flux's letter dated 16th July 1956, [the solicitors acting for Crabb's mother] *an extract from the records of the Principal Probate Registry, records the grant on 10th July 1956 of letters of administration to Beatrice Crabb of Nynehead Cottage, Towersey, near Thame, Oxfordshire, widow, "the lawful mother and only person entitled to the estate of the said intestate."*
Gross value £1205-9-9
Net value £374-19-11

Wednesday, 18 July 1956

The Head of Naval Law, W R Lewin, wrote to the lawyers representing Cdr Crabb's mother explaining that the Admiralty will be paying her £100.

At the same time, they enclosed a list of Cdr Crabb's belongings which had been found in a wooden box at HMS *Vernon* and which would be forwarded to her.

A LIST *OF EFFECTS BELONGING TO THE LATE COMMANDER L.K.P. CRABB, O.B.E., G.M., R.N.V.R.*

  2 Lounge Suits
  1 Mess Undress Jacket, Vest and Trousers
  1 Blue Blazer
  1 Uniform Suit
  1 Pair Rubber Half Boots

  1 Pair Canvas Shoes
  2 Pair Black Shoes
  3 Blue Linen Collars
  1 Uniform Cap
  2 Sheets
  2 Pillow Cases
  1 Rubber Sailing Suit
  1 Great Coat
  1 White Ensign

  1 Block of Quartz
  2 Wire Coat Hangers
  3 Wallets

Thursday, 19 July 1956

Following the disappearance of Cdr Crabb, MI6 and the Admiralty urgently needed to fabricate a believable cover story due to the questions coming from the Russians, the furore being stirred up by the politicians in the House of Commons, the anxious inquiries from his friends in London and the sudden interest from the national newspapers,.

After such a catalogue of errors in trade craft during the spying operation itself, the cover-up needed to be absolutely watertight.

But was it?

Crabbgate — the bungled cover-up

On 17 June 1972, five men broke in to the Democratic National Committee HQ at the Watergate office complex in Washington DC, USA. It was of course an illegal though government-inspired operation and merited some form of prosecution. However, the ensuing cover-up and investigation escalated the issue to an unprecedented level of adverse publicity which in turn led to no less than a constitutional crisis and the resignation of President Nixon.

The moral of the story is that the original 'sin' paled into insignificance compared to the public backlash over the subsequent bungled cover-up.

A new term was thus coined – 'Watergate'.

From that day since, whenever any government makes a mess of attempting to cover up a misdemeanour, real or imagined, the word 'gate' is attached to a key word to generate the working title, examples being Irangate, plebgate etc., etc.

And so now we have 'Crabbgate'.

In this case, the original spying mission itself has fallen into insignificance compared to the spectacularly bungled attempt at a cover-up. It led to the resignation of the head of MI6 together with many other senior government officials and, together with the Suez crisis, contributed to the eventual resignation of the Prime Minister, Sir Anthony Eden and the fall of his government.

The time-line of the principal events unfolded as follows.

Saturday, 21 April 1956

Two days after Cdr Crabb's disappearance, Marshall Pugh decided to make his own enquiries into his whereabouts. He contacted the *Daily Mail* News Editor in London and asked him to get one of his reporters in Portsmouth to check at the Sally Port Hotel, where he (and about six other friends) knew Cdr Crabb had been staying. The News Editor in turn contacted Peter Marshall, an aspiring young freelance journalist who ran a small news agency in Portsmouth (see the Foreword). He was a regular contributor to the paper, as well as many others in Fleet Street, mainly on naval matters.

Peter Marshall duly went along to the Sally Port Hotel. When he entered, there was nobody in reception, so he helped himself to the Visitor Registration Book. He quickly noted that Cdr Crabb and Smith had stayed two nights. The manager, Mr Richman, appeared and Marshall explained he was trying to find Cdr Crabb. Richman was unable to help him any further, so Marshall returned to his office in his apartment at 3 Southsea Terrace and reported back to the News Editor at the *Daily Mail*.

Marshall was immediately instructed to grab a photographer, return to the Sally Port Hotel and take a picture of the Visitor Register. So within an hour, Marshall had collected photographer Bert Lemmon, who ran a small photographic shop and studio in Arundel Street, and returned to the Sally Port Hotel. They were surprised to discover that in the intervening one hour, the pages in which Cdr Crabb and Smith had written their details had been torn out and the next page bore a hand-written receipt from Superintendent Jack Lamport: *"Previous page removed by J. Lamport, Supt. Portsmouth Police."*

Peter Marshall in 1957 interviewing the commander of the USS *Nautilus* for the BBC on its arrival at Portland. It was the first nuclear submarine to visit the UK.

It appears that, without first checking with MI6 in London, Lamport had been instructed to remove the evidence of Crabb and Smith's brief stay at the Sally Port Hotel. Detective Constable Bernie Wright was sent to collect Lamport from his home and take him to the hotel immediately, where he tore out two sheets (4 pages) from the register. Lamport instructed Wright that he was never to repeat what he saw him do.

Before Bert Lemmon got a chance to photograph the receipt the hotel proprietor returned and snatched the book away from them saying he had been instructed to say nothing further. When this news was received back at the *Daily Mail* in London, the editor immediately smelled a rat.

On his own initiative, Peter Marshall made further enquiries at the naval diving school in HMS *Vernon*, but the officers there were unable to help apart from saying that they knew Cdr Crabb and that he occasionally borrowed diving equipment from them. Indeed, Peter Marshall was told that Crabb had visited as *"recently as the previous month when he had been issued with a complete set of diving gear ... "*. He was encouraged by the *Daily Mail* to make further enquiries through his local contacts, but it took another week before the coincidence of the missing frogman and the Russian visit began to add up. Marshall quickly established himself as the principal reporter covering the Crabb story in Portsmouth, which soon escalated to involve dozens of reporters arriving from Fleet Street (see Appendix 14) as well as international radio and TV correspondents. Marshall has since written:

It was, of course, an amazing experience to be at the centre of such a major long-running news story – but the bottom line was that my earnings over the period ran into previously unimaginable

thousands of pounds. On a personal level, it enabled me to move from my flat in Southsea Terrace to buy one of the most sought-after houses in Old Portsmouth – Semaphore House in Battery Row, overlooking the entrance to Portsmouth Harbour.

In a document released in the National Archives, Detective Superintendent Lamport claimed:

On the 21st April 1956 [name obscured] *informed us that the missing man was named Commander CRABB, that he had stayed at the Sally Port Hotel, Old Portsmouth, with another man named Bernard SMITH, and it was desirable if possible that these names and addresses should be removed from the hotel register. After discussion I went to the hotel where I saw the proprietor Mr RICHMAN. I told him that a gentleman who had stayed at his hotel had been engaged in some secret naval exercise and was missing and that it was desirable to ensure that particulars in his register should not become public. Mr RICHMAN was very co-operative and after I had examined the register he consented to my suggestion that I should remove a double page, which I did. The pages in the register were not numbered and it was only by checking dates that it could be seen that a part was missing. I asked Mr RICHMAN and his wife not to disclose the matter to anyone, and they agreed. No mention was made of the Official Secrets Act and no threats were made.*

MI6 counter-claimed that Lamport had acted on his own initiative (i.e., not at the request of MI6), when he removed the pages from the hotel register. Lamport cleverly deduced that it would be difficult for anyone to know the pages had been removed, and then only if anyone examining the consecutive dates recorded in the remaining pages.

Unfortunately, from a secrecy point of view, he left a receipt in the Visitor Register recording the fact that he, Detective Superintendent Lamport of Portsmouth Police, had removed the double pages. Keeping secrets was clearly not his forte. Within minutes, the *Daily Mail* journalist Peter Marshall discovered Lamport's receipt.

This exercise, considered to be just one of many examples of poor trade craft, was to play a significant role in subsequent events. However, it is worth noting here that Hugh Gaitskell, the leader of the opposition in Parliament, made the important point on 14 May 1956 identifying yet another *faux pas* by the Portsmouth Police:

The Portsmouth Police came in – in fact, they seized part of the register, although, under the Aliens Order, it was the property of the hotel keeper who is under statutory duty to preserve it. It is indeed very hard, therefore, to see what right the police officers had to make the hotel keeper break the law in this way.

Tuesday, 24 April 1956

Maitland Pendock, Cdr Crabb's employer in London, also became concerned about his continued absence. He had been expecting Crabb back in London by Friday at the latest. He first rang the Sally Port Hotel only to discover that Smith had returned, picked up both their belongings, paid both bills and left. He next called Lt Cdr John Crawford at his home in Leigh Park, Bedhampton near Havant to ask about Cdr Crabb's whereabouts. This suggests that Cdr Crabb had told Pendock that he would be meeting Crawford while on his visit to Portsmouth. Crawford then made enquiries at the Admiralty but failed to get a satisfactory reply. He was ordered to say nothing and to refrain from contacting Pendock.

Wednesday, 25 April 1956

Rear Admiral Inglis, Director of Naval Intelligence (DNI) obtained the approval of Vice-Admiral Sir William Davis KCB DSO, Vice Chief of Naval Staff (VCNS) for the Admiralty to admit their sponsorship of Cdr Crabb's diving operation. The Admiralty realised that they needed to concoct a credible cover story but stalled any overt action due to the continued presence of the Soviets as their guests. They took the decision that *"the top priority was to prevent the story breaking while the Russians were still in England."* They had to keep it secret for just another two days.

Thus it became essential to prevent the concerns of Cdr Crabb's employer, friends and family becoming public. Vice-Admiral Sir William Davis sent Captain Sarell RN to see Maitland Pendock at his offices in Seymour Place. He met Pendock at 17.00 hours.

Sarell took Pendock around to his flat in Dorset House in Gloucester Place near Regent's Park and over a few whiskies explained that Cdr Crabb had disappeared underwater while carrying out some trials of secret underwater apparatus for the Admiralty in the Portsmouth area. Sarell instructed him not to talk about it. Pendock explained that he had already started to make enquiries about Cdr Crabb's whereabouts soon after he failed to return to London on the Friday (20 April). After calling Lt Cdr Crawford, he had contacted Miss Ruth Drew, a friend in the BBC for advice. She put him on to a Mr Fallon, formerly the Head of the River Police. Pendock had been about to meet Fallon later in the evening when Sarell had first contacted him. He agreed to tell Fallon that he had received information about his missing friend and had no need to make further enquiries.

One of Pendock's reactions was that Cdr Crabb may have committed suicide. This was possibly because Cdr Crabb was known to suffer from bouts of depression. It seems that Cdr Crabb's biographer, Marshall Pugh, came to the same conclusion. In a touching and inquisitorial article he wrote ten years after Cdr Crabb's disappearance, he stated:

... Crabb spent his last lonely year searching the bars of his past for his lost identity, a hungry hero in a time of peace and plenty ... the evidence fades as fast as the legend grows.

Pendock further explained that Cdr Crabb's landlady at 2a Hans Road had been in touch with him enquiring about Cdr Crabb's whereabouts. Sarell got him to agree to contact her and tell her that Cdr Crabb had gone away and would not be returning. He would call in to collect Cdr Crabb's effects and pay off his rent. He did not anticipate any problems in doing so as the landlady knew him well as one of Cdr Crabb's friends.

A number of business clients had also called Pendock to try to get in contact with Cdr Crabb regarding outstanding orders. Pendock said that Cdr Crabb looked after that side of the business and his loss was going to be a blow. Sarell had done quite an efficient job of keeping the lid on Crabb's disappearance as far as Pendock was concerned.

Sarell returned to the MI6 Head Office at 54 Broadway which was disguised as the Minimax Fire Extinguisher Company at 19.30 hours to give his report: *"He was able to give us some valuable details regarding CRABB's family and associates."* One of these was his cousin and close friend Mr Honniball, of the solicitors Piper, Padfield & Honniball of 102 High Street, West Wickham in Kent.

The ex-MI6 HQ at 54 Broadway near St James' Park underground station as it appears today.

Thursday, 26 April 1956

Marshall Pugh rang the secretary of the Deputy Chief of Staff at MI6 and warned him that their actions were likely to provoke publicity rather than prevent it. As a result, Captain Sarell invited Pugh to his apartment for a chat. He arrived at 17.30 hours. Sarell explained that the Admiralty would make a formal announcement as soon as Cdr Crabb's mother had been informed and he was *"asked for his silence"* until that time.

Friday, 27 April 1956

This was the last day of the Soviet visit. The talks in London had gone reasonably well though there had been some unfortunate exchanges outside the official programme. Bulganin and Khrushchev returned to Portsmouth by train, boarded the *Ordzhonikidze* and the three warships left Portsmouth Harbour at 14.15 hours. There must have been sighs of relief all around. The story had still not leaked to the newspapers.

MI6 and NID had already been busy concocting their cover story with Captain Sarell's assistance and by 10.30 hours they had drafted the statement which it was proposed the Admiralty should use when answering any questions. Later that day Sarell was sent by the Admiralty to inform Cdr Crabb's ailing mother, Mrs Beatrice 'Daisy' Crabb, living in a tiny cottage in Towersey near Thame in Oxfordshire, of his presumed death. He first called Mr Honniball at 15.00 hours and asked him to let Mrs Crabb know of his impending visit. Honniball set out by car at 16.30 hours and arrived at the home of Mrs Crabb at 18.00 hours. Sarell was already there and he repeated the cover story of Cdr Crabb's disappearance.

Sarell returned to London and saw Rear Admiral J G T Inglis, Director of Naval Intelligence (DNI) at about 20.00 hours. He was told *"… there was now an approved Admiralty statement although no announcement was to be made."* Sarell telephoned Pugh at midnight and passed the message on, at the same time emphasising that the Admiralty still wanted to minimise any publicity.

Saturday, 28 April 1956

Captain Sarell conferred with the DNI and at 10.30 hours set off to discuss matters with Mrs Margaret Crabb, Cdr Crabb's ex-wife, at her home at Erin Cottage, St Margaret at Cliffs, near Dover. She had to be given the cover story and told to keep quiet. He also needed to confirm that she had actually divorced Cdr Crabb. He arrived at 13.00 hours and

discovered that Mrs Crabb had reverted to her previous name of Mrs Player, from her first marriage. He was surprised by her suggestion that *"Cdr Crabb had deliberately disappeared in order to evade his creditors and an impossible burden of debt."* She also stated that she had not seen Cdr Crabb since their divorce.

Sunday, 29 April 1956

Captain Sarell picked up a telephone message from Pugh at 23.00 hours. He telephoned him back and Pugh told him the press were on to the story and he had provided them with an obituary of Cdr Crabb.

The press were soon on to the Admiralty and in answer to their questions they produced the previously prepared false cover story to explain away Cdr Crabb's disappearance. Their brief was as follows:

Cdr L K P Crabb, OBE, GM, RNVR, who was specially employed in connexion with trials of certain underwater apparatus, has not returned from a test dive and must be presumed drowned.

2 The above is NOT to be volunteered to the Press but can be used in answer to any pertinent Press enquiry which may arise.

3 If pressed by the enquirer, it can be admitted that the location was in Stokes Bay, Portsmouth area.

4 Similarly, if pressed, it is to be admitted that he became missing, presumed drowned, on 19th April.

5 If asked whether the next of kin has been informed, the answer is yes.

A subsequent statement released by the Admiralty asserted that Cdr Crabb did not return:

… from a test dive which took place in connexion with trials of certain underwater apparatus in Stokes Bay, in the Portsmouth area, about a week ago.

Monday, 30 April 1956

Speculative reports about Cdr Crabb's disappearance first appeared in the press. *The Times,* as did most of the other papers, dutifully regurgitated the Admiralty press release:

The Admiralty stated last night: 'He did not return from a test dive which took place in connexion with trials of certain underwater apparatus in Stokes Bay, in the Portsmouth area, about a week ago.'

Stokes Bay near Gosport was a popular trials area for the RN diving trials teams. It is a long, arching pebbled beach conveniently close to HMS *Vernon* in Portsmouth and there were extensive Admiralty facilities in the immediate area. These were established during WW2 and were closely associated with the preparations for D-Day. The adjacent Solent provided relatively sheltered water. For better or for worse, the Admiralty had now committed themselves to a blatantly false cover story to explain Crabb's disappearance.

The seeds of Crabbgate had been sown.

Wednesday, 2 May 1956

Daily Mail reporters were the most pro-active in investigating Cdr Crabb's disappearance. It was the young journalist Peter Marshall who led the field having been the first to turn up at the Sally Port Hotel late in the evening of 21 May and discovered that the pages had been removed from the hotel register by the Portsmouth police. The secret that Cdr Crabb and a man called Bernard Smith of the Foreign Office had stayed there had already been blown. The Chief of Naval Information acknowledged this on 11 May 1956 in a note to the DNI: *"The Daily Mail was the first to find this out but its first edition 'scoop' of this fact started the 'rat race'"*.

PRESUMED DEATH OF PIONEER "FROGMAN"

LOST IN TEST DIVE

Frogman GM dies on secret test

Press headlines for the Admiralty's cover story: *The Times* (*above*) and the *Daily Mail* (*below*)

Thursday, 3 May 1956

The press interest was rapidly gathering momentum and the morning papers gave considerable publicity to the hotel register incident. An all-out, national press campaign was soon underway (see Appendix 14). The *Daily Mail* reported:

It was revealed that Detective-Superintendent Jack Lamport, head of Portsmouth CID has torn four pages from the register of the hotel in which Commander Crabb stayed.

Lamport had also ordered that the staff remained silent on the matter. MI6 reluctantly conceded:

It was obvious that all hope of keeping the matter quiet must now be abandoned and that Ministers should be told without further delay.

Incredibly, the government had been completely kept in the dark up to this point. MI6 realised that they were now into a 'damage control' phase of the rapidly floundering cover-up. It was 'all hands to the pumps'. MI6 had that horrible sinking feeling. They had no alternative but to put their hands up and come clean.

Friday, 4 May 1956

The Minister of State for Foreign Affairs, Mr Nutting, went along with the First Lord of the

Mr Richman, the owner of the Sally Port Hotel, indicates where the Portsmouth police had removed four pages from his Visitors' Register.

Admiralty, the Rt Hon Viscount Cilcennin, to break the bad news of Cdr Crabb's disappearance to the Prime Minister Sir Anthony Eden. Eden was predictably furious. The first he had heard of the failed spying mission had not been through official channels but from the newspaper coverage. He had been placed in an invidious position. He had no alternative but to sustain the secrecy and the cover-up. But the guilty parties were not going to go unpunished. In his address to the House of Commons he said with tangible embarrassment:

It would not be in the public interest to disclose the circumstances in which Commander Crabb is presumed to have met his death. While it is the practice for Ministers to accept responsibility,

I think it is necessary in the special circumstances of this case to make it clear that what was done was done without the authority or knowledge of Her Majesty's Ministers. Appropriate disciplinary steps are being taken.

The reluctance of the Admiralty to provide further information inevitably and immediately led to imaginative conspiracy theories being developed in the press. The *Daily Mail* was first off the mark:

Has Commander Crabb's body been found and buried secretly to hide the purpose of his mission and the cause of his death?

The press could smell a cover-up and they relished their investigations, focusing their combined inquiries on Crabb and Smith. MI6

Britain admits it: Crabb was there

The *Daily Mail's* headline announcing the demise of the government's cover-up story.

---

took evasive action and recorded: *"Smith and his wife were moved from London to the country..."*

Now that the British press had exposed Cdr Crabb's failed mission, the Soviet politicians understandably decided to exploit the disaster for their own ends. Having not initially considered the matter worthy of official comment, they could now see the self-destructive machinations in Parliament and the press. Predictably they snatched the opportunity for a propaganda coup. They hand-delivered a note to the Foreign Office in the evening of 4 May 1956 which was more of an observation than a protest.

... at 7.30 hours on April 19, three sailors of the Soviet vessels discovered a diver swimming between the Soviet destroyers at their moorings at the South River Jetty. The diver, dressed in a black light-diving suit with floats [sic] on his feet, was on the surface of the water for the space of one or two minutes and then dived again, under the destroyer Smotryashchy.

The absence of any overt reaction to the sighting by the Russians is worth noting. A Soviet Embassy spokesman explained to a *Daily Mail* reporter, *"We were in a British Port and our regulations forbid any action being taken in these circumstances."*

The government finally put its hands in the air and reluctantly admitted that their Stokes Bay cover story was not true. The *Daily Mail* reported on 12 May that on 4 May:

Britain has admitted in an official Note to Russia that the frogman seen by Soviet sailors in Portsmouth Harbour on April 19 "was to all appearances Commander Crabb"

The government's cover story had held up for only four days.

Tuesday, 8 May 1956

Sydney Knowles took a very personal interest in the mystery and he went to Portsmouth to try to investigate Cdr Crabb's disappearance himself. He was gently advised to desist.

Cdr Crabb's former wife, Mrs Margaret Crabb also decided to make her own enquiries. She travelled to Portsmouth from her home in St Margaret's Bay near Dover with her 11-year-old son Michael. She was quoted as saying: *"I want Michael to know what happened to Buster".* She telephoned for a meeting with the C-in-C, Admiral of the Fleet Sir George Creasy, but was refused an audience. She only got as far as his secretary when her request was promptly turned down. Later, she spent an hour in the evening with Portsmouth's Deputy Coroner, Mr Peter Childs, in an unsuccessful attempt to initiate an Inquest.

At the same time the Admiralty tried vainly to reinforce their cover story about Crabb disappearing in Stokes Bay. They sent two inshore minesweepers to search the area while *"scores of helicopters flew low over Stokes Bay".*

Back in London, MI6 was busily tying up other loose ends. After obtaining the agreement of the Admiralty and MI5, they sent an officer around to Pendock's office at 124 Seymour Place. He found the office was besieged by an army of reporters. He slipped inside and paid Smith's bill for £4.18.6 in cash for the two tables he had previously bought from Crabb. As soon as he left the premises the officer was accosted by the journalists but MI6 were pleased to note later that *"contact was broken satisfactorily".*

Wednesday, 9 May 1956

The political attacks on the Prime Minister were relentless. In response to the growing conspiracy theories, questions asked in Parliament included:

Has the body, in fact, been recovered and secretly buried and is there any truth in suggestions that Commander Crabb might have been taken aboard a Russian cruiser (here during the B and K visit) and is now in Russia?"

The Prime Minister had himself been kept in the dark about Crabb's dive and disappearance. So he took immediate action. He needed to get to the bottom of the confused affair and he commissioned his most senior and respected civil servant, Sir Edward Bridges KG GCB GCVO MC PC FRS, Permanent Secretary to the Treasury and Head

Sir Edward Bridges, Permanent Secretary to the Treasury and Head of the Home Civil Service. He carried out the investigation into the Crabb affair for the Prime Minister.

of the Home Civil Service, to undertake an urgent and definitive investigation into who had said what, when and to whom:

PRIME   MINISTER'S   PERSONAL MINUTE, SERIAL No. M.104/56
TOP SECRET
SIR EDWARD BRIDGES
I wish you to carry out on my behalf an enquiry into the circumstances in which Commander Crabb undertook an intelligence operation against the Russian warships in Portsmouth Harbour on April 19.
Your enquiry should include the following points:-
(a) what authority was given for the operation,
and (b) why its failure was not reported to Ministers until May 4.
My object is to establish, by independent enquiry, what the facts are and where responsibility lies.

A CIA report dated 14 May 1956 stated:
On May 9 the USSR Embassy in London received the following note from the Foreign Office of Great Britain:
The Foreign Office of Great Britain conveys its respects to the Embassy of the Union of Soviet Socialist Republics, and has the honor to give the following answer to the Embassy's note dated May 4:
As has already been publicly stated, Lieutenant Commander (Kapitan Tretyevo Ranga) Crabb was carrying out diving tests, and is supposed that he perished during these tests. The diver detected from the Soviet warships, and, as stated in the Soviet note, swimming between the Soviet destroyers, was, in all probability, (PO vsei vidimosti) Lieutenant Commander Crabb.
His presence near the destroyers was without any permission whatsoever, and Her Majesty's Government expresses regret over this incident.

This is a very significant acknowledgement by the government that it was Cdr Crabb who was observed between the Soviet destroyers. In so doing, the government was embarrassingly admitting that the cover story of Cdr Crabb dying in Stokes Bay was not entirely factually accurate and beginning to unravel.

The *Daily Express* newspaper claimed they had authentic proof from contacts in Portsmouth that the operation had been launched by MI6. The government's bungled cover story was in shreds.

Thursday, 10 May 1956

The *Evening News* carried a story that the Navy had been observed dredging both sides of Kings Stairs, which included South Railway Jetty. This has to be assumed to have been part of the activities to search for Cdr Crabb's body. At the same time the Dockyard police Superintendent Joe Beckett received the order: *"No unauthorised divers to approach the South Railway Jetty"*. There were clearly concerted efforts to search for Crabb's body around this time and over the following weeks. This would undoubtedly have included an eventual search under South Railway Jetty by divers.

Then W R Lewin, the Head of Naval Law at the Admiralty, sent a description of Cdr Crabb to the Chief Constable, City Police, Portsmouth:

I am commanded by My Lords Commissioners of the Admiralty to inform you that on 19th April 1956 Commander L.K.P.Crabb, O.B.E., G.M., R.N.V.R., while undertaking diving operations in the Portsmouth area, failed to return from a dive and must be presumed to be drowned. His body has not been recovered.

2. Owing to tidal conditions, it is possible that Commander Crabb's body may be brought to the surface or washed ashore at a considerable

distance from the area in which he was diving. A description is attached at the annexure to this letter, and I am to request that you will be good enough to arrange that if a body which may answer to that description is found, the Admiralty may be informed at once.

The following note describing the body was enclosed:

ANNEXURE TO ADMIRALTY LETTER N.L.1811/56 OF 9TH MAY 1956
[should be 10th May]
DESCRIPTION
Name:Lionel Kenneth Philip CRABB
Age: 46 [he was actually 47, dob 28.01.1909, died 19.04.1956]
Height: 5 feet 7 inches [it was actually 5 feet 6 inches]
Build: Medium
Hair: Brown
Eyes: Brown
Nose: Prominent
*   Tufts of hair on cheek bones*
Believed to have been wearing:
*   Two-piece Heinke suit*
*   Breathing apparatus pattern 5562*
*   Service-type face mask*
*   Service-type swim fins*

This is a very important note because it identifies the breathing apparatus (Pattern 5562) that Crabb was known by the authorities to have been wearing, having had the opportunity to interview Franklin and others who assisted in Crabb's mission.

The search was on in earnest for Crabb's body. Finding it was of the highest priority. MI6 would have already been making plans as to what they should do with it, if or when they found it.

Stoker Sydney Knowles was scheduled to be interviewed by ITV that evening but he was silenced at the last minute under a 14-day rule which banned discussion on a subject that was still before Parliament. Likewise, the BBC radio Home Service withdrew a 4-minute recording of an interview of Cdr Crabb which was made in London just two days before he disappeared. It had been intended to include it in a children's programme called *Conquest of the Depths* written by James Gleeson and produced by Tom Waldron. It did not go unnoticed by the *Daily Mirror* who revealed the censorship in an article headlined: *"BBC cut voice of lost frogmen".* The government was pulling all the strings it could to keep Crabbgate out of the public's eyes.

The government's cover story continued to disintegrate. The *Daily Mirror* pointed out:

One thing is clear from Sir Anthony Eden's House of Commons statement yesterday about the missing frogman:

This is the BIG COVER-UP for a BIG POLITICAL BLUNDER.

THE FROGMAN BLUNDER

Above: The *Daily Mirror's* front page headline.

Frogman Blunder
THE BIG COVER-UP

The *Daily Mirror's* headline refuting the government's cover-up.

Friday, 11 May 1956

The Russians maintained the pressure on the government and for the first time their newspapers *Pravda* and *Izvestiya* carried feature articles about Cdr Crabb. Interestingly, they stated that Cdr Crabb had carried out two dives under their vessels, on both 18 and 19 April. So perhaps the Russian searchlight activity on the evening of the 18th was connected with their suspicion of an earlier Crabb dive after all.

Clearly the Russians had not swallowed one iota of the Stokes Bay cover story.

Sunday, 13 May 1956

The Russians were on a roll. The CIA reported that on 13 May the Soviet newspaper *Pravda* had published an interview with Rear Admiral V F Kotov, the commander of the Soviet naval squadron that had visited Portsmouth. Kotov is quoted as stating:

At 07.30 GMT on Apr. 19 three sailors of the destroyer Sovershenny, which was anchored next to the cruiser Ordzhonikidze in Portsmouth Harbour, spotted on the surface of the water between the Soviet destroyers a diver in a black, light diving suit. On his head he wore a mask with a quadrangular cut for the eyes. On his feet were rubber flippers.

They had no intention of allowing the British government, the Admiralty and MI6 to get away with their Stokes Bay cover story.

Monday, 14 May 1956

The Prime Minister suffered another onslaught during a two-hour debate in the House of Commons on Cdr Crabb's disappearance. The leader of the Labour Party, Hugh Gaitskell, was unrelenting in his criticism and questioning.

With considerable annoyance Sir Anthony Eden complained:

I deplore this debate and I shall say no more ... I have not one word more to say than I announced on Wednesday ... I am not prepared to discuss these matters in this House.

In the Public Gallery, quietly listening to what the Prime Minister had to say were two smartly dressed figures, Admiral the Earl Mountbatten, the First Sea Lord, wearing a dark grey lounge suit and Mountbatten's political chief, the white-haired Lord Cilcennin, the First Lord of the Admiralty. Mountbatten was taking a personal interest in how Crabbgate was playing out. The Labour MP George Wigg noticed Mountbatten's presence. He stood up, pointed dramatically at the public gallery and called out:

The man responsible is the First Sea Lord: he should be thrown out!

The *Daily Mirror* waded in on 15 May 1956 with the front-page headlines:

The Frogman Blunder – The silent man in the Commons last night – Does Mountbatten know the answer?

The government's policy was to close down communications completely and hope that Crabbgate would simply go away with the passage of time. That was wishful thinking. There was no chance of that happening.

The Kremlin unexpectedly came to Sir Anthony Eden's rescue over the Labour Party's onslaught in Parliament and counter-attacked Gaitskell. They had their own axe to grind with the Labour Party. The *Sunday Express* revealed that Krushchev had used the pages of *Izvestia* to vent his feelings:

The leader of the Labour Party, Gaitskell, proposes to make sharp criticism of the Government in the name of his party. The

Labour leaders wish to make use of this incident to distract the attention of the public from their own actions during the stay of Mr. Bulganin and Mr. Krushchev – actions which were not well-wishing towards the Soviet Union.

Meanwhile, in anticipation of Crabb's body eventually being discovered, the Chief Constable of the crime office in Chichester wrote to all local police authorities in Portsmouth area warning them that should Crabb's body surface, *"It is absolutely essential that the finding of the body is not to be disclosed to the press."*

But why of all police forces, Chichester police? And why would the police not want the public to know about the discovery of Crabb's body? The information would have to become public eventually. The reason was that MI6 and the other associated authorities wanted to be able to stage-manage the 'discovery', not only when, but also where. There was no sign of Crabbgate coming to a conclusion any time soon and the anticipated reappearance of Crabb's body was of mounting concern.

Tuesday, 29 May 1956

Sir Edward Bridges circulated the Prime Minister and other parties with a note that began:

Two problems remain to be dealt with:-
(a)   the establishment of or presumption of death ...
... The first is the most important. The matter cannot be left where it is because royalties from a biography about to be published will accrue to the estate.

This confirms that the government placed the highest priority on establishing the fact that Cdr Crabb was definitely dead. In effect, they desperately needed to find the

Daily Mirror

TUES MAY 15 1956

2⁰ FORWARD WITH THE PEOPLE
No. 16,305

THE FROGMAN BLUNDER

THE SILENT MAN IN THE COMMONS LAST NIGHT

DOES MOUNTBATTEN KNOW THE ANSWER?

THERE was a silent figure in the Gallery of the House of Commons last night. He was:

FIFTY-FOUR-YEAR-OLD ADMIRAL THE EARL MOUNTBATTEN, THE FIRST SEA LORD.

Wearing a dark grey lounge suit, he sat in the front row of the Peers' Gallery listening to evasive replies from Sir Anthony Eden, the Prime Minister, in the debate on the Frogman Blunder.

Sitting next to him was the white-haired figure of Lord Cilcennin, aged fifty-two, First Lord of the Admiralty—Mountbatten's political chief.

They heard Sir Anthony say:

"I deplore this debate and I will say no more." . . . "I have not one word more to say than I announced on Wednesday." . . . "I am not prepared to discuss these matters in this House."

Without Authority of Ministers

Sir Anthony repeated that what was done in the affair of Commander Crabb was done without the authority of Ministers.

He emphasised: "That includes ALL Ministers and ALL aspects of this affair."

The first official statement that Commander Crabb was presumed dead was issued by the Admiralty. That was on April 29 —ten days after Crabb disappeared in Portsmouth harbour.

The Service chief at the Admiralty is Lord Mountbatten.

IS HE THE ONLY MAN IN THE WORLD BESIDES THE PRIME MINISTER WHO KNOWS THE FULL FACTS OF THE MISSION AND THE FATE OF COMMANDER CRABB?

The Commons Debate is reported on the Back Page

The *Daily Mirror* front page noting Admiral Mountbatten's interest in the Prime Minister's debate in the Commons.

body. Furthermore, it appears that at this stage, at least Bridges did not know what had happened to Cdr Crabb's body and the government agencies were making plans as to what to do in the meantime. This is also the last document that has been disclosed which refers to the subject of *"the establishment of or presumption of death"*. The correspondence on the subject so far released comes to an abrupt halt at this juncture. Why is there no further correspondence on this subject?

The inference is that sometime after 29 May, the government was informed that Cdr Crabb's body had in fact been found. From that time onwards, MI6 would have been plotting the public 'discovery' of the body and clearly that particular correspondence awaits disclosure.

Friday, 29 June 1956

The conspiracy theorists were fed a tasty morsel by the mischievous Soviets when the West German newspaper *Bild Zeitung* published an article purporting to claim that Crabb had been captured by the Soviets and was actually imprisoned in Moscow. The following has been extracted from a report in the *Portsmouth Evening News*:

It stated that a Soviet officer told a Left Wing French politician at a Moscow banquet: "We have got Crabb … he is our legitimate prisoner" The Soviet officer stated Crabb almost got away, but was captured after a struggle.

Crabb had swum as far as the destroyer Smotriaschi when Soviet swimmers grabbed him "at the last moment". … Cdr Crabb was prisoner number 147 in Lefortown Prison, Moscow. He had been asked to work for the Soviet Navy … the Soviet officer had asked the French politician to tell Cdr Crabb's former wife that he is well but would not be seen in London "for some years …

We had an undoubted right to arrest Crabb. The water around our ships had been declared extra-territorial by Marshal Bulganin and Mr Krushchev for the period of our visit. We therefore had the right to arrest a spy caught redhanded and to take him to the Soviet Union for investigation."

The newspaper said the French politician then asked if that meant a trial was pending. The officer answered "That is possible. Crabb is at the moment in solitary confinement. He has been given the number 147. Officially he has no name."

The official alleged that Crabb had confessed, after long interrogation, that he had been attempting to find out about secret devices on the Soviet ships.

An investigating judge Colonel Mjasakov, had offered Crabb a post with a special department of the Soviet Navy for ten years, which would have been about the same length of sentence for spying. After that he could go back to Britain.

Admiral Tribuz, Chief of Soviet Naval Intelligence had interviewed Crabb and given his word of honour as an admiral that the offer would be fulfilled to the letter if Crabb accepted.

The Soviet officer said the admiral would probably agree that Crabb should not work against Britain.

The Soviet officer said Crabb had not yet accepted the offer.

Asked: "Is the pay not high enough for him?" he replied "No, it is not that. He is being offered £1,000 a month. I have heard that Crabb wants permission from the British Government to enter into our service for the expected period of his sentence."

Crabbgate was growing another dimension. Not only had the cover story been blown out of the water, but now a new saga was developing around the possibility that Crabb was alive and in Russia.

From the time of the first appearance of the cover story to this day, the press both in UK and abroad have maintained a constant flow of articles debunking the cover story and publicising the ongoing mystery surrounding Cdr Crabb's disappearance. A string of books has been written on the subject expounding on the machinations of MI6, not to mention countless other publications which refer to the mystery (see Appendix 14). The reputation of MI6/SIS has taken, and thanks to the extended period of secrecy, continues to take a pounding as a result.

The Leader of the Opposition, Hugh Gaitskell denounced the government's secrecy with a cutting question:

Are you aware that, while we would all wish to protect public security, the suspicion must inevitably arise that your refusal to make a statement on this subject is not so much in the interests of public security but to hide a very grave blunder?

The Russians have also enjoyed keeping the debacle simmering. As Nicholas Elliott of MI6 pointed out:

… rumours of Crabb's fate have for decades been kept alive in the world press, some doubtless spread as part of KGB's disinformation exercises … Stories have appeared with regularity in the press in many countries with the objective of discomforting MI6 and the British government, to the effect that the unfortunate man had been captured by the Russians as a result of the incompetence with which the operation had been carried out and that he is now in Russia. It has been a typical example of Soviet disinformation.

Crabbgate is an ongoing farce. This self-imposed penalty is destined to haunt MI6/SIS for every minute of the 100 years of the embargo on the records.

Did Commander Crabb dive on his own?

In reply to the following question put to the Admiralty:

What precautions are normally taken in a trial of this nature and were they taken on this occasion?
The Admiralty replied:

Normally two divers would be used and a safety boat would be in attendance.

This is consistent with the arrangements taken on the Royal Naval dive where two, or perhaps three pairs of divers carried out the investigation, operating from a diving tender. However, while it appears that Cdr Crabb operated from a launch from HMS *Maidstone*, there has not been any evidence disclosed that would indicate he had a buddy diver.

If Cdr Crabb had been diving with a buddy diver, he would have been on a 'buddy line' in order to have been able to remain in contact with him in bad visibility water. In such a case, when Cdr Crabb got in to trouble, he could (and surely would) have been recovered by the buddy diver.

The author's conclusion is therefore that on the balance of probabilities Commander Crabb dived alone.

How did Commander Crabb die?

There are many conflicting versions of the manner of Cdr Crabb's death. A sample of the conspiracy theories has already been given. The following focuses on the likely mechanism of Cdr Crabb's death.

Cdr Crabb could have been immobilized by the operation of the powerful sonar equipment on any one or all three of the vessels, followed by drowning or asphyxia. Indeed, there were several anti-diver options open to the Russians. It is most unlikely that the Russians would have wanted to take any such drastic action, not least because it could have endangered the lives of RN divers carrying out 'legitimate' work in the vicinity.

One report claimed that a Russian sentry on board one of the warships shot and killed Cdr Crabb when he appeared on the surface alongside one of the ships. This is almost certainly untrue since the ships were under constant and close surveillance for the entire period of their stay. Such an event would definitely have been observed.

According to the late Mike Borrow OBE, who had met several Soviet naval officers in the ensuing years, including an assistant naval attaché who had been serving on the *Ordzhonikidze* at the time of Cdr Crabb's dive, they had always taken it for granted that Royal Navy divers inspected all their ships while visiting UK ports. Peter Wright (*Spycatcher*) stated that the KGB even had advance notice of Cdr Crabb's intended dive. Chapman Pincher (*Treachery*) has stated that "*... Soviet Intelligence had a month's advance warning of Cdr Crabb's operation.*"

It is perhaps unfortunate that Cdr Crabb's handler in MI6 was Nicholas Elliott. He happened to be a staunch friend and supporter of Harold Adrian Russell 'Kim' Philby who was later to be unmasked as a Soviet agent and who ultimately defected to Russia. Philby, as the MI6 agent responsible for offensive counter intelligence in Spain and Gibraltar during WW2, was well aware of Cdr Crabb's background from his knowledge of Operation Tadpole, Cdr Crabb's operations against the Italian frogmen in Gibraltar during WW2.

While it is possible that details of the Cdr Crabb diving operation in Portsmouth were leaked to Russia via this route, it is unlikely, since Philby had been forced to resign from MI6 at the end of 1955 (though later foolishly re-instated) due to his association with Burgess who had already fled the country along with

Russell 'Kim' Philby of MI6 and one of the 'Cambridge Five' Soviet agents.

Maclean. As a result, Philby had fallen under suspicion as being the 'third man'.

The more likely route was via Sir Anthony Blunt, another of the notorious Cambridge spies. Cdr Crabb had been attending social meetings with Blunt and his associates in Tite Street, Chelsea and other locations in London in the weeks leading up to the diving operation in Portsmouth. Other venues included Blunt's apartment on the top floor of Home House, 20 Portman Square in W1. This was the Courtauld's Institute of Art of which Blunt was the director between 1947 and 1974. At some stage MI5 concealed a listening device in the connecting wall between No 20 and No 21 but the exact timing is not known. Tomas Harris's home in Garden Lodge Studio, Logan Place in South Kensington was another likely setting for Blunt's meetings. Harris was a wealthy half-Spanish art dealer with connections to Burgess and Philby.

At the end of the day, it is academic exactly who it was that tipped off the Soviets. To them, the diving operation had but little significance.

The Soviets themselves had equivalent interest in the design of Royal Navy vessels. When six British warships had visited Leningrad the previous year, in October 1955, *"… they were subjected to intensive intelligence probes by the Russians, including the use of divers"*. And Britain did not bother to make any complaints about it to the Soviets.

In the event, the Soviets made no more than a nominal fuss about the observed diver activities near their vessels in Portsmouth, at least initially. They certainly did not exploit the matter for any political advantage or allow it to interfere with the main diplomatic objective of their visit.

It should be no surprise that Cdr Crabb died while on his diving mission. The most likely cause of death was simple drowning. He was seen on the surface by three Russian sailors. One said that Crabb was struggling on the surface and trying to grab a handhold on the side of the ship before sinking away. Exactly what induced the drowning in the first place could be any one or more of a gamut of reasons, all of which were avoidable had Cdr Crabb been young and fit.

Cdr Crabb was a prime contender for oxygen poisoning as he was diving at or deeper than the safe limit for the use of pure oxygen.

He could have been incapacitated by natural causes, such as a heart attack brought on by exhaustion. Indeed exhaustion is the most likely candidate since he had swum at least 200 metres which for him was near his limit.

As described earlier, another possible explanation could have been a 'soda lime cocktail'. This was a classic mode of failure of an oxygen set with the single hose arrangement whereby in the event of water leaking into the mouthpiece and running down into the Protosorb canister, a highly caustic foam can be produced which expands up the breathing hose and can enter the mouth and even lungs of the diver. The result is a painful chemical burn of the naso-pharynx that renders the breathing apparatus unusable, with possible fatal consequences.

Add to this his lack of physical fitness, his advanced age, his lack of sleep, his drinking session(s) the previous evening with consequent hangover, his dehydration, his heavy smoking, his lack of breakfast (low blood sugar), the cold water (hypothermia) and you have a recipe for disaster, not to mention a massive lapse in trade craft.

So the simple explanation of how Cdr Crabb died is most likely by drowning brought on by exhaustion.

Were the CIA involved in Commander Crabb's diving operation?

The original idea that the Central Intelligence Agency (CIA) of the USA were involved in the Cdr Crabb/MI6 operation arose out of Pat Rose's and Sydney Knowles' observations that Bernard Smith, who accompanied Cdr Crabb from London to Portsmouth and stayed at the Sally Port Hotel with him, spoke with an American accent. Knowles had nicknamed him "GD" because of his *"annoying habit of prefixing everything and everyone with "God-damned"".* The Soviets also suggested that Cdr Crabb had been working for the CIA. The Member of Parliament for Gorton, Manchester, Mr Zilliacus, went on record to suggest:

The most likely explanation is the possibility that Commander Crabb, who had retired but was still taken on from time to time for special jobs, had on this occasion been employed by the United States secret service with the complicity of their – and his – contacts in the British secret service.

The author's enquiry to the CIA requesting information about any involvement in the Cdr Crabb affair under the US Freedom of Information Act drew the following unhelpful response:

In accordance with section 3.6(a) of Executive Order 13526, the CIA can neither confirm nor deny the existence or non existence of records responsive to your request.

A letter from the Admiralty to Sir John Lang hurriedly sent immediately following the Inquest,

... every particle of evidence in our possession points conclusively to the fact that this very gallant gentleman died as he had lived in the service of our country and of no other.

The Admiralty commented:

Statement seems to have been aimed at earlier puff that Crabb was working for American agency.

A newspaper reported on 12 June 1957:

Shortly after the inquest on the "unidentified man" a spokesman of the US Navy in Britain denied that Comdr Crabb was working for the US intelligence service at the time of his disappearance.

Looking objectively at the diving operation, there does not seem to have been any advantage in including a CIA operative directly. It would have been an entirely unnecessary complication to an already ill-prepared mission. This is especially so since the whole operation depended heavily on Cdr Crabb's personal contacts and local influence in Portsmouth. Cdr Crabb's associate would have had to have been a *bona fide* MI6 agent. Indeed, the National Archives disclosures in 2015 state that Smith had been working for MI6 since 1950. It is of course not outside the realms of possibilities that Smith was seconded to MI6 from the CIA.

Dick White who took over as head of MI6 after the hasty departure of Sinclair said:

The government had little confidence in SIS. I had to keep the service afloat and regain that confidence. Crabb was typical of an intelligence service which rushed into operations, often encouraged by the Americans, and did them rather badly.

The CIA do, of course, have a file on the Cdr Crabb case. But that has not yet seen the light of day. One of the privileged few who has seen it (in June 1960) was the US Under Secretary of State for Political Affairs,

Livingstone 'Livie' T Merchant who thanked Allen W Dulles, the then Director of the CIA for its loan, in a letter disclosed in 2003.

In view of this and the lack of any convincing evidence, in the author's opinion the CIA were almost certainly not directly involved in Cdr Crabb's diving operation. However, it is very likely that MI6 would have been in close communication with the CIA regarding the operation and might possibly have been encouraged to undertake the operation by the CIA in the first place.

The Royal Navy / Naval Intelligence diving operation

The releases of previously classified information on the Cdr Crabb affair under the Freedom of Information Act in 2006 and 2015, have revealed that the Naval Intelligence Division commissioned a duplicate investigation of the Soviet cruiser using probably three pairs of naval divers about the same time. However, the details of the naval operation have not been disclosed. One of the reasons given in the disclosed documents was:

… the disclosures could provoke comment about the lack of discipline in the Royal Navy which permitted the second operation to take place at all.

Vice Admiral Sir Norman Denning, Secretary/DPBC of the Admiralty wrote a Secret letter on 11 April 1972 in which he stated:

… it is a fact that a naval team from "Vernon" did separately from Crabb who was [words redacted] – *dive under the Russian ships …*

It appears that following the disastrous failure of Cdr Crabb's dive on 19 April, the Admiralty overcame their original reluctance to use serving RN divers and the NID were given the go-ahead. They simply could not afford to miss the opportunity to examine the Soviet cruiser while it was on their doorstep in Portsmouth harbour.

NID had a choice of four top diving teams based at HMS *Vernon*. The team of diving instructors led by Lt Franklin, the Home Station Clearance Diving Team (HSCDT), led by Lt Cdr Peter Roberts, The Acceptance Trials Team led by Lt Cdr Joe Brooks and the Development Trials Team led by Lt Mark Terrell.

Lt Cdr Joe Brooks DSC was at the time in command of the Clearance Diving Acceptance Trials Team at *Vernon* (as opposed to the Development Trials Team attached to the Underwater Countermeasures & Weapons Establishment in Havant, where Cdr Crabb had worked). The latter team developed equipment that the former then tested before it was introduced into service. Several sources claim that Joe Brooks was in charge and also the lead diver of the RN team who investigated the cruiser. Brooks himself *"enthusiastically did not deny"* being involved to his friends. He and his team were based on board HMS *Deepwater* (Appendix 7) permanently berthed at HMS *Vernon* shore establishment which was also the operational base of the other three teams. Joe Brooks had previously distinguished himself during WW2 when he carried out a daring and successful attack in Bergen, Norway with X-craft X.24, for which he had been awarded the DSC.

Cdr Crabb and Brooks were old friends. One of Brooks' sons has said he remembers his father and Cdr Crabb chatting one evening at their home, shortly before the fatal dive. Unfortunately, he didn't recall the content of the discussion, so we will never know if Cdr Crabb ever revealed his planned operation to Brooks.

Cdr Crabb was actually eligible to work directly for Naval Intelligence. They had *"two kinds of delicate intelligence operations,"* those that directly involved service personnel and gear and those that employed non-service personnel and equipment. Cdr Crabb's name was on the list of divers *"not in the service".*

It has been reported that the RN operation commenced on Saturday 21 April, a week after the three vessels had tied up. The divers entered the water at the stern of the aircraft carrier HMS *Bulwark* which was berthed at Pitch House Jetty, 60 metres further up and north of Kings Stairs, where it had been tied up since 1 April. The ideal time for their dive would have been between 13.00 and 15.00 hours. They could have drifted south with the

Lt Cdr Joe Brooks, the Officer in Charge of the Acceptance Trials Team at HMS *Vernon*.

outgoing tide, carried out their survey over low water slack and returned in a northerly direction with the incoming tide.

They dived from a dockyard diving tender tied up at the stern of the carrier. Copper-helmeted divers (*"steamers"*) appeared to be undertaking routine maintenance work on

The Royal Navy diving teams based on HMS *Deepwater*.
(CDs = Clearance Divers)

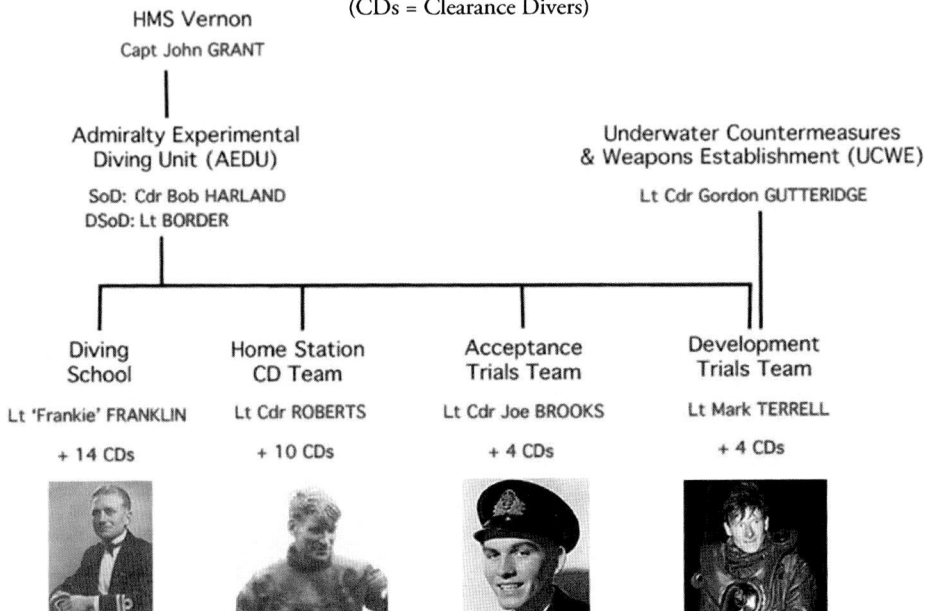

HMS Vernon
Capt John GRANT

Admiralty Experimental
Diving Unit (AEDU)

SoD: Cdr Bob HARLAND
DSoD: Lt BORDER

Underwater Countermeasures
& Weapons Establishment (UCWE)

Lt Cdr Gordon GUTTERIDGE

Diving School	Home Station CD Team	Acceptance Trials Team	Development Trials Team
Lt 'Frankie' FRANKLIN	Lt Cdr ROBERTS	Lt Cdr Joe BROOKS	Lt Mark TERRELL
+ 14 CDs	+ 10 CDs	+ 4 CDs	+ 4 CDs

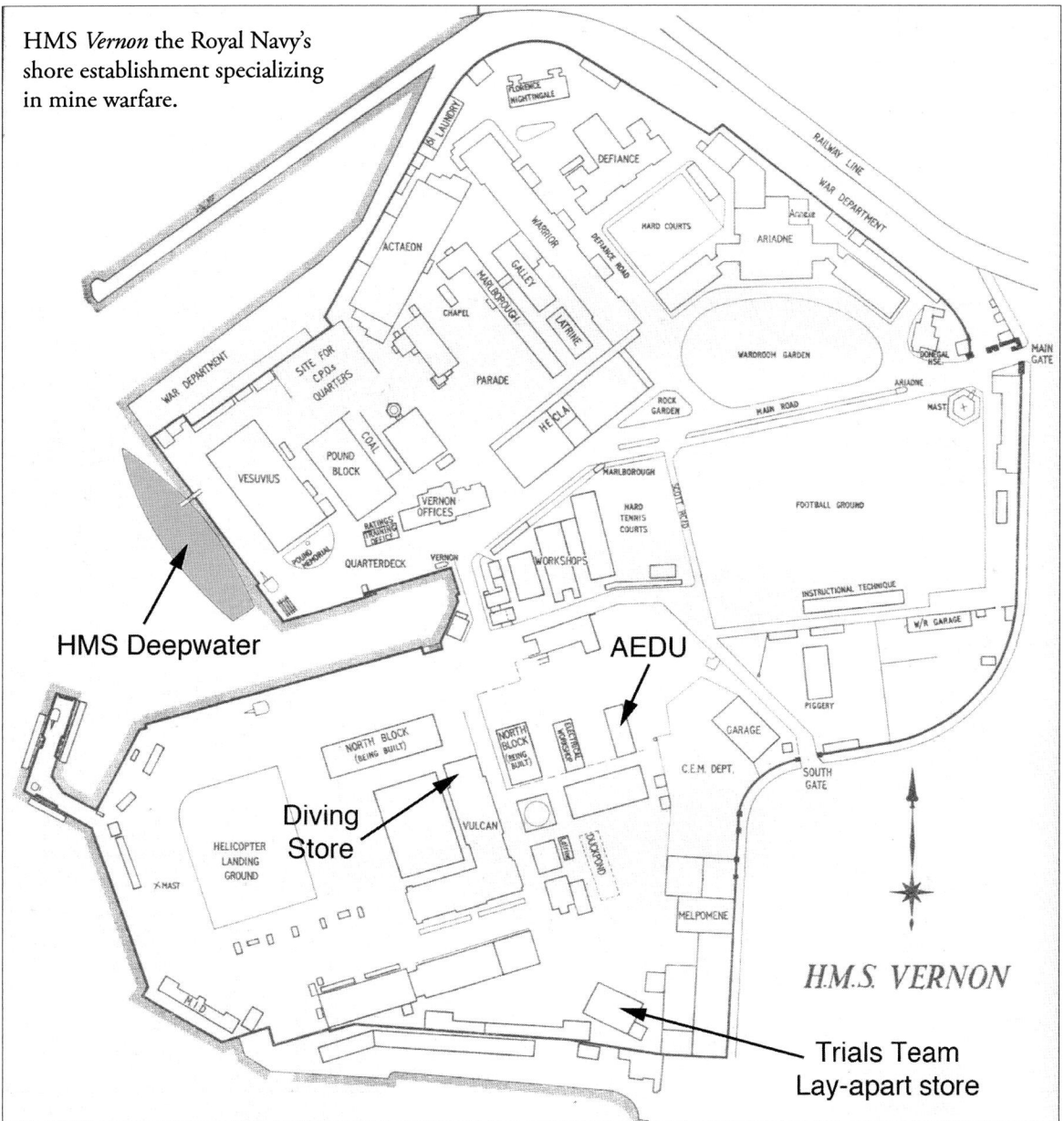

HMS *Vernon* the Royal Navy's shore establishment specializing in mine warfare.

HMS Deepwater

AEDU

Diving Store

Trials Team Lay-apart store

HMS *Deepwater*, the home of the Royal Navy's diving school based at HMS *Vernon*.

the carrier's propellers. The diving tender, flying the NATO Flag Four diving flag, was in full view of the Soviet cruiser. This was the Dockyard's civilian diving team consisting of two standard divers, two attendants and four pump handlers. They normally operated from an unpowered 30-foot ex-naval cutter, which had to be towed to its working location. However apart from their cover operations for the RN divers, they had been stood down for the duration of the Soviet visit.

Out of sight, two or perhaps three pairs of RN 'frogman' divers slipped over the side, turned in the opposite direction and swam south just beneath the surface until they reached the Soviet cruiser's hull. Each pair was connected together by a 10-foot (3m) buddy line. From there Brooks and his partner swam the length of the hull as far as the two propellers and stern. They met no other divers during their dive and they all returned safely to the diving tender alongside HMS *Bulwark* without any incident. It was said that they came across swim lines ('jackstays') strung across the cruiser's hull, connected at each end to the bilge keels on either side of the hull. These would have been previously laid by the Russian divers to provide guides for their divers to follow while conducting their finger-tip searches in zero visibility. The name of Petty Officer Macrae-Clifton has been suggested as one of the other divers.

The *Daily Express* reported:

Red divers were at work under the Russian cruiser during most of their stay at the South Railway Jetty in Portsmouth Harbour. It was said then that they were working on a defect or obstruction in a water intake.

Another reporter said her hull was patrolled at frequent intervals by Soviet frogmen.

In a letter sent to the Private Secretary at 10 Downing Street, presumed to be from Lt Cdr Brooks, on 27 March 1981, he mentioned:

I was in charge of the Naval operational team who successfully surveyed the undersides of the Russian ships at the time to ensure that all was either 'safe' or 'unsafe' … There were others [note plural] *apart from myself, who did the underwater work …*

He refers to the *"Russian ships"* [note plural] so it appears all three hulls were investigated. The reference to *"safe or unsafe"* is curious. One interpretation of this is that one of the objectives of the dive was intended to establish whether there was any nuclear radiation coming from the cruiser.

On 23 April, four days after Cdr Crabb's disappearance, Russian divers were sent down at the stern of the cruiser. They operated from one of the ship's own boats which tied up between the cruiser and the jetty. A newspaper reported:

They were operating from a ship's boat, and no-one knew what was their purpose. The boat was between the jetty and the cruiser, and the proceedings were watched by a small cluster of Russians on the quarter-deck, and by others on the jetty near the sentry at the gangway. Passing Dockyard men looked on, but nobody had his curiosity satisfied.

One could speculate that this was in response to suspicions raised on board by the RN diving activities near HMS *Bulwark* over the weekend. The previous day (22 April), the *Ordzhonikidze* had been opened to the public and crowds 30 to 40 deep milled around the single gangway leading on to the cruiser. For the Dockyard police it was a nightmare afternoon. The cruiser was quickly packed with sightseers. On the quayside, three policemen and an English-speaking Russian tried to

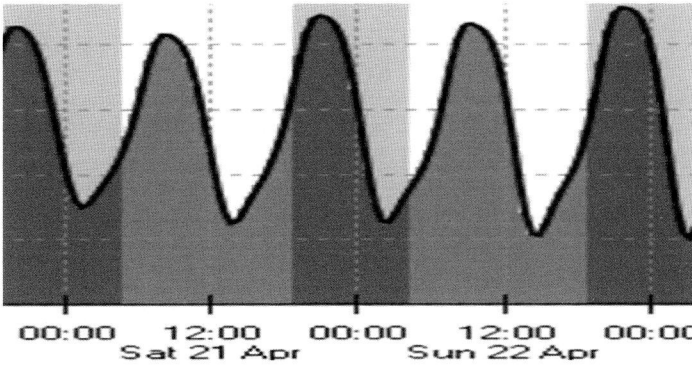

Graph showing the times of high and low tides over the weekend when the Royal Navy probably carried out their investigation of the Soviet ships.

The Soviet warships tied up at the South Railway Jetty with HMS *Bulwark* berthed ahead of them.

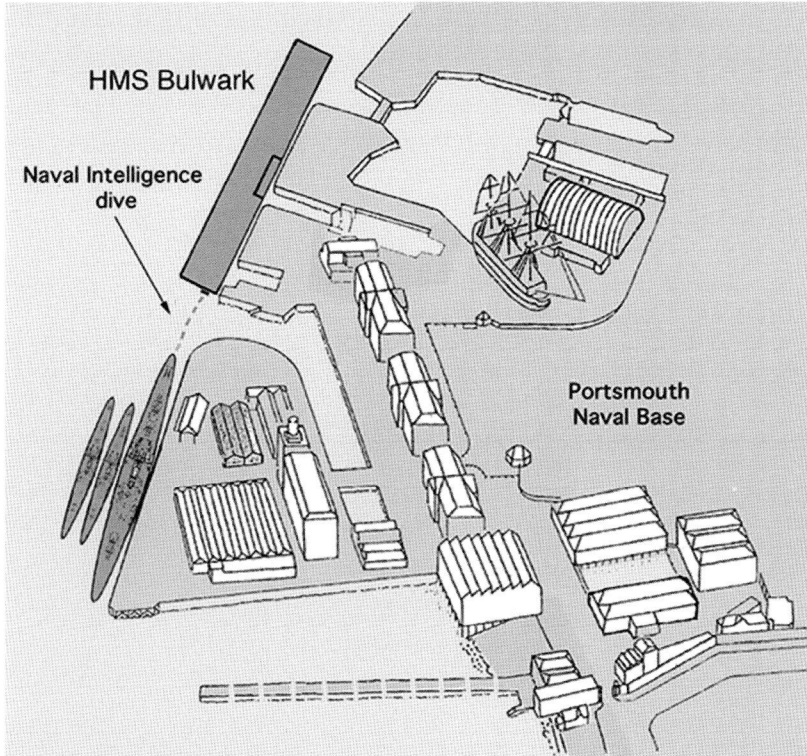

The location of HMS *Bulwark* and the path of the Royal Navy divers.

control the crowds. The Russian sailors would certainly have been kept busy trying to keep control of the crowds on board. Perhaps the opportunity was taken at this particular time to send in the naval diving team and perhaps also this is the reason for the Russian divers to check the stern the following day.

Perhaps more likely, it was in response to having observed Cdr Crabb surfacing four days earlier.

The purpose of the Russian dive could well have been to check that no monitoring devices had been attached to the ship's hull by British divers.

Despite the obvious interest of the British military in the Soviet warships and the noted frogman activity, the Soviet crews became increasingly relaxed during their stay in Portsmouth. This was undoubtedly assisted by the many social activities that were organised for them during their stay while the politicians were busy in London.

An example of this laid-back attitude was provided by Nigel Butlin who lived a few doors up from the Sally Port Hotel at 53 High Street. He was a nephew of Billy Butlin, the holiday camp pioneer. As a boy he used to own a small rowing boat which he kept in The Camber, a small dock just a few hundred metres south of South Railway Jetty. He and a young friend used his boat to row over to the Soviet warships and throw copies of magazines, women's fashion magazines in particular, up to the sailors. In return, the Russians threw them small souvenirs such as badges and rings. On one occasion the two boys were actually invited on board. They climbed a ladder at the stern and spent about twenty minutes being shown around by the Russian sailors.

So far we have covered the circumstances surrounding Cdr Crabb's disappearance. The next step is to review his reappearance, or rather his body's reappearance. It reappeared twice.

PART 3

COMMANDER CRABB'S BODY

The appearances of the body

On 14 May 1956 the Chief Constable of the crime office in Chichester wrote to all the local police authorities in the Portsmouth area warning them that should Cdr Crabb's body surface:

It is absolutely essential that the finding of the body is not to be disclosed to the press.

Does that sound as if he was expecting a body to be found? And why should Chichester Police suddenly get involved? It is interesting to note:

1 It was the Chichester Police Station that took this initiative and not Portsmouth.
2 Chichester Police Station belonged to a different force (West Sussex) and therefore had no prior involvement in the incident.
3 The body was eventually found in Chichester Harbour.
4 The Admiralty had noted earlier that *"If the body turns up ... there will have to be an inquest – in the place where the body is found."*
5 The Chief Constable and Coroner at Chichester were noted by MI6 to be *"very co-operative"*.

These events appear suspiciously to suggest that the scene was being prepared for Crabb's body to be 'discovered' in Chichester Harbour.

Body No 1

On the evening of Saturday, 3 November 1956, nearly seven months after Cdr Crabb's disappearance, Harry Cole of Bosmere Gardens, Emsworth, who worked for the Admiralty but was also a part-time fisherman, trawled up a dead body in his nets while fishing from his boat *Raven* outside Emsworth Harbour. The time was around 19.00 hours and it was a dark and blowy evening. He was on his own and he said he had difficulty recovering the body into the boat. The body was caught up in the wing of his 12-foot beam trawl. The body was covered with writhing prawns that were particularly thick over the face. The exposed part of the face was black. He was reported to have said he:

... gripped with both hands two breathing tubes which passed over either shoulder and around the back of the diver's neck. No bottles were present or at least observed. During these efforts, the head

became detached and fell away[3], into the sea, as did the body [he] was left holding one only of the breathing hoses together with a mouth piece.

He could see that it was the body of a diver in a rubber dry suit and it was still wearing a breathing apparatus. The suit appeared white but when scraped or rubbed it showed black underneath.

He eventually lost the body and retained only part of the breathing equipment which he eventually threw away. Cole claimed to have reported his experience to a local Emsworth police officer named Brown but strangely no official statement was taken at the time. Cole informed the police again three months later, on 7 February 1957. He casually mentioned it while reporting the recovery of an abandoned dinghy. In a statement to police sergeant Hoare dated 13 June 1957 he described the equipment he recovered.

Detective Sergeant George Brown (above) and Detective Superintendent Alan Hoare (below)

THE NEWS
PORTSMOUTH

TUESDAY, MARCH 23, 1965.
No. 27,298   (87th Year)   4d.

Havant man breaks nine-year silence

'I FOUND FROGMAN'S HEAD IN HARBOUR'

New light on Cmdr. Crabb's disappearance

After nine years of silence, a Havant security officer has revealed to an Evening News reporter that he holds the key to the mysterious disappearance of frogman, Cmdr. Crabb.

Mr. Harry Cole (45), of Bosmere Gardens, Emsworth, who is employed at a Havant factory, told our reporter that he found a frogman's body—he is confident it was Cmdr. Crabb's—in Chichester Harbour three months after Cmdr. Crabb had been reported missing.

In this picture, taken in 1945 from a de-mined ship off Venice, Commander (then Lieutenant) Lionel Crabb is seen (right) with C.P.O. Charles Canning and a group of Italian frogmen.

The headlines in The News, Portsmouth, on 23 March 1965.

3   A police report states gruesomely that heads of bodies tend to become separated from trunks within 4-6 weeks of immersion due to putrefaction of the body tissues.

I tried to get the object aboard but owing to the weight it broke away and I was left with a piece of rubber tube, a long rubber strap and a collar. Attached to the collar was a lead weight about four inches by four inches by half an inch.

Cole was interviewed much later by a reporter from *The News* (23 March 1965). He explained that he had been fishing in Chichester harbour when at about midnight he felt a *"terrific weight"* in his trawl. He was quoted as saying:

I immediately stopped and pulled it in and saw there was something in it. I thought it was a big skate, because they sometimes get caught in the front of the trawl. I made a grab for this thing in the trawl, got hold of it, and gave a tug. Then I suddenly realized that I had a head in my hands. I dropped it but I still kept hold of a mouthpiece, tube, a piece of metal, and a belt which goes around a man's chest. The head and the body dropped away straight down to the seabed.

Cole also drew a sketch to illustrate what he thought the equipment looked like. The sketch is not particularly accurate and it does not conclusively identify exactly what type of apparatus it was. However, the sketch shows a single hose connected centrally to the rubber *"collar"* (assumed to be the breathing bag/counterlung) and a single valve to one side and a weight in a pouch.

Unfortunately, further statements Cole made many years later conflicted with his original version given above. He described two breathing hoses and ball-shaped weights and the discovery was made in the evening.

Cole has been quoted as saying that after he lost the body it would undoubtedly be fished up again because anything heavy on the sea bed in that particular part of the harbour tended to remain in that area. If that were the case, then it would add to the attraction of the location

to the intelligence agencies for ensuring the eventual discovery and recovery of the body.

Body No 2

On Sunday, 9 June 1957, 14 months after Cdr Crabb's disappearance and seven months after the first body had been trawled up from the sea bed, a body was again discovered, this time floating in Chichester Harbour, 230 metres off Pilsey Island. It was found by the crew of a small trawler named *Red Goose*, six tons, from Bosham. There were three fishermen aboard, John Seymour Randall and two brothers, Ted and Bill Gilby. Randall, who lived at Snow Goose, Cutmill, Bosham, had a retail fur business in Portsmouth, by coincidence, near the Sally Port Hotel. They noted the rubber suit was dirty grey, there were rust marks around the legs and deep indentations clear of undergrowth where a breathing set may have been attached. They made the body fast and trailed it behind their boat. They headed for a deserted part of the beach at Pilsey Island where they placed the anchor ashore with the body still floating in the shallows. They called up the RAF at Thorney Island on their radio and reported their discovery. They were told to await their arrival.

The RAF telephoned the police at Southbourne and at 12.00 hours PC Ronald G Williams went to the RAF base on Thorney Island. He and the RAF Medical Officer were transported to the body by members of the 1107 MCU detachment in an old WW2 40ft assault landing craft (ALC 48) which was used for inshore and harbour rescue. They included Jim Knight, LAC Ray Howes and one other. Another launch and a helicopter also attended.

When they arrived they found the body on the beach. Two men from the helicopter

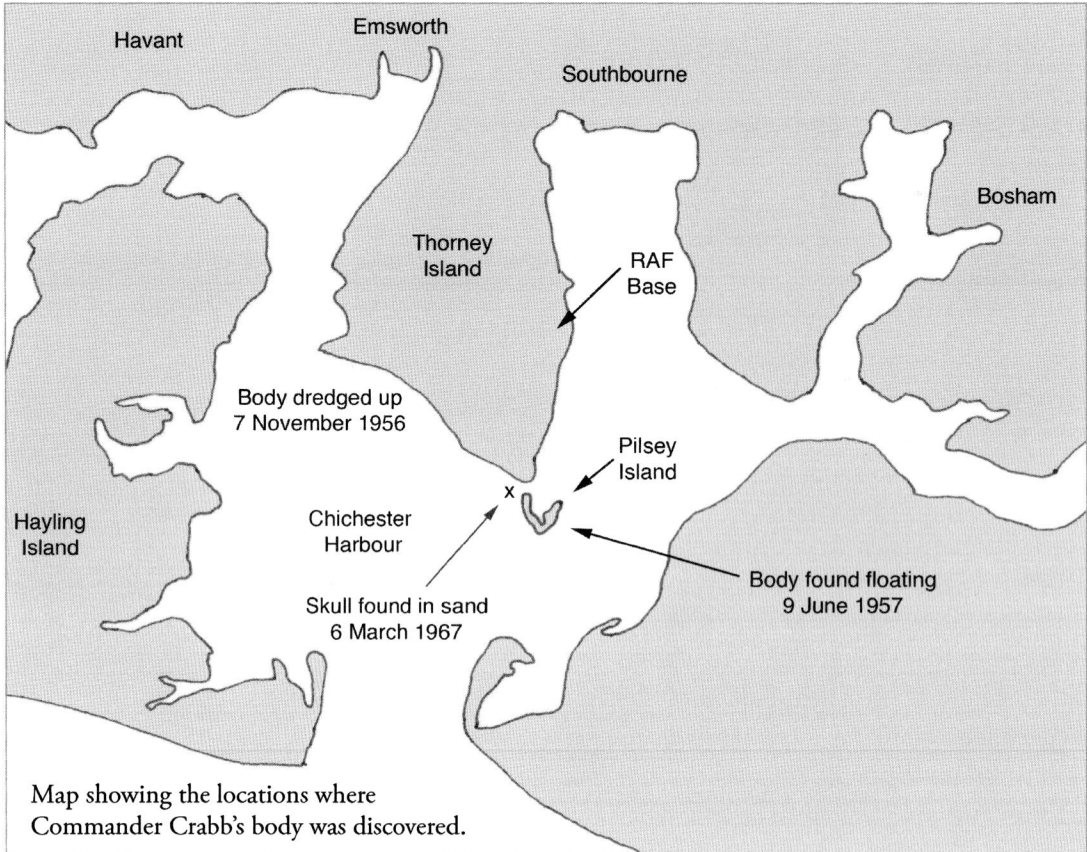

Map showing the locations where
Commander Crabb's body was discovered.

John Randall and Bill Gilby. Two of the fishermen who
recovered Commander Crabb's body.

examined the body after which it was recovered onto the landing craft's lowered front ramp. It was clear at the time that the head and hands were missing and in the cavity where the head had been were *"hundreds of small crabs and other such creatures. The odour was abominable."*

The RAF landing craft returned to the Marine Craft Section (MCS) and was able to run almost up to West Thorney Road as it was high tide. Waiting for them was a group of RAF Officers including Group Captain Boxer, Station Commander of RAF Thorney Island, four men in long dark overcoats, an RAF ambulance, local police and many unknown onlookers.

The RAF crew who recovered Commander Crabb's body on board ALC 48.

The body was initially taken to the mortuary at Chichester Hospital. Then on Tuesday, 11 June, it was transferred to Bognor Mortuary which was more modern and had refrigeration facilities. The diving suit along with the other items of clothing were retained at Chichester Police Station.

Nearly ten years later another body part turned up quite unexpectedly. On 5 March 1967 two boys playing on the sands near Pilsey Island found part of a human skull almost completely buried. They reported it to the RAF on Thorney Island and a little later, the Chief Technician at RAF Thorney Island handed it

The Mortuary in Spitalfield Lane, Chichester where Cdr Crabb's body was first taken. The mortuary keeper, Mr Tracey White, 50 years, was ordered by the police not to go back there until further notice.

The police station in Chichester where
Commander Crabb's diving clothing was taken.

in to the Police. Police Constable Colin Turrell who was stationed at Southbourne Detachment (which covered the area of Chichester Harbour) took a statement at 11.00 hours in the Main Guardroom at RAF Thorney Island. After expert examination, it was considered to be of the right sex, age and condition as to have been from the body previously recovered in 1957 and identified as Cdr Crabb. The lower jaw was missing and the upper jaw retained just seven teeth. The teeth were found to be in poor condition, but none had any fillings.

The present whereabouts of this skull are unknown though a photograph of it has been retained in the Chichester Public Record Office.

It appears the authorities carried out a thorough search of the area. A young lad named Steve Miller along with a few friends happened to be cockling on the sands on the east side of Pilsey Island and he noticed that

over on the west side, at the high water mark, canvas screens had been erected and official-looking men milled around the area.

Sadly, no trace of the breathing equipment that Cdr Crabb had been wearing appears to have been saved. This has led to speculation as to the nature and source of the breathing equipment.

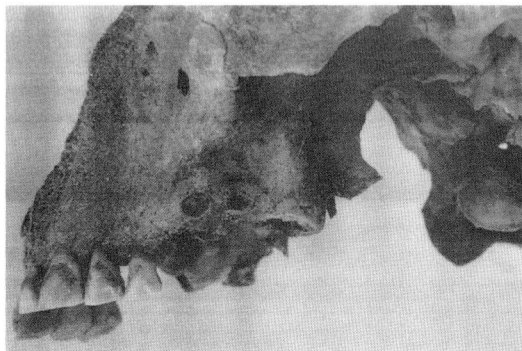

The remains of a skull discovered in the sand near Pilsey Island in 1967. It was considered to be consistent with the age of the body recovered in 1957.

What breathing apparatus did Commander Crabb use?

The evidence as to which oxygen breathing set Cdr Crabb used is conflicting. An oxygen set of some sort would definitely have been used because it did not give off tell-tale bubbles. It was also relatively light-weight, compact, had a long endurance and was more suitable for underwater swimming (as opposed to walking heavy on the sea bed).

Lt Cdr Gordon Gutteridge has stated:

The breathing set he used was a WW2 Italian one which he acquired dishonestly and by subterfuge from a serving officer who was responsible for preserving historic diving gear.

Lt Cdr Gutteridge was a close friend of Lt Cdr Franklin who actually helped to dress Cdr Crabb, together with Lt Cdr Crawford and Petty Officer Lofty Gordon who Cdr Crabb made a point of meeting during visit to Portsmouth. This should have placed him in a good position to know what set Crabb had actually used. But he was probably wrong.

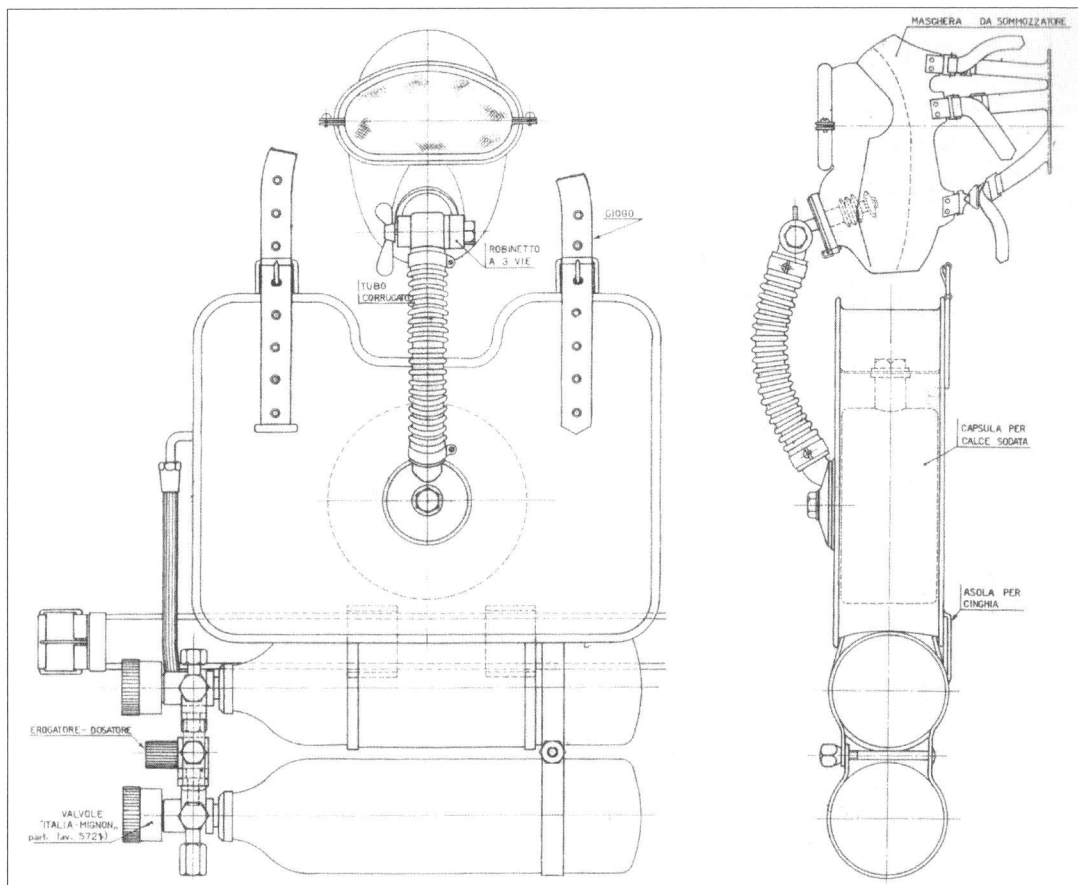

Design drawing of the Italian ARO oxygen rebreather. (From: *Palombari della Marina Militare Italiana*)

If the equipment had been Italian, then the issue of recharging the oxygen cylinders is raised. The oxygen cylinders would have been incompatible with the standard RN recharging system. There were two ways of overcoming this. The first would have been to have produced adaptors to connect the Italian cylinders to the RN decanting cylinders and booster pump; or second, by modifying the Italian set to accept RN oxygen cylinders. Either option was possible and would most certainly have been previously arranged in order to evaluate the performance of the apparatus.

Another possibility was that Cdr Crabb wore the contemporary oxygen breathing equipment in use in the Royal Navy – the Shallow Water Breathing Apparatus (SWBA).

The SWBA (Pattern 5562) could be rigged in one of two modes: Shallow Diving (booted diver) with a maximum depth of 33 feet or Swimming (diver wearing fins, frogman-style) with a maximum depth of 25 feet. It used a single breathing hose, the lead weights were small, ball-shaped, weighing 12 ounces each, held in a pouch or an optional, 12-pound slab weight hung on the back (for booted diving). The set carried two oxygen cylinders with a total capacity of 147.6 litres for normal operation and an extra, emergency cylinder with a further 73.8 litres of oxygen. For shallow

The Italian frogman oxygen rebreather favoured by Commander Crabb. It was produced by Pirelli and called the "ARO Pirelli LS 801" (From: *Palombari della Marina Militare Italiana*)

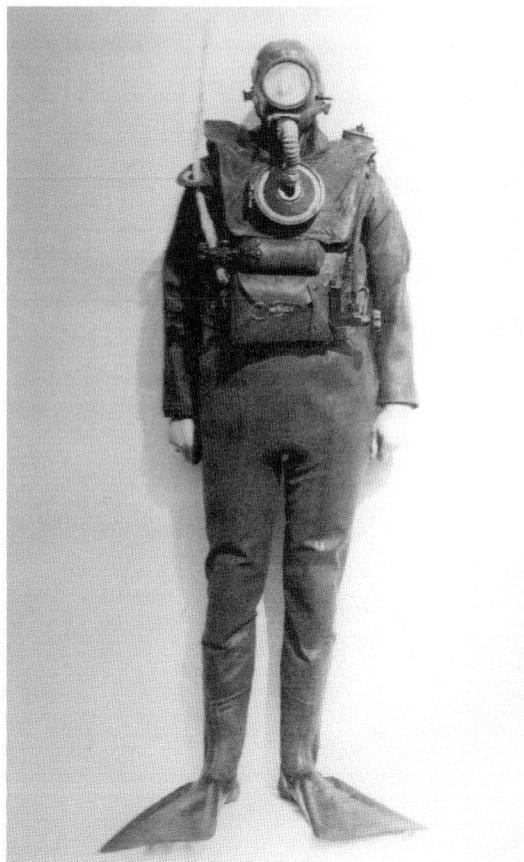

The Shallow Water Breathing Apparatus (SWBA) Pattern 5562, rigged for swimming.

water diving the oxygen was supplied as a continuous bleed via a reducer valve and for underwater swimming the oxygen was supplied manually by the operation of a manual valve. The carbon dioxide absorbent canister carried a 2-pound charge of Protosorb. It was stated at the time of its introduction to have a maximum endurance of two hours. If Commander Crabb had used this set, he would have used it in the "swimming" rig with the manual gas feed. Assistant Scientific Officer, George Allpress, who worked at AEDU in HMS *Vernon* remembered Commander Crabb asking about the loan of a SWBA.

A statement by Petty Officer 'Lofty' Gordon would tend to support the SWBA option: "*… the diving equipment Crabb used was supplied by the Naval Diving School at HMS Vernon …*" Lt Cdr Franklin who was in charge of the Diving School at HMS *Vernon* also stated that the breathing apparatus was a naval set from HMS *Vernon*.

Furthermore, in view of Franklin's statement that the breathing set used by Cdr Crabb had a maximum endurance of two hours, it is the author's opinion that on the balance of probabilities the set used was the contemporary SWBA Pattern 5562 rigged for swimming (i.e. a manually operated oxygen supply).

The most credible indication of the actual breathing set used by Cdr Crabb is in the description provided to the Police by the Admiralty at the time when they were looking for his body, already quoted above:

ANNEXURE TO ADMIRALTY LETTER N.L.1811/56 OF 9TH MAY 1956
> *Believed to have been wearing:*
> > *Two-piece Heinke suit*
> > *Breathing apparatus pattern 5562*
> > *Service-type face mask*
> > *Service-type swim fins*

In all probability therefore, it would seem that Cdr Crabb used a contemporary Royal

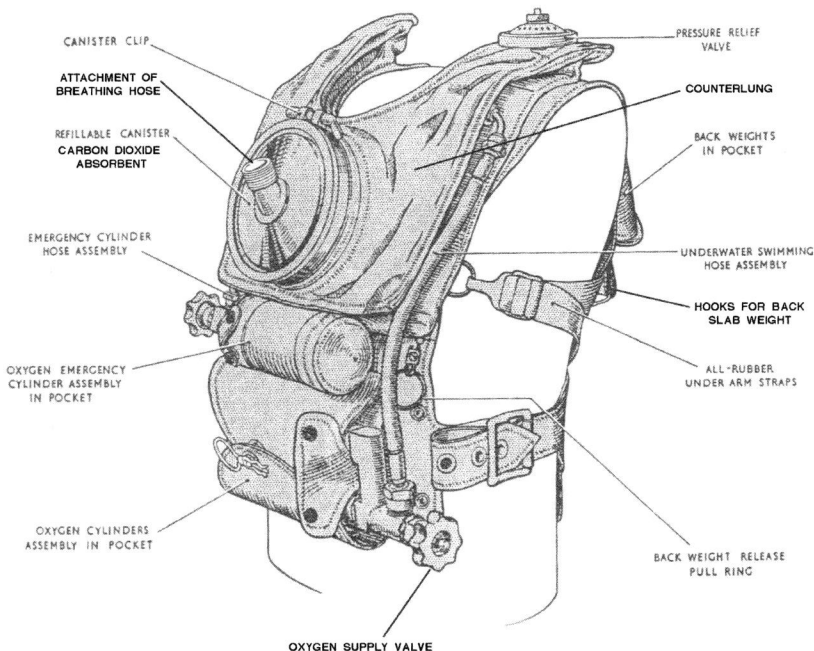

CANISTER CLIP

ATTACHMENT OF
BREATHING HOSE

REFILLABLE CANISTER
CARBON DIOXIDE
ABSORBENT

EMERGENCY CYLINDER
HOSE ASSEMBLY

OXYGEN EMERGENCY
CYLINDER ASSEMBLY
IN POCKET

OXYGEN CYLINDERS
ASSEMBLY IN POCKET

OXYGEN SUPPLY VALVE

PRESSURE RELIEF
VALVE

COUNTERLUNG

BACK WEIGHTS
IN POCKET

UNDERWATER SWIMMING
HOSE ASSEMBLY

HOOKS FOR BACK
SLAB WEIGHT

ALL-RUBBER
UNDER ARM STRAPS

BACK WEIGHT RELEASE
PULL RING

Drawing of the Shallow Water Breathing Apparatus (SWBA) Pattern 5562, rigged for swimming.

Navy oxygen breathing set known as the Shallow Water Breathing Apparatus (SWBA) Pattern 5562 rigged for swimming and that it came from the diving school on HMS *Deepwater* at HMS *Vernon*.

With the body of a diver clad in a rubber diving suit safely in the hands of the Chichester Hospital, it should have been a routine matter to confirm its identity. Confirmation that it was Cdr Crabb's body was the government's highest priority. Sadly the issue was not that straight forward and there was possibly room for doubt. The government, the Admiralty and MI6 subsequently conspired to get the result they wanted. Crabbgate was still fully operational.

The SWBA, worn by PO McKinlay.

The Autopsy and Inquest –
Was it Commander Crabb's body?

Following the discovery and recovery of the body, events unfurled in quick succession.

The body was discovered on 9 June 1957 and initially taken to the public mortuary in Spitalfield Lane, Chichester. There Dr Donald Plimsoll King, Chief Pathologist at St Richards Hospital, Chichester, carried out the autopsy the following day, on 10 June, which lasted about two hours. The police photographer, DC Malcolm G Barrett was called in to photograph the dissected body at 9.45 am on the 11 June. As mentioned previously, the body was then moved to the mortuary at Bognor Regis which had refrigeration facilities. The Inquest was officially opened at the Court House in Chichester on 11 June. It lasted just two minutes. The Coroner's officer, PC Dennis Castleden, simply accounted for the clothing found on the body and the Coroner, George Frederick Leslie Bridgman

Dr Donald Plimsoll King, Chief Pathologist at St Richards Hospital, Chichester. He carried out the autopsy on Commander Crabb's body.

Police photographer, Malcolm Barrett (before his promotion to DC) and his notebook record for 11 June 1957

adjourned the proceedings for two weeks. This was a normal procedure.

Dr King carried out a further examination of the body at Bognor Regis on 14 June, having been advised that there should be a distinctive, 'Y'-shaped scar on one of the legs, which he had failed to notice during his first examination.

His report included:

Above the waist, parts of the body, including the skull, had disappeared although certain bones, including the left humerus and both scapulae, *remained. The abdominal cavity was empty except below the waist-band of the suit. The organs had undergone extensive post mortem change including a change known as adipocere, but they were recognisable … He also found there was a condition called valgus which was a condition of the toes in which the big toe, which was the hallux, was turned outwards. The joint of the big toe was enlarged and disjointed. With regard to the hair on the body the pubic hair was intact and the colour was clearly a light brown and in certain lights when*

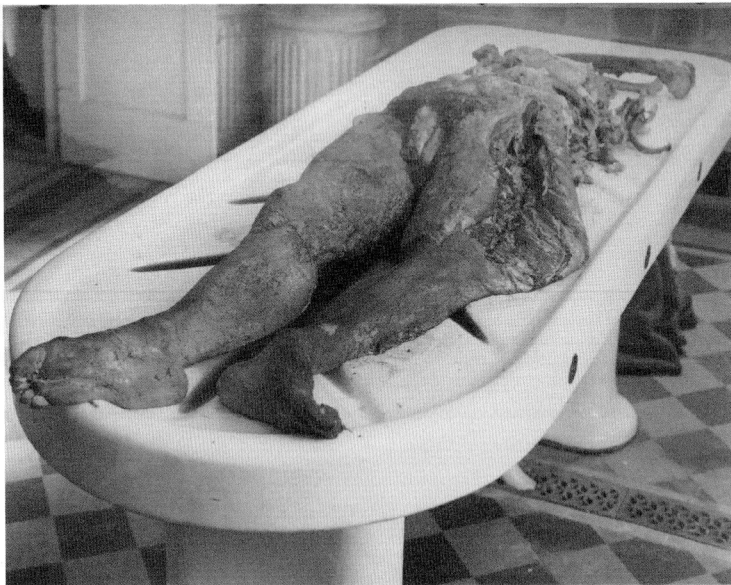

The upper part of the body and arms have been largely eaten away by scavenging sea creatures which had access via the openings into the rubber suit at the neck and sleeve cuffs. The left femur (thigh bone) has been dissected out and placed at the head of the table.
Photograph: DC Malcolm Barrett

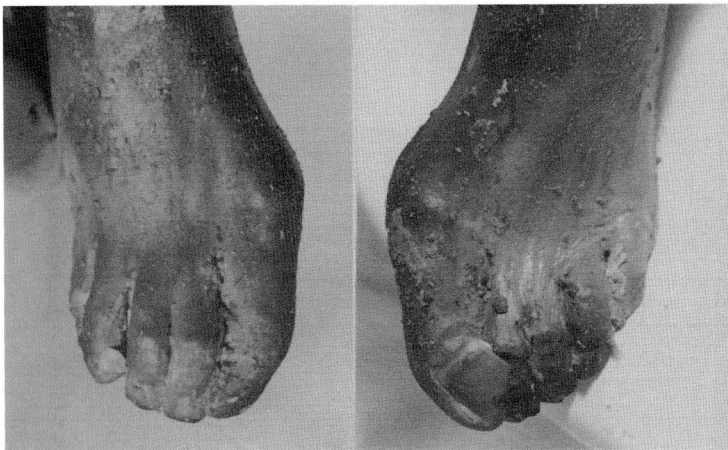

The feet of the corpse. While probably deformed or 'straightened' by being squeezed inside the swim fins, the *hallux valgus* condition is still quite obvious.
Photograph: DC Malcolm Barrett

dry it had a gingerish tinge. The legs were in a good state of preservation and he would describe them as muscular and well formed and, apart from the feet, there was no deformity. They were quite straight.

From the adipocere, he concluded that the body had been in the water for at least six months and could well have been in the water for at least fourteen months.

On the 14th June 1957, he went to the Mortuary and examined the remains again. He looked at the left knee and saw a scar.

At the request of the author, Consultant Orthopaedic Surgeon James Calder TD MD FRCS (Tr & Orth) FFSEM, has examined the photographs of the feet and concluded:

Yes he does have hallux valgus deformity … He also has a degree of interphalangeus (which means that there is a valgus deformity at the inter-phalangeal joint of the great toe which accentuates the overall deformity and makes the bunion on the medial side of the metatarsophalangeal joint appear more prominent).

Detective Constable Malcolm G Barrett of Chichester Police Station wrote the following account of his involvement in 2008:

The body was removed to the public mortuary in Chichester, located beside the Hope Inn in Spitalfield Lane. I was not present.

I went to the mortuary at 9.45 am on Tuesday, 11th June 1957, with Det Sgt George Brown, to take photographs of the post mortem. I drove up to the green double gates but was hampered by the press, who seemed to think I had a Mrs Crabb in the back of my photographic van. (I did not). The post mortem examination was conducted by Dr King, a Consultant Pathologist from St Richard's Hospital, Chichester. Those present were Detective Superintendent Alan Hoare, Detective Sergeant George Brown (my senior officer) and Mr Figg the Mortician.

By this time it was suggested that the body of the frogman may be that of Commander Lionel "Buster" Crabb, RNVR Ret, who went missing in April, 1956 while diving in Portsmouth Harbour during the visit of the two Russian leaders – Khrushchev and Bulganin.

The remains were laid out on the mortuary slab; all garments had been removed. The hands and head were missing along with most of the chest area – destroyed by decomposition. The lower part of the body was in fairly good condition. A preliminary examination revealed that the man was about 5 feet 2 inches tall (gauged from the length of the thigh bone).

He had hammer toes and his pubic hair was ginger. I took five photographs of these remains.

The remains were then removed to the public mortuary at Bognor Regis to be placed in the refrigerator, as the mortuary at Chichester did not have this facility. The clothing, minus the head gear, consisted of the main frogman's suit, which bore rust marks, a one-piece faded red cotton item of underwear, a pair of swimming trunks and flippers, was taken to Police Headquarters, Kingsham Avenue, Chichester. They were spread out to dry on the grass at the rear of the photographic studio.

An amusing incident resulted from this – apparently the Chief Constable, Mr R P Wilson, complained to the Chief Clerk, C/Inspector Watson that there was an awful smell of drains permeating into his office, which was situated above the studio. On hearing of this the clothing was hastily gathered up and taken to a lockup garage for examination, where the following day I carried out an examination with Det Cons L Clausen. It was noted that all labels had been removed from every garment. Ultra violet and infra red were used on all garments, but nothing was revealed.

Mrs Crabb, the Commander's former wife, was asked to identify the body in my absence

Detective Constable Len Clausen

but she was unsure, although she specifically mentioned a scar below the Commander's left knee. As a result of this remark , the Pathologist cut out the area of the knee, including the scar and it was taken to be photographed at the Police photographic department at Chichester, prior to being returned to Bognor Mortuary and replaced with the other remains.

The clothing was removed to an old barn on the Police Station site, which was later demolished and replaced by new garages, and that was the last I saw of any of it.

I did not attend the Inquest, but I recall the Coroner said that the body was that of Commander Lionel Crabb, and he recorded "An Open Verdict".

A more recent piece of evidence has come to light which further supports the conclusion that the body recovered from Chichester

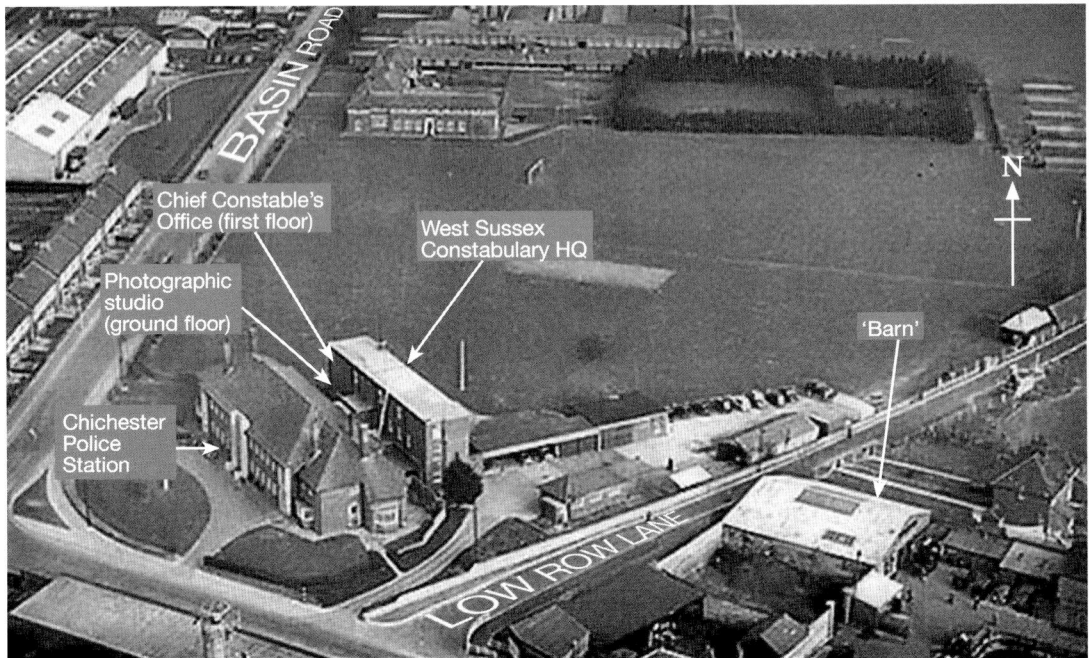

Aerial photograph of Chichester Police Station from the 1950s.
Note the photographic studio and the 'barn' where Crabb's diving clothes were last seen.

harbour was that of Commander Crabb. It also concerns the nature of the corpse's feet.

Frederick 'Rick' Grimes was a diver/electrician at the Admiralty Research Laboratory (ARL) in Teddington at the same time as Crabb (1949-1951). When a collection of Grimes' diving kit and archives was donated to The Diving Museum at Gosport, it included a pair of fins which Grimes claimed had previously belonged to Crabb (then a Lt Cdr) during his time at ARL.

These fins were a pair of Owen Churchill fins, of American manufacture, and the type used and supplied by the RN. They are the same type as the pair which Cdr Crabb had been wearing on his fateful dive. However, the right fin had been cut away in the area over the top of the instep. This was clearly an attempt by the wearer to alleviate the pain and discomfort caused by the stiff fin when worn by someone with a particularly high instep.

Close inspection of the photograph of the corpse in the mortuary at Chichester Hospital clearly shows the feet had a pronounced instep, also confirmed by Dr James Calder, the Consultant Orthopaedic Surgeon.

Dr King's report also included the following details:

Length of feet 8.74 inches (22.2 cm)
Moderate degree of bilateral hallux valgus
    [also referred to as a 'bunion']
He was circumcised
Small man, about 5ft 6ins

The subsequent attempts at the formal identification of the body by witnesses unfortunately produced conflicting results.

Cdr Crabb's former wife, Margaret Crabb, then 43 years old, viewed the body at Bognor Mortuary on 11 June 1957. She had initially driven from her home in St Margaret's Bay to

One of the fins claimed by diver Frederick Grimes to have belonged to Lt Commander Crabb while at ARL. Note the cut away area.

Chichester but found the mortuary closed. The body had just been removed to Bognor Regis mortuary. The police took her to Bognor where after only thirty seconds of viewing the body she declared *"I am sorry. I cannot say yes or no."* She could not identify the feet as those of Cdr Crabb although she was not able to say definitely that they were not his feet. While she had stated that he had hammer toes, the feet had been distorted by the long immersion and confinement in the fins. She described him as a short man, not as tall as she, her height being 5 feet 5 inches. His legs were very straight and muscular and the hair on his body was very light brown inclined to ginger. In private she stated to friends it was definitely not his body, even though she had been told it was and that she had been urged to agree it was.

The body was viewed by Lt William Young 'Mr Mac' McLanachan, a Diving Officer at HMS *Vernon* and an old friend of Cdr Crabb's, at 16.00 hours the same day at Bognor Regis.

McLanachan stated he *"cannot definitely identify the body as that of Commander Crabb"* but *"that the feet are similar inasmuch that they are small and appear to be slightly splayed."*

Cdr Gutteridge has stated:

It was a little surprising that McLanachan, who did not know Crabb well, was chosen for this unpleasant task whereas I, who lived in Chichester, was serving at the Underwater Countermeasures & Weapons Establishment where Crabb last served and probably knew Crabb in his later life better than anyone except his wife, was not asked to be involved in any identification ... for which I was most grateful.

Petty Officer Ron McKinlay CGM viewed the body and he agreed it was that of Cdr Crabb.

The Inquest was reopened on 26 June 1957 at 15.00 hours at the Court House, Chichester. It was held in camera (i.e., not open to the public). There was no jury and it lasted for less than one hour.

Witness statements included those of:
— Dr Donald Plimsoll King, the pathologist who conducted the autopsy
— John Seymour Randall, one of the fishermen who found the body
— Police Constable Ronald George Williams, who attended at the recovery of the body
— George William Bostock, a civil servant who kept records of RNVR officers
— Miss Amy Frances Thomas, the manageress of Cdr Crabb's flat in Hans Road, London
— Mrs Margaret Elaine Crabb, Commander Crabb's former wife
— Eric James Blake, a director of Heinke & Co Ltd who made Cdr Crabb's diving suit
— Sydney James Knowles, Commander Crabb's former diving colleague
— Colin Grey Turner, a shoe specialist
— Detective Superintendent Alan Hoare,

Lt William Young McLanachan MBE BEM who viewed Cdr Crabb's body.

Inquest witness, Amy Frances Thomas, the manageress of Cdr Crabb's flat in London.

who had been in charge of enquiries concerning the body

The Admiralty and MI6 were successful in preventing Franklin and Smith, who were the actual last persons to see Cdr Crabb alive, from being called as witnesses and absolutely no reference was made to them by the Coroner in his conclusions. The same goes for Lt McLanachan who had been called on to identify the body. Indeed it appears from the documents available and contrary to all normal practice, not one representative from the Royal Navy or MI6 was called to give evidence. A note from the Head of Naval Law to Chief of Naval Intelligence prior to the Inquest suggests it was rigorously choreographed:

The body will be identified by the evidence of the following:

(a)   Crabb's wife …

(b)   Heinke's …

(c)   A man in Newcastle …

The Coroner is aware of the background to the case and is not asking for the appearance of any embarrassing naval witness …

The answer to all questions continues to be that we have nothing to add to what the Prime Minister said in the House of Commons in May 1956 …

Rear Admiral J G T Inglis, Director of Naval Intelligence, has stated that The Coroner and Chief Constable were *"being most co-operative"*. A government document stated that *"The Home Office think they would be able to persuade him* [the Coroner] *to avoid awkward questions."*

Controversially, Sydney Knowles was adamant that it was not the body of Cdr Crabb. He claimed he was shown the body and he was told by the Chief Inspector of Police:

We know this is not the body of Commander Crabb but I want you to say it is the body of Commander Crabb.

But Knowles' description of the body differs markedly from the others. So much so it draws serious doubt on whether he did actually see it. In his book *A Diver in the Dark* he claims that when he saw it, it was still wearing the rubber dry suit though it had been cut open to display the body. Surprisingly, he described the suit as the type used by the navy which was a one-piece suit and was fitted with an urinal port. He also described the remains of a heavy duty submariner's sweater. This all conflicts with the evidence of the Admiralty given to the

The Court House at Chichester where the inquest was reopened, as it appears today.

Eric Blake, the Managing Director
of C E Heinke & Co Ltd.

Ron Collins
of C E Heinke & Co Ltd.

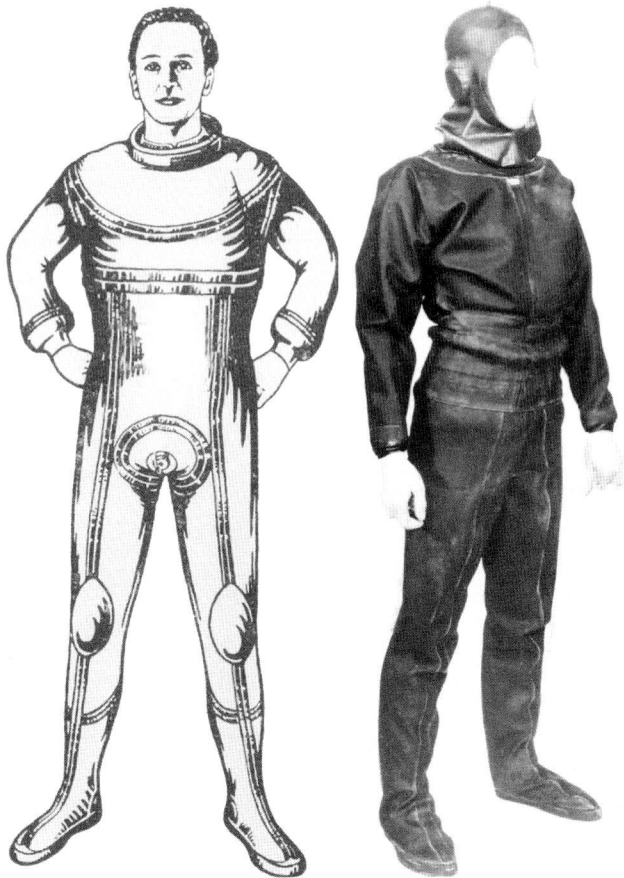

Right: The type of one-piece Royal Navy
dry suit with urinal port that Sydney
Knowles claimed he saw on Crabb's body.

Far right: The Heinke two-piece "Delta"
dry suit of the type found on the body
as described by McLanachan, Blake and
Collins. The illustration actually shows
the hood-attached version whereas
Commander Crabb used one with a neck
seal and a separate hood.

Police on 10 May 1956 (above) and that given by Franklin, McLanachan as well as Eric Blake (Managing Director) and Ron Collins of C E Heinke & Co Ltd regarding the other clothing described below. In the author's view Knowles' version is therefore unreliable.

Interestingly, Knowles had once quoted Cdr Crabb as saying *"Syd, when I die I don't want to have bed-socks on, I want to have my flippers on."*

Knowles was shown photographs of the feet of Cdr Crabb and *"He was not able to say from the photographs shown to him whether the feet are those of Crabb".*

If Knowles was shown photographs of Cdr Crabb's feet, why would he not have been able to undertake the same exercise when he allegedly saw the actual body. This throws further doubt on Knowles's claim that he actually saw the body.

He said he looked closely for two scars he knew of on Cdr Crabb's legs but found none. He described how Cdr Crabb had sustained an inverted 'Y' scar on the side of his left knee. The mention of a distinctive 'Y' scar sent the pathologist back to Bognor to examine the body. He located it on the knee, cut out the section of skin bearing the scar and sent it to the Chichester Police Station to be photographed. There, police photographer Malcolm Barnett pinned it onto a board and photographed it in the presence of DC Clausen.

This conflicts slightly with the evidence in the police file at Chichester. The photograph of this piece of skin removed by the pathologist does indeed appear to bear a 'Y' scar. However, it appears from an accompanying drawing that it was not an inverted 'Y'. Furthermore, according to police photographer DC Malcolm Barrett, it was Commander Crabb's ex-wife who raised the subject of the scar.

Knowles added that Commander Crabb

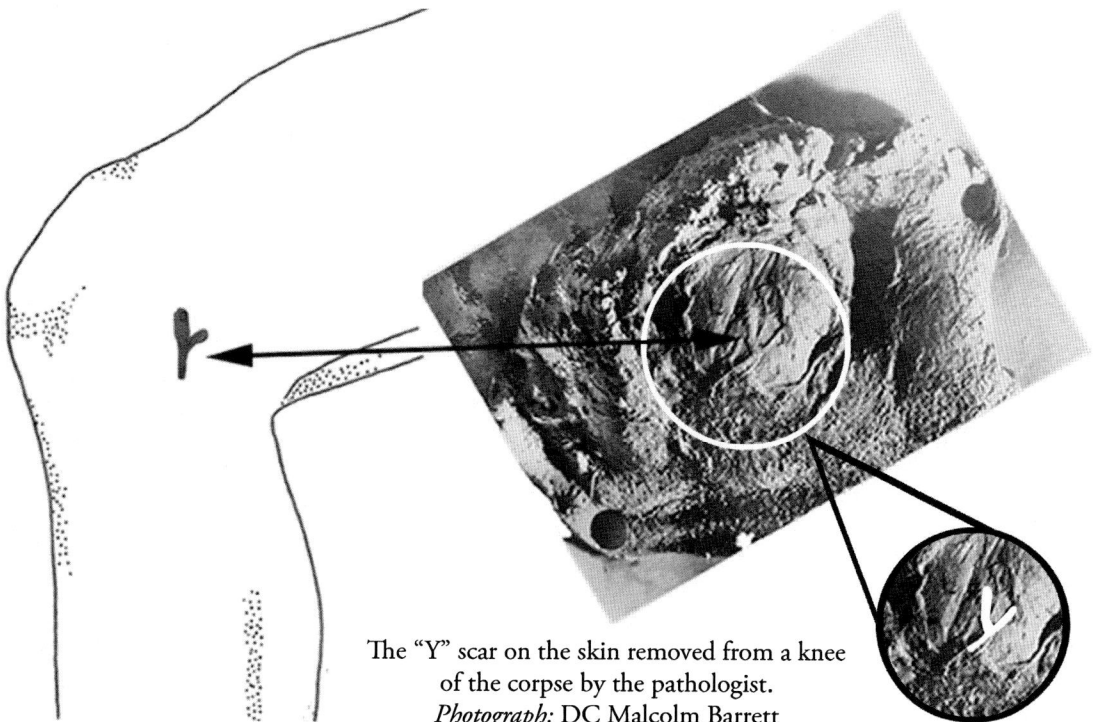

The "Y" scar on the skin removed from a knee of the corpse by the pathologist.
Photograph: DC Malcolm Barrett

used a two-piece dry suit with a neck seal instead of an attached hood. He used to wear maroon swimming shorts and two sets of combination underwear to wear alternately, one khaki in colour and the other blue. He also used blue socks.

Further examination of Knowles's claim in his book *A Diver in the Dark* to have seen Cdr Crabb's body adds more doubt that this actually did take place. He says that he was visited by two men from MI5 who invited him to help identify the body in Chichester. Cdr Crabb's body was only at Chichester mortuary from the afternoon of 9 June to 11 June (say 48 hours or less) after which it was transferred to Bognor mortuary. This does not give much time for Knowles to have been identified as a suitable witness, be visited by MI5 personnel (why not MI6 for whom Cdr Crabb had been working?) and to have ridden his motorcycle from Preston to Chichester. Knowles states that when he saw the body it was still dressed in the rubber dry suit, though it had been cut open by the pathologist. This does not ring true as the pathologist would surely have carried out his detailed inspection of the body before anyone else was invited to view it. In which case it would not have still been dressed in the dry suit when Knowles alleges he saw it. Furthermore, the *Lancashire Evening Post* reported on their discussions with Knowles on 14 June 1957:

"Last night [13 June 1957] *Mr Knowles was in touch with the coroner's office in Bognor Regis ... He was told that if he was required the CID would get in touch with him sometime today. Early this afternoon he had not heard anything."*

Lt McLanachan viewed the diving equipment at Chichester Police Station on 11 June 1957. It included:

1 Frogman's two piece suit, in good condition but with marine growth, marked HEINKE LONDON inside waist band; soles similarly marked 9-10; two piece; inside of left leg and at feet large areas of rust

1 pair swim fins similar to RN pattern (marked Pattern 3386)[4]

2 sorbo pads

1 pair Maroon bathing trunks; "Just men"

1 pair nylon socks; St Michael brand, size 10-12

1 pair blue stockinette combinations (top half missing 18"zip)

1 pair nylon combinations, top torn

1 piece of undervest

Not mentioned in the official reports but noted briefly in a newspaper report:

In preliminary examination it was found that the ends of connecting straps were all that remained of the headgear and breathing apparatus ...

Eric James Blake, Managing Director of C E Heinke & Co Ltd, identified the two-piece suit with neck seal which he said was the type that had been sold to Cdr Crabb on 11 October 1955. He said Cdr Crabb always expressed a preference for a suit with a neck seal rather than one with a hood attached.

Ron Chamberlain of Siebe Gorman & Co Ltd has referred to his friend Ron Collins, a manager at C E Heinke who stated that the suit found on the body:

... was a Heinke Dry Suit and quoted the Number inside ... confirmed that that Numbered Suit was supplied to Buster Crabb.

This conflicts with the statement of Eric Blake. If the suit had been numbered, then this information should have been provided

---

4   "Pattern 3386" is the Admiralty Pattern number for the fins so they actually were naval fins and not just *"similar to RN pattern"*. They were actually copies of the American Churchill fins.

by Blake at the Inquest. I have not seen any official reference to such a number having been observed.

Detective Superintendent Alan Hoare described *"marks of rust"* around the legs making it *"apparent that the body had been held by being caught on an underwater metal object"*.

Police photographer, DC Malcolm Barrett, has also stated that there were no identifying marks or labels on the dry suit. The suit was also examined under both ultraviolet and infrared lighting.

Lt Cdr Franklin, having seen the clothing found on the body has stated:

It appears to me to be similar to the clothing which Crabb was wearing when I assisted him over the side of the boat and in my own mind I am convinced that it is the same clothing.

Newspaper reports suggested:

There was a strong suspicion amongst some defence chiefs that the body had not been in the water 14 months.

Might this suggest that the body had been kept in cold storage at Fort Monckton by MI6 for a period of time following its recovery and before being dumped in Chichester Harbour?

Pat Rose, Cdr Crabb's 'fiancée' at the time of his disappearance, never accepted that Cdr Crabb had died during the dive or that the body recovered was that of Cdr Crabb. But she never actually viewed the body.

Nevertheless, the Coroner subsequently returned an open verdict on the cause of death and said he was satisfied that the remains were those of Cdr Crabb. There was no evidence of the cause of death. He was sufficiently satisfied with the evidence to issue a formal Death Certificate. Once again, this was exactly what the Admiralty and MI6 wanted, and some might again suggest, actually arranged.

In his summing up the Coroner stated *"Cdr Crabb, who was last seen by witnesses on April 17th 1956 in London ..."*

How truthful was that? It was so blatantly untrue it defies credibility.

What about Lt Cdr Albert Franklin, Cdr Ted Davies, Bernard Smith, Chief Constable Arthur West, Chief Detective Superintendent Jack Lamport, PC John Edwards, Mary Barnett, Edward Richman, Cdr Emmerson, Lt Cdr John Crawford, Senior Commissioned Boatswain 'Lofty' Gordon, a messful of officers in HMS *Vernon* and pubfuls of drinkers in the Keppel's Head hotel, The Bear Hotel, the Sally Port Hotel and the Country House pub, to mention just a few?

Even Rear Admiral Inglis of NID knew that was not the case. He had stated in a Top Secret letter:

I am afraid the lawyers have concluded that it is inevitable that [Redacted, but actually Lt Cdr Franklin] *of the Diving School should give evidence in person at the inquest as he was the last person on our side to see him alive.*

The Coroner was obviously persuaded to bend to the wishes of NID/Admiralty and in a despicable display of irresponsibility and unprofessionalism, failed to call Franklin as a witness. The conduct of the Inquest fell so far short of an acceptable standard that its credibility and even legality are seriously questionable. This could constitute an additional reason for the extended embargo of 100 years on the release of information.

Perhaps it is more than just 'embarrassment' that the government wishes to cover up. It could well be downright criminality.

After the formal declaration, if it was not the body of Cdr Crabb and he had indeed ended up in Russia, then the Russians had a first class opportunity for a propaganda coup by parading Cdr Crabb for all the world to see. What could be more embarrassing for the British government than for their Coroner to declare he had Cdr Crabb's body and then for Russia to miraculously resurrect him in Moscow? The fact that this did not happen supports the view that it was the body of Cdr Crabb in the mortuary. Indeed the Russians themselves did not claim to have him (see Appendix 11).

On the other hand, the fact that the body recovered from Chichester Harbour was almost certainly planted there by MI6, it did also provide the opportunity to plant a replacement body. Furthermore, it was not entirely outside the capability of an intelligence agency to produce a suitably decomposed and similar replacement body. While a substitute body provides an interesting and even tempting theory about MI6's clandestine capabilities, the author agrees with the Coroner's conclusion that the remains were indeed those of Cdr Crabb.

To summarise, the evidence that it was Commander Crabb's body included:

- The body was wearing a frogman's dry suit made by C E Heinke & Co Ltd, exactly the same size, type and pattern which the company had recently sold to Cdr Crabb.
- The types and colours of the underclothing worn under the dry suit were the same as that known to have been worn by Cdr Crabb.
- No other deaths of divers had previously occurred in the area.
- The size and proportions of the body matched those of Commander Crabb.

- The feet and shoe size of the body matched those of Commander Crabb.
- The feet exhibited a condition known as "hallux valgus" from which it was known that Commander Crabb suffered.
- The feet showed a high instep, which it was known Commander Crabb had.
- A "Y"-shaped scar found on the leg of the body matched that known to have existed on Commander Crabb's leg.
- The pubic hair was ginger, the same as that of Commander Crabb.
- The body was circumcised – nobody challenged this.
- The putrified condition of the body including adipocere was consistent with that which would have been expected for the period that Cdr Crabb had been lost.
- The body had previously been found wearing an oxygen breathing apparatus, consistent with that which Commander Crabb would have used.
- The body was found about ten miles from where Commander Crabb was last seen alive.

In the author's opinion, based on the above evidence, on the balance of probabilities, the body was that of Commander Crabb.

With a Death Certificate issued, the way ahead was clear for the funeral. But even this poignant and very personal ceremony was stage-managed by the authorities. They wanted to be sure it was as secret as possible.

The Funeral

A Requiem Mass was celebrated in Portsmouth Roman Catholic Cathedral for Commander Crabb at noon on Friday, 5 July 1957.

The funeral was organised by James Gleeson, co-author of *The Frogmen* on behalf of Cdr Crabb's mother and paid for by the Admiralty. Marshall Pugh, Cdr Crabb's biographer also attended. But such was the Admiralty's sensitivity, there were no naval honours allowed. Attendance by serving personnel was ordered to be unofficial and out of uniform. This directive was most unpopular with Cdr Crabb's naval colleagues, many of

whom were decorated for gallantry during WW2. Estimates of the number of people who attended vary between 50 and 80. Most of them were women. The six bearers of the coffin, all in civilian clothes, included Lt Cdr Bill Filer MBE GM, Lt Cdr Bill McLanachan MBE BEM, Lt Barry Barrington MBE and Lt Cdr Harry Wardle.

The gravestone inscription was dictated by the Admiralty and they refused to include Cdr Crabb's awards for gallantry, namely his OBE and GM. This was particularly hurtful to his grieving mother.

A letter from Neil F Cairncross to the Cabinet Registry sent on 1 July 1957 explained the reason that Cdr Crabb was not given a naval funeral was because he *"was not a serving naval officer at the time when he met his death"*. This was despite the fact that he died while in the RNVR, in the employment of MI6 and the Admiralty itself paid for the funeral and also the £100 he was due, to his next of kin, his mother Beatrice Crabb. Furthermore, Marshall Pugh has also stated that he had received an official assurance that Cdr Crabb *"had died on service"*.

This only fired up the escalating curiosity and suspicions of the nation's newspapers.

The family mourners were headed by Cdr Crabb's mother, Mrs Beatrice Crabb. She was a small and frail lady. Cdr Crabb's former wife 43-year-

Commander Crabb's coffin and bearers outside Portsmouth Cathedral.

Portsmouth Roman Catholic Cathedral where Cdr Crabb's funeral was held.

Left:
Cdr Crabb's hearse leaving
the Cathedral on its way
to Milton Cemetery.

old Mrs Margaret Crabb did not attend and neither was there an official representative of the Royal Navy. His coffin was draped in a Union Jack. On top lay his sword stick along with a card bearing a French inscription taken from Joan of Arc's sword in Rheims Cathedral. Roughly translated it said: *"I was there at the fight, so I will be there at the glory".*

Following Mass, Cdr Crabb's body was interred at Milton Cemetery, Portsmouth. The entire cemetery was closed to the public for the duration of the burial ceremony. The funeral cortège made its way slowly past the Lodge at the entrance to the cemetery. It was witnessed by Reg Stone, 27 years, who was standing in the Lodge doorway watching the solemn procession. He happened to be staying there with his ex-guardian, Robin Phillips, the Superintendent of the three Portsmouth cemeteries. The burial was to all intents and purposes carried out in secret. Following the brief ceremony, the coffin bearers retired to The Gravedigger's Arms to drink to the memory of their brave departed colleague.

Lt Cdr Wardle who was one of the coffin bearers.

Cdr Crabb's grave is in a section of the cemetery designated for Roman Catholics. Floral tributes included a wreath in the shape of an anchor from his mother. It was formed mainly from carnations and roses in red, white and blue. The card read, *"In everlasting love and memory of my dear son."*

At the graveside, and bravely the only man in uniform, was a Royal Marine who blew the Last Post on his bugle.

The author has been informed that it is the most-visited grave in the cemetery by far. The grave itself is maintained in good condition.

Perhaps one day Commander Crabb's remains will be re-interred in the Naval Cemetery at Haslar, Gosport and this time, with full military honours.

The present condition of Commander Crabb's grave, looking in a westerly direction.

The Grave

Has the gravestone been relocated?

There have been some suggestions that the gravestone of Commander Crabb's grave has been moved to a new location in order to prevent the possibility of an exhumation to clarify the identity of the body or to deter trophy hunters. Furthermore, it has been suggested that this happened in 1981 when a Mrs Walsh, a relation of Cdr Crabb's mother, arranged to have the headstone newly inscribed.

The story was recanted by M and J Welham in their book *The Crabb Enigma*. To support their account, the authors quoted evidence which indicated the original gravestone faced to the west while the present gravestone faces to the east.

In order to investigate this possibility, the present author examined an early photograph showing the gravestone in its original location.

Note the length and orientation of the shadow cast by the rectangular stone vase. In order to estimate the time of day this photograph was taken, as well as the orientation of the grave, a similarly shaped object was placed on the ground to compare the shadow cast at various times of the day. The long axis of the grave is aligned in the traditional east-west direction. So the model stone vase was placed with one side parallel to the east-west orientation as shown in the photograph.

An early photograph of Commander Crabb's grave, looking in an easterly direction. Note the shadow cast by the central stone vase.

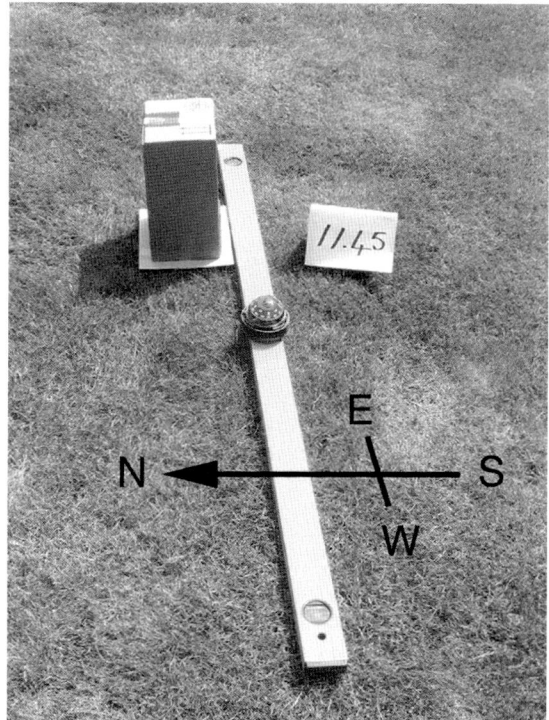

Note the shadow cast by the model at 11.45 hours (BST).

Note the shadow cast by the model at 20.45 hours (BST).

A shadow at a similar angle to that in the original photograph was cast in the morning at 11.45 hours and in the evening at 20.45 hours. The shadow cast in the morning was of a similar length to the one in the original photograph, while the shadow in the evening was many times longer. The conclusions drawn are that the original photograph was taken at about 11.45 hours BST and that the gravestone was therefore originally located at the easterly end of the grave.

The gravestone on the present grave is placed at the westerly end of the grave. So it appears that the gravestone has been moved from one end of the grave to the other and rotated 180 degrees.

The traditional Christian orientation of a body in a grave is with the head to the west and the feet towards the east. A photograph of the burial in 1957 confirms that this was the arrangement adopted when Cdr Crabb's coffin was placed in the grave.

It therefore appears that the original headstone was placed at the feet (east) end of the grave. Why this was done is not known. The situation has been remedied by placing the re-inscribed headstone at the head (west) end of the grave, consistent with the other graves in the same row.

This, on its own, does not however prove that the gravestone has or has not been moved to a different grave location.

In order to establish if the grave site itself has been changed, the author has compared photographs taken during the burial to

Commander Crabb's coffin being lowered into the grave. The photographer's view is looking towards the east. Note the 'head end' of the coffin is nearest to the photographer, at the western end of the grave.

A recent photograph taken of the grave by the author. The view is looking to the east.

photographs taken more recently by himself as well as checking the Burial Registers at the Cemetery.

Note the cross-shaped headstone of Alfred Francis Bulkley lying on the left foreground in the older photograph and standing upright in the recent photograph.

Furthermore, by reference to the original Burial Registers, it can be seen that Cdr Crabb's grave (Row 16, No 10; in April 1957) was between those of the Pini family (Row 16, No 9; in April 1953) and the Renouf family (Row 16, No 11; in June 1959), and immediately behind, to the east of Michael

Commander Crabb's burial entry in the Register of Graves.

Register of Purchased Graves, entry at No 833, page 100. The grave was purchased on 5 July by Beatrice Crabb, Nynehead Cottage, Towersy, near Thame, Oxford: Commander Crabb's widowed mother.

Register of Graves entries for George Alfred Bulkley, Row 17, No 9 and Michael Ryan, Row 17, No 10 located behind and to the west of Commander Crabb's grave.

In the foreground: The graves of Renouf (Row 16, No 11), Commander Crabb (Row 16, No 10), and Pini (Row 16, No 9).
Behind: Ryan (Row 17, No 10) and Bulkley (Row 17, No 9).

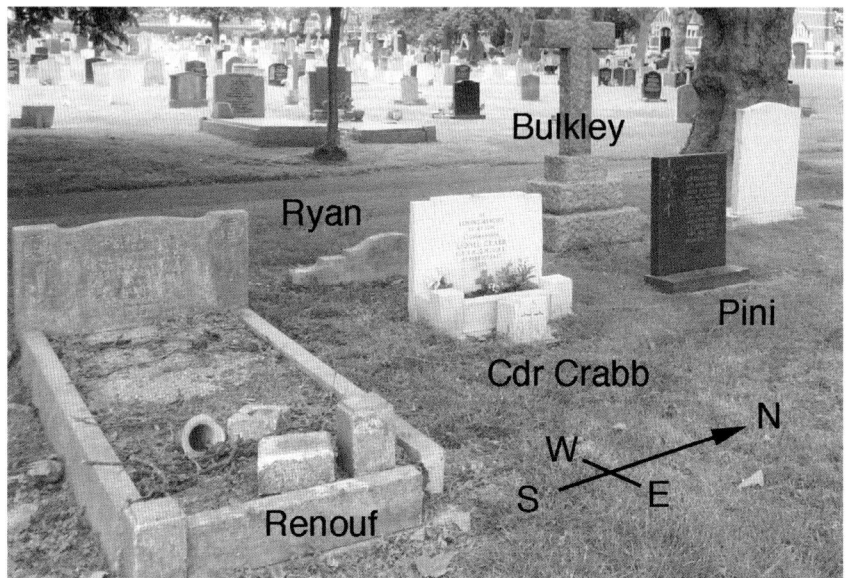

Ryan's grave (Row 17, No 10), all in Plot M. These entries are chronological.

Note that Cdr Crabb is registered as buried in Plot M, Grave No 1275, Row 16, No 10. Also in the column *"If purchased, No. of entry in Register of Purchased Graves"* the number and page reference is: 833/100. In the 'Description' column it is recorded that the original headstone was produced by Bull & Son and that it was later renovated by Barrells (undertakers).

There is no record of any other member of Cdr Crabb's family assuming ownership of the grave following the death of Beatrice Crabb, though any surviving blood relative would be entitled to do so.

In conclusion, it is clear that the grave site of Cdr Crabb has not changed since the original burial on 5 July 1957 though for some unknown reason the headstone was first placed at the easterly, feet end and later relocated to the westerly, head end.

The inscription on the gravestone

The original inscription on the gravestone read:

IN
EVER LOVING MEMORY
OF
MY SON
COMMANDER CRABB
"AT REST AT LAST"

The authorities did not permit Cdr Crabb's mother to have any other inscription. It was a great disappointment to her. The recognition of his awards for gallantry were not allowed to be included. However, it appears that in 1981 Mrs Walsh, a relation of Cdr Crabb's mother, arranged to have the headstone newly inscribed. This time Cdr Crabb's affiliation to the Royal Navy and awards for gallantry were added.

The present inscription on the gravestone reads:

IN
LOVING MEMORY
OF MY SON
COMMANDER LIONEL CRABB
R.N.V.R. G.M. O.B.E.
AT REST AT LAST
1956

Strictly speaking, the OBE should have been placed before the GM as Orders take precedence.

While the government tried its best to suppress the entire episode of Cdr Crabb's fatal dive, the Prime Minister quietly dispensed his severe punishments to those he decided were responsible for Crabbgate, based on the Bridge Enquiry and well outside the glare of publicity.

Subsequent events

The bungled cover-up that followed Crabb's fatal dive was responsible for an upheaval in the Conservative government. Suffice it to say, the Prime Minister, Sir Anthony Eden, was highly displeased and there was a major shake-up in the various departments implicated. Many heads rolled, to a large extent discretely. The Prime Minister's displeasure would of course have been incurred by the Naval Intelligence diving operation as well as the MI6/Crabb operation, since both went ahead against his directive and without his knowledge. However, it seems that MI6 bore the main brunt of the Prime Minister's wrath, presumably because it had not only been a catastrophic failure, but it had permanently damaged his hold on power and the whole saga had been played out in public.

Sir Anthony Eden released a statement on 14 May 1956 stating that:

It would not be in the public interest to disclose the circumstances in which Commander Crabb is presumed to have met his death. I think it necessary, in the special circumstances of this case, to make it clear that what was done was done without the authority or the knowledge of Her Majesty's Ministers. Appropriate disciplinary steps are being taken.

Sir Anthony had commissioned an immediate, in-house, top secret investigation into the affair on 9 May to be conducted personally by the Head of the Civil Service, Sir Edward Bridges. He was instructed to investigate the Cdr Crabb intelligence operation. There was no mention of the Royal Navy/Naval Intelligence operation. The detailed report was on the Prime Minister's desk by 18 May.

The Prime Minister approved the disciplinary measures to be taken against individuals in the Admiralty and Foreign Office in the light of the Bridges Enquiry. They were carefully co-ordinated so that the axes would fall on Wednesday, 27 June 1956. On 26 May 1956 Sir Edward Bridges had commented:

It looks as if the PM is determined to try and pin all the blame on the Admiralty and DNI in particular.

Perhaps the reason for this direction of blame was because the Prime Minister would by then have known that the Admiralty had not only sponsored the Cdr Crabb operation, but having failed in that mission, had then gone on and conducted their own covert diving operation under the Soviet cruiser using serving naval divers.

Rear Admiral John G T Inglis OBE,
Director of Naval Intelligence,
was censured.

Rear Admiral John G T Inglis OBE, Director of Naval Intelligence, was censured as well as having been *"rather downright rebuked"* by the Right Honourable Viscount Cilcennin the First Lord of the Admiralty. But he kept his job until he retired in 1960. He was promoted to Vice-Admiral in 1958.

The Rt Hon Viscount 'Jim' Cilcennin, First Lord of the Admiralty, himself resigned on 1 September 1956. He had previously volunteered his own resignation to the Prime Minister on 13 May 1956 as a means of minimising the embarrassment to the government. Viscount Hailsham slipped seamlessly into his place.

Sir John Lang GCB, Permanent Secretary of the Admiralty, was told he had been *"guilty of an error of judgement"* in not keeping his

Sir John Lang GCB, Permanent Secretary of the Admiralty was told he had been guilty of an error of judgement.

Minister informed as well also as having been *"rather downright rebuked"* by the First Lord of the Admiralty. But he kept his job and remained a prominently successful civil servant until his retirement in 1961.

Admiral Mountbatten claimed he knew nothing of Cdr Crabb's mission. He was out of the country throughout the affair, on a tour of South East Asia and Australia, including Royal Australian Navy establishments. He did not arrive back in Britain until 27 April. He claimed to have instructed his Vice Chief of Naval Staff, Vice-Admiral Sir William Davis, that no such operation should be undertaken. Sir William Davis denied ever receiving the instruction. In the House of Commons, the labour MP, George Wigg pointed his finger accusingly at Mountbatten saying:

The man responsible is the First Sea Lord. He should be thrown out! Nothing in the Navy happens unless you want it to … they wouldn't have dared do it if they thought you would disapprove.

Major General Sir John 'Sinbad' Sinclair (aka "C"), Chief of MI6, took full responsibility for *"the operation which had failed with such lamentable consequences"*. He was *"reluctant to see any part of it fall on any of his subordinates"*. He 'fell on his sword' and took early retirement. He was relieved swiftly by MI5's Sir Dick White on 1 July 1956. Several other senior members of MI6 closely associated with Sinclair also 'retired' around the same time.

Sir John Bruce-Lockhart KCMG, CWE, the MI6 officer responsible for obtaining the clearance of the Foreign Office for the operation which failed through a misunderstanding with the FOA Michael Williams, appears to have got off scot-free and was even later promoted to Deputy Chief of Secret Service (DCSS).

Admiral Mountbatten inspecting the novel diving equipment of Royal Australian Navy divers at their base at NOWRA, Jervis Bay, New South Wales on 10 April 1956.

Michael S Williams CMG, the Foreign Office Adviser (FOA) who had failed to prevent the operation going ahead and failed to communicate the details to the Foreign Office was *"moved"*. However, his onward career was unaffected and he was knighted KCMG in 1968.

Bernard Sydney Smith was *"severely censured"* and lived up to his title, namely being a 'Temporary Officer'. He was purportedly an academic, fluent in Russian and German with an MA from Trinity College, Oxford. It appears he left MI6 shortly after the Cdr Crabb operation. One account relates he ended up as a history lecturer in Swarthmore College in Pennsylvania, USA while Frank Bicknell of MI6 stated he was moved into the BBC Overseas Service.

Sir Ivone Kirkpatrick, Permanent Secretary, Foreign Office was also told he also had been *"guilty of an error of judgement"* in not keeping his Minister informed. He only managed to hang on until he retired in February 1957.

Lt Cdr Frankie Franklin was initially moved sideways from HMS *Vernon* to UCWE in Havant. He moved out of his apartment in Southsea and into a house a few hundred metres from where Lt Cdr Crawford lived in Bedhampton. When UCWE moved to the Admiralty Underwater Weapons Establishment (AUWE) at Portland, Dorset, Franklin followed suit. However he was given no further promotions.

Lt Cdr Joe Brooks's career advanced no further. It was not helped when he accidentally blew both his legs off in an attempt to dispose of a basking shark which was interfering with some diving trials off Falmouth later the same year. He miraculously survived the incident though two civilians in the same boat were killed outright. He was invalided out of the Navy in April 1959. He went on to a very successful career running a commercial diving company based at Havant (Mobell Marine Ltd).

Nicholas Elliott in MI6 appears to have escaped censure and remained until his retirement around 1968.

In MI6 two officers were *"severely censured"* and three or four others were merely *"censured"*.

Major General Sir John 'Sinbad' Sinclair (aka "C"), Chief of MI6 took early retirement.

MI5's Sir Dick White took over as Chief of MI6.

Sir Ivone Kirkpatrick, Permanent Secretary, Foreign Office was told he had been guilty of an error of judgement.

Some careers simply came to a grinding halt; all of course carried out discretely with clinical civil service precision.

Two years after Commander Crabb's disappearance, Lt Cdr Joe Brooks (minus his legs) was in Malta advising on the filming of *The Silent Enemy* starring Laurence Harvey, the well-known film re-enacting Cdr Crabb's epic (though largely fictional) diving operations against Italian frogmen at Gibraltar during World War 2.

The next time a Soviet warship visited Portsmouth Harbour on a goodwill visit was on 28 May 1976, twenty years after Commander Crabb's disappearance. It was the turn of the 5,200-ton destroyer *Obraztsovyi*.

On the bridge stood Lt Cdr Cyril Lafferty RN, himself an experienced Clearance Diver, who was acting as a liaison officer with the destroyer's captain. As the ship edged its way through the narrow entrance in to the harbour, the Soviet Navigation Officer nudged Lt Cdr Lafferty's elbow and pointed out of the window to starboard, to 'The Point' at Old Portsmouth where the Coal Exchange and Still and West public houses stand. He then placed his finger on the equivalent location on their navigation chart on the table before them and read out the Russian text. Lafferty explained he couldn't speak Russian, so the Navigation Officer translated it for him:

"It reads: Crabb Point."

PART 4

CONCLUSIONS

What was Commander Crabb's cause of death?

On the balance of probabilities, it is most likely that Cdr Crabb died during his dive. Only this possibility is considered here. It is most likely he died shortly after briefly surfacing when he was observed by three of the Soviet sailors at around 07.30 hours. The author's own enquiries to a reliable and senior Russian source returned their official opinion that Cdr Crabb probably drowned while investigating the hull of the *Ordzhonikidze*.

The cause of his death could have been due to any of several individual reasons or any combination of two or more of them, possibly aggravated by poor physical fitness, cold, low blood sugar, dehydration, hang-over, residual blood alcohol and lack of sleep, including:

- Oxygen poisoning
- Carbon dioxide poisoning
- 'Sodalime cocktail'
- Heart attack
- Exhaustion
- Drowning

It is unlikely to have been due to lack of oxygen as he had only been underwater for about 30 minutes.

What were the movements of Commander Crabb's dead body?

The author has dived around all parts of the Solent from 1964 to 2016. This always involved careful planning to exploit the tides to the best advantage. Based on this experience, the author could not understand how a negatively buoyant body could drift along the sea bed, out of Portsmouth harbour, eastwards along the Solent into deep water and then turn left and drift 'uphill' into the shallows of Chichester harbour. So some considerable time and effort has been spent researching the potential movements of Commander Crabb's body.

His body would have been negatively buoyant in order to carry out that type of diving operation. This means he would have had to fin continually in order to maintain constant depth without sinking. It is also likely that his breathing set counterlung deflated or flooded causing him to become even more negatively buoyant. This would have occurred if the mouthpiece had fallen out of his mouth, as was most likely once he became unconscious. Indeed, he was seen to sink after his brief surfacing between the two Russian destroyers. Lt Cdr Franklin has stated:

The weight and nature of the [breathing] *apparatus were such that if, through maladjustment subsequent to entering the water or through some physical failure on the part of the wearer, he becomes unconscious, it is most unlikely that the body would rise to the surface so long as the apparatus remains in place.*

Two possibilities exist as to what would have happened to his body after it sank. It was either:

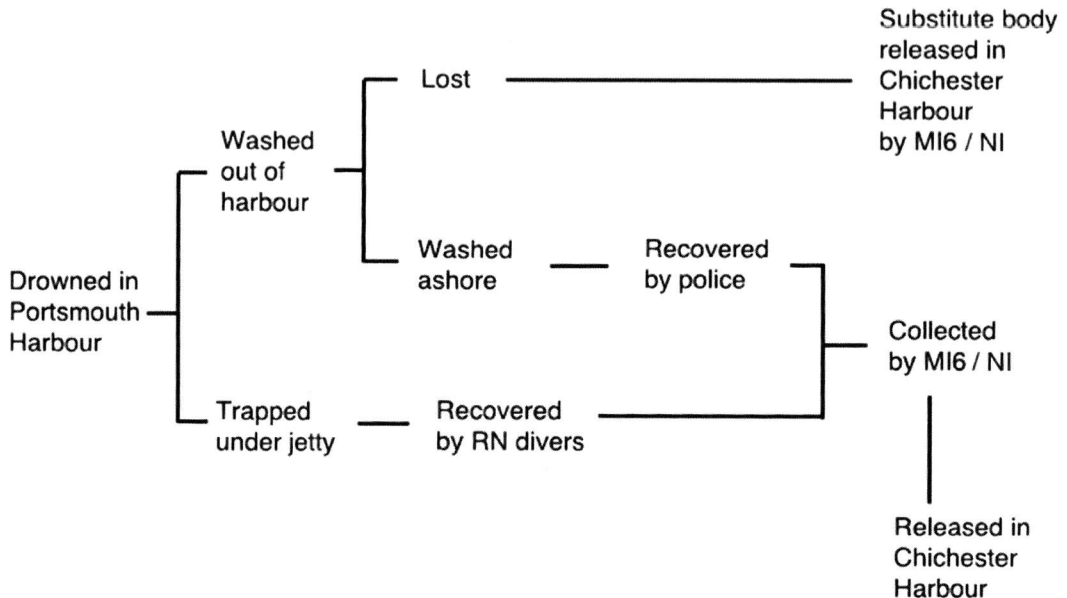

Conjectural possibilities of the fate of Cdr Crabb's body.

1. carried by a tidal eddy under the piled structure of the jetty and there became entangled in debris, or

2. washed out of the harbour by the ebbing tide.

1. Trapped under South Railway Jetty

It is known that under that particular jetty the sea bed was strewn with all kinds of debris including coils of steel cable that could easily snag and entrap a diver. An Admiralty diver has stated that there were large coils of rusting steel cable under the jetty, possibly scrap cable placed there to minimise any scouring by eddies from ships' propellers, or simply just dumped. This would have provided one of the possible opportunities for the rust marks to be deposited on Cdr Crabb's legs as noted following the recovery of the body.

It would have been logical and certainly expected that the authorities would have wanted to check whether Crabb's body had ended up under the jetty.

A local newspaper reported on Thursday, 10 May 1956:

… there has been dredging on both sides of King's Stairs. This is probably routine work, although no-one will deny that it could be for the purpose of searching for a body or for equipment.

G F Marshall, Chief Engineer in Charge at the Dockyard gave his opinion on the practicalities of a search for Cdr Crabb's body under South Railway Jetty in a note dated 25 May 1956. Dredging would take 10 days at a cost of about £3,500. It went on to suggest:

There is practically no silt on the dredged berth and the bottom is hard clay. The underside of the jetty is encumbered with wire ropes and other debris. The tidal stream on ebb and flow sets in

South Railway jetty today.

towards the jetty and there are local eddies which maintain northward flow after high water …

Diving Inspection – very laborious owing to debris. A quick look along the front of the jetty could be done in 5 days (1 week) probably at a cost of about £60. A proper inspection of the whole of the space under the jetty would take 3 or 4 weeks or perhaps even more at £50/60 a week.

If anything is there I would personally think its most probable location is caught up in the debris near the front of the jetty.

An official note observed:

An inspection of the space <u>under</u> the jetty would be a dangerous operation because of obstructions, wire ropes, old anchors etc.

It appears that the dredging operation was not successful and the second option of using divers was next undertaken.

The late Surgeon Vice Admiral Sir John Rawlins has stated that he was on a Shallow Water Diving course at HMS *Vernon* shortly after Crabb's disappearance. The course

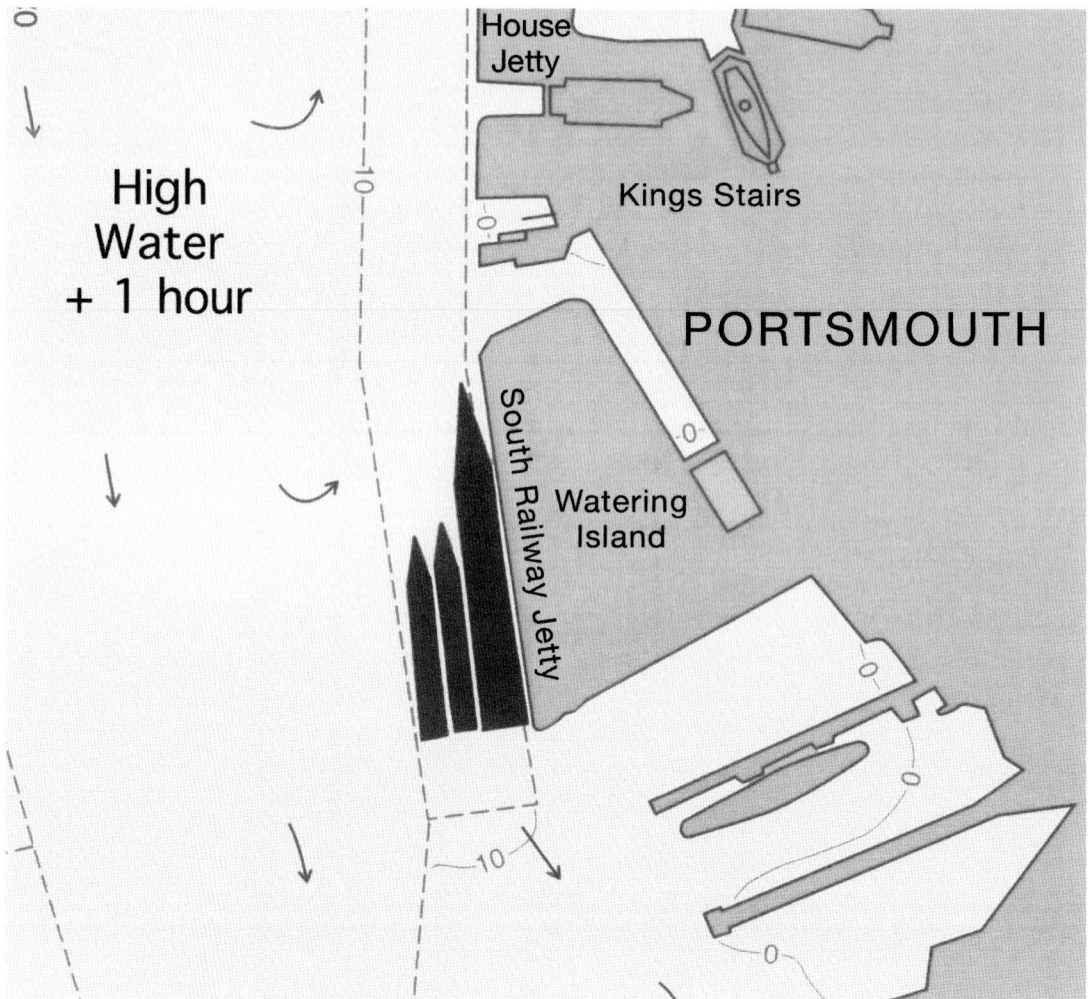

Illustration to show tidal stream one hour after high water in Portsmouth Harbour.
Note the eddy that would take a body under the pilings at South Railway Jetty.

instructor was PO J N 'Nutty' Hallam. It commenced on 7 May 1956 and finished on 25 May 1956. One of the exercises he and his fellow trainees were required to undertake while on course was to assist in a search for *"anything interesting"* under the same jetty. Even if any trainee divers failed to find a body, it would have been reasonable to order a thorough search by qualified Clearance Divers or the Special Boat Section (SBS) in due course. If Crabb's body had ended up under the jetty, then it is almost certain it would have been recovered by naval or SBS divers. In the author's opinion, this is the most likely turn of events.

If the body was found, it would not have been in the interest of the navy or the government to release the information where and when it was found. Indeed, as has been already mentioned, on 14 May 1956 the Chief Constable of the crime office in Chichester wrote to all local police authorities in Portsmouth area warning them that should Crabb's body surface:

It is absolutely essential that the finding of the body is not to be disclosed to the press.

The authorities clearly wanted to be able to control the eventual disclosure of the reappearance of the body and under circumstances that best suited them.

2. Washed out of the harbour

If the body had been washed out of the harbour, then it appears it would have disappeared into the English Channel. Sir Edward Bridges recorded:

Owing to the shape of Portsmouth Harbour and the tides it was not likely that the body would reappear.

A report by a forensic hydrographic expert in the tidal drift of dead bodies, Mr Matthew French, CMarTech, FCInstCES, FIMarEST, FRGS, MRIN, commissioned by the author, dated 05.06.2014, has concluded:

• *It is most unlikely that the body would have left the main channel out of Portsmouth Harbour once it was in the water until it reached the two forts* [Horse Sand and No Man's Land].

• *It is most unlikely, if not impossible, for a negatively buoyant body exiting Portsmouth Harbour to leave the channel between Southsea castle and the forts and then travel eastwards and on into Chichester Harbour.*

• *In my opinion, assuming that the body exited Portsmouth Harbour, it was carried by the tidal stream past the two forts and into the English Channel. From there, it could not have entered Chichester Harbour.*

The inescapable conclusion is that the body recovered from Chichester Harbour did not arrive there by natural means. Which begs the questions *"Who put it there and why Chichester Harbour?"*

Why Chichester Harbour?

It is almost certain that the body recovered from Chichester Harbour was that of Commander Crabb. But how did it get there?

On 14 May 1956, the Chief Constable of the crime office in Chichester wrote to all local police authorities in Portsmouth area warning them that should Cdr Crabb's body surface it was not to be disclosed to the press.

It is curious that the Chichester police in neighbouring West Sussex, rather than Portsmouth police, should have taken this initiative and come up with this directive. Why, of all the police forces, should the Chichester police in West Sussex get involved by sending out the order not to disclose the finding of a body? It is a strange coincidence that the body was eventually discovered in the jurisdiction of the Chichester police force and where the Chief Constable and Coroner were, according to MI6, *"most co-operative"*. Interestingly, by another strange coincidence, Lord Mountbatten was the Commodore of the Emsworth Sailing Club, at the head of Chichester harbour.

In the author's opinion the most likely explanation for the re-appearance of Cdr Crabb's body in Chichester Harbour was not due to any tidal drift but to have been orchestrated by one of the security agencies, most likely MI6. The body was placed in one of the heavily-fished tidal creeks in Chichester Harbour with the intention that it would, at some time thereafter be netted, dredged up or washed ashore.

The most likely scenario that could fit the above supposition would be that the Royal Navy or SBS conducted a search for Cdr Crabb's body under South Railway Jetty sometime after the Soviet ships had left. It would certainly have been the logical action to take and there is evidence that it did. If Cdr Crabb's body had been recovered either by divers or dredging activities, the security agencies would not have been in a hurry to declare their find. It would not have suited them at the time to reveal either that they had found it or where they had found it.

At the time they were still hoping the public had swallowed the cover-up story that Cdr Crabb had been lost off Stokes Bay. The best solution would have been to quietly release the body at an uncontroversial location where it was likely to be found, a respectable time after the departure of the Soviet warships and after the press feeding frenzy had died down. Chichester Harbour provided an ideal choice.

But in the meantime where could MI6 find a secret and secure location to store the body?

What happened at Fort Monckton?

It was fortuitous that MI6's premier field operations training centre was based at Fort Monckton, just over a mile from the entrance to Portsmouth Harbour, on the sea front at Gosport (Appendix 9). It is still there today and nondescriptly called *"No1 Military Training Establishment"*. Cdr Crabb's body was delivered there a little while after his disappearance. It was brought by boat to the beach in front of Fort Monckton and carried in to the parade ground through the sally port located in the centre of the twenty-two obsolete gun ports. Captain Barry Dodd RN, director of the establishment took personal charge of the arrangements. This confirms that the body had been successfully recovered and it means that the body must have been deposited later in Chichester Harbour by MI6.

All this goes to illustrate the extraordinary but not entirely unsurprising lengths to which the intelligence agencies are capable of going to mislead the public. It also provides an additional reason why the embargo on the documentation has been extended to 100 years.

Fort Monckton in Gosport, The No1 Military Training Establishment.

The beach in front of Fort Monckton.

This information is not amongst that which has been disclosed to date. Could it be that the continued secrecy is due to the additional embarrassment the disclosure of such a clandestine operation is too much for the government to bear? Surely not in this day and age?

But why would anyone want to take all that trouble to produce Commander Crabb's, or even a fake body in the first place?

The answer lies in a report dated 29 May 1956, when the Admiralty stated:

Two problems remain to be dealt with:-
(a) the establishment of or presumption of death;
(b) payment for the action involving Crabb's death.
The first is the most important. The matter cannot be left where it is …

The re-appearance of Cdr Crabb's body would tie up these tedious loose ends, generate the much-needed Death Certificate, simplify the proceedings and allow the books to be closed.

Or so they hoped.

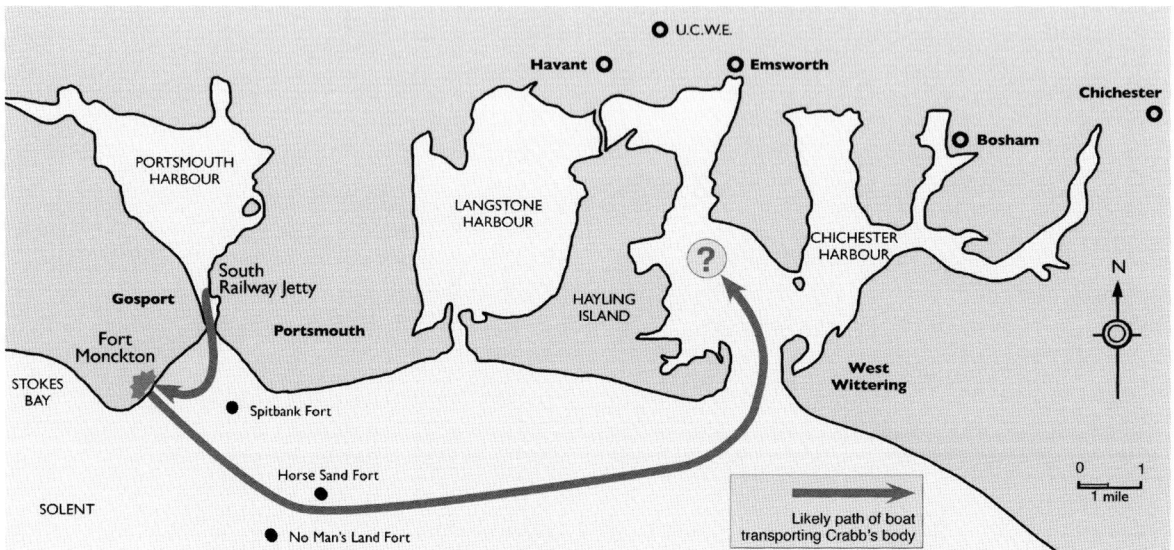

The movement of Cdr Crabb's body as determined by the author.

Failures in MI6 "trade craft"

The official and highly intrusive investigations into the failed Cdr Crabb covert diving operation by Sir Edward Bridges and MI6 identified significant flaws in the trade craft of a number of MI6 officers.

The diving operation should have been completely 'unattributable', meaning that if it failed there would have been no connection with any official governmental organisation. The list of failures in trade craft identified by Bridges included the following:

1   Bernard Smith, *"... the operator in immediate charge of the operation, should not have signed his real name and address in the Hotel register."*
[An official document described this as no less than *"criminal folly"*.]

2   *"Commander Crabb should not have been allowed to spend so much time in Portsmouth where he was likely to meet people he knew."*
[This included the social visit to HMS *Vernon* and later to wander around Portsmouth after the first dive. Cdr Crabb's visit to Havant to see Lt Cdr Crawford and PO Lofty Gordon was not listed as one of the unnecessary activities. This increases the likelihood that this was a necessary exercise, probably to do with the provision of the oxygen breathing set.]

3   *"He was brought to Portsmouth on the 17th April with a view to the operation being carried out on the following morning when the Russian ships anchored* [sic] *at Portsmouth. But Mr D* [Davies] *Mr Smith's*

superior officer, soon saw that our own security precautions would make it necessary to postpone the attempt until a later date. This postponement could have been avoided if the operation had been more fully discussed with the Security Service."

4   *"Again, from ... what Crabb said about his work for MI6 to some of his associates in civil life, there seems some reasons to doubt whether he was altogether a wise choice for this kind of work."*
[Also, bearing in mind Cdr Crabb's poor health and physical fitness, his heavy drinking and smoking habits, his choice as the most suitable candidate to carry out the mission was clearly flawed.]

5   *"... Mr D* [Davies] *and Mr Smith ... both agree that proper precautions had not been taken to make the operation unattributable and to provide an adequate cover story in the event of a mishap."*

Another criticism was aimed at the requirement for a canvas awning to be installed on the launch from which Cdr Crabb dived, to ensure secrecy. This facility should have been appreciated beforehand. The method of finally arranging it exposed poor planning.

Other lapses in trade craft which were not considered worthy of attention in the official report included the failure of Cdr Crabb to carry out practice dives beforehand in order to check and improve his physical fitness to dive and to establish his correct weighting requirements.

Nicholas Elliott's version of events

If anyone could provide a definitive version of Crabb's fatal diving project it should be Nicholas Elliott, MI6's Chief of the London Station, who was responsible for 'masterminding' the entire operation. Elliott wrote down his version in his book *With My Little Eye* published in 1993, 25 years after his retirement.

Sadly, what he wrote is superficial and not particularly revealing. There are so many errors and inaccuracies that its value is questionable. The following quotations are offered to support this conclusion.

… the Soviet cruiser Ordzhonikidze, which anchored in Portsmouth Harbour …

Possibly splitting hairs here, but the cruiser was berthed, i.e. tied up alongside at South Railway Jetty and did not anchor in the harbour.

Commander Lionel Crabb was … the best frogman in the country, probably the world.

Elliott concedes on the very next page *"He almost certainly died from respiratory trouble, being a heavy smoker and not in the best of health …"*. Elliott also fails to mention Cdr Crabb's poor swimming ability, his advanced age, his alcohol dependency, his over-weightness, his lack of physical fitness and his lack of preparedness. While acknowledging his distinguished career, Cdr Crabb was certainly not the best frogman in the country at that point in time.

The Soviet admiral … said … that his officer of the watch had reported that a diver had been seen in trouble round the stern of the ship that morning …

A diver was seen between the bows of the two accompanying destroyers and not at the stern of the admiral's ship.

… the Commander-in-Chief … launched every form of enquiry, news of which not surprisingly reached the press.

Not so. The press got on to the story through the investigation of journalists Marshall Pugh and Peter Marshall after Cdr Crabb's employer Maitland Pendock raised concerns about his failure to turn up for work back in London.

They found out Crabb's name and got on to his estranged and neurotic wife;

Crabb was not married or separated at the time, he was divorced.

There was no discussion of finance.

Cdr Crabb's mother, his next of kin, was paid £100 by MI6 which was the agreed payment with Cdr Crabb for his diving operation. Finally, Elliott concluded with a very strange anecdote which makes little sense:

There was a surprising sequel to the Crabb tragedy. Shortly after he disappeared, a man was approached by an officer in naval uniform in a Portsmouth pub. The officer, after a drink or two, confided that he was a naval frogman who had done a run under the Ordzhonikidze just for the hell of it and had taken some photographs. They appeared to be valuable but if he handed them in and confessed he would be court-martialled. What should he do? The man, with commendable presence of mind, said he would give him 30/- for them and a large Scotch. The deal was done and the Admiralty got some of what they wanted. The problem though was to explain how the pictures had been obtained – or not to explain. And that will remain a secret.

This has to be total misinformation. In any case it fails to acknowledge the subsequent successful and official diving investigation carried out by the Royal Naval Clearance Divers at the behest of the Naval Intelligence Division.

Can the continued secrecy over Commander Crabb's disappearance be justified?

The bungled cover-up of Cdr Crabb's diving operation has grown into a more controversial issue than the original spying mission itself, justifying coining the term "Crabbgate".

The fiasco over the bungled cover story of Cdr Crabb's disappearance has sparked an entire industry of publications which grows incessantly. The enforced secrecy has had a paradoxical effect. It has fed the fire of public curiosity. The piece-meal disclosure of previously classified documents has ensured the flames have been regularly fanned and grow higher and higher.

As if Crabbgate was not bad enough, it has opened a Pandora's Box of embarrassing issues for the government and its security agencies. These all combine to escalate their chagrin. The list of issues include:

1   The misunderstandings over clearance for the operations

The lack of communication between the security agencies, namely NID and MI6 within themselves as well as with their overseeing government departments caused a total failure in carrying out the Prime Minister's instructions. The most notable was a serious misunderstanding between Sir Michael Williams the Foreign Office Adviser (FOA) inside MI6 and Sir John Bruce-Lockhart (in charge of Central & Western Europe, CWE, MI6 operations including all anti-Russian activities). This placed the Prime Minister in an invidious position and led to his being verbally mauled in Parliament. Together with

the ensuing Suez crisis, it contributed to no less than the fall of the conservative government.

2   A "bad project" with poor trade craft

As described above, the poor planning and management of the operation revealed serious inadequacies in the professional standards of many officials. There was a glaring failure to ensure the operation would be 'unattributable' in the event of its becoming public.

3   The death of Commander Crabb

The tragic fatal accident that befell Cdr Crabb could justifiably be called an accident looking for somewhere to happen. While it is easy in hindsight to criticise the choice of Cdr Crabb for the operation, the criticism is however still valid. This by no means diminishes in any way whatsoever the gallantry and undaunted devotion to duty displayed by Cdr Crabb himself who gave his life for his country and deserves special recognition for his courageous attempt.

4   The lateness in informing Ministers

The government ministers including the Prime Minister himself were not informed of the catastrophic event of 19 April until 4 May, and then only after the press had exposed the affair. Sir Edward Bridges stated it was because *"… the Admiralty regarded the Foreign Office as responsible for the operation, while the Foreign Office thought the Admiralty were responsible".*

The Prime Minister was *"incandescent"* with rage at the delay in being informed.

5   The bungled cover-up

The cover story produced by the Admiralty which was intended to prevent the connection being made between Cdr Crabb's disappearance and the Soviet visit and the involvement of MI6 was blown clean out of the water within days of its unveiling. The national newspapers had a field-day dismantling the cover-up (and still do today). Roger Hollis, Deputy Director General at MI5 conceded: *"… the chief risk against which one had to plan in mounting clandestine operations in this country are not the enemy or the object of the intelligence, but the British press"*.

6   The MI6 plot to dump the body in Chichester Harbour

Having found Cdr Crabb's body under South Railway Jetty, MI6 took over the arrangements for it to be 'discovered' in Chichester harbour. This was chosen as the most convenient location, being a respectable distance from Portsmouth harbour and in the jurisdiction of a *"co-operative"* Coroner and police force.

7   The alleged illegality of the Inquest

The most cursory examination of the conduct of the stage-managed Inquest reveals a string of the most questionable and some might even call criminal practices adopted by the Coroner, the Admiralty and MI6.

The government's dubious policy to maintain the cover-up as best it could has had the paradoxical effect. A whole industry of

associated publications has grown up and is thriving as a result.

Ironically, the mounting embarrassment is not only associated with those directly involved in the Cdr Crabb affair, but now implicates today's intelligence agencies and their questionable historical secrecy policy. It is extremely difficult to understand why the files should remain closed for 100 years.

Let us review the official reasons given for the continued secrecy claimed by the government:

1. *"exceptionally sensitive … disclosure of which would be contrary to the public interest on security grounds;"*

What could possibly still be a sensitive issue today? The politics between the UK and the then Soviet Union are old hat. The Soviet Union no longer exists. The stories of the Cambridge Five are not only in the public domain, but the subject of popular books and television programmes. All the military technology being investigated by the intelligence agencies at the time is now in the public domain. It is old technology. The technology of 1956 is the stuff of museum exhibits. Technology has moved on significantly in the intervening sixty years. The subject can no longer be claimed to be *"exceptionally sensitive"*.

2. *"containing information supplied in confidence, disclosure of which would … constitute a breach of faith"*

This is a catch-all, nebulous, philosophical statement. When would the requirement for secrecy ever expire under such a principle? The 'Top Secret' information already declassified and disclosed by the Public Record Office in 2006 and 2015 was itself given in confidence, disclosure of which already presumably constitutes a breach of faith. If disclosure means

A selection of books covering the story of Cdr Crabb's diving operation.

breach of faith then nothing would ever be disclosed. If it is reasonable that it would expire after the death of the individuals involved, then it has already expired. See below.

3. *"disclosure ... could cause distress or embarrassment to living personnel ..."*

Has not the embarrassment been caused already? Is not this continued publicity over the meaningless secrecy rubbing salt in the wound? Or is it, as Kim Philby has boasted to his Soviet paymasters, that the British security agencies dared not accuse members of the 'upper class'. Maybe that remains the case.

It may be as simple as the out-dated mentality of an antediluvian Civil Service.

And who are the *"living personnel"* who are still around following Cdr Crabb's disappearance over 60 years ago? Prominent contenders for embarrassment would include the following (in alphabetical order with their hypothetical age in 2019):

Sir John Bruce-Lockhart (CWE) in MI6 would be 105 years old.

Rt Hon Viscount Cilcennin, First Lord of the Admiralty would be 116 years old.

Sir Anthony Eden, the Prime Minister would be 122 years old.

John Elliott, MI6, Head of London Station would be 103 years old.

Rear Admiral Inglis, Director of Naval Intelligence Division (113 years old).

Sir Ivone Kirkpatrick, Permanent Secretary of the Foreign Office (122 years old).

Sir John Lang, Permanent Secretary of the Admiralty (123 years old).

Lord Louis Mountbatten, Admiral of the Fleet (119 years old).

Major General Sir John Sinclair, Head of MI6 (122 years old).

Sir Dick White, Director General of MI5 (113 years old).

Michael Williams, Foreign Office Adviser inside MI6 would be 108 years old.

The author knows of no living person who had any responsibility for Commander Crabb's spying mission or the botched cover-up.

In any case, which is the greater evil?

1. To conceal the embarrassment of any deceased individuals responsible for sending Cdr Crabb to his death? or

2. To suppress the distinguished reputation and gallantry of Cdr Crabb who gave his life for his country while on active service?
   To deny him his burial with full military honours?
   To cause distress to all of Cdr Crabb's family, friends and Royal Navy colleagues?
   To incur the bewilderment, distaste and distrust of millions of the British public?

It can be argued that the three reasons put forward by the government as detailed above are simply no longer valid. It may be further argued that if the account given in this book is within a gnat's whisker of the truth, then what is the point of maintaining the secrecy?

The elephants in the room

One of the most enigmatic and outstanding mysteries of the Crabb affair is the apparently inexplicable reason behind the 100-year embargo on the Crabb and RN files.

One hundred years is an extraordinarily long period over which to keep information secret. In order for this to be considered necessary, there is perhaps a very major issue that cannot be disclosed. So we are not talking about the relatively trivial embarrassment over a failed spying mission or even a failed cover-up. These blunders have been wallowing in the public domain for decades.

There is presumably something else; something that demands the highest possible level of restriction on public knowledge. So what is it that can still be so critical that it cannot be disclosed?

Could it be the farcical or perhaps even criminally conducted inquest?

In our search for the truth during the enforced absence of the facts, we can only speculate, however unpleasant an exercise that may be. Possible contenders that have been put forward in the past include the following.

Was Cdr Crabb a Soviet spy?

There are strong associations linking Cdr Crabb with active communists including members of the infamous Cambridge five: Kim Philby, Donald Maclean, Guy Burgess and Sir Anthony Blunt (the fifth has not been definitively identified, but John Cairncross is a popular contender).

Cdr Crabb's cousin Kitty Jarvis was a Personal Assistant to Sir Anthony Blunt. Cdr Crabb worked for a period of time in an art gallery owned by Blunt. He met Blunt socially while he lived at the Cavendish Hotel and later, where he also met Maclean and Burgess. Sydney Knowles has spoken of parties, referred to as the *"Last Suppers"* in Tite Street, London, he attended with Cdr Crabb where he met Blunt, Marshall Pugh and a variety of communists. The connection between the *"Last Supper"* and the *"Cambridge Apostles"*, an exclusive society club in Cambridge University springs to mind. Knowles has stated that Blunt was referred to as the *"Queen Mother"* ostensibly because he was the curator of the Queen Mother's paintings at Clarence House,

Kitty Jarvis, Commander Crabb's cousin who was a Personal Assistant to Sir Anthony Blunt.

although is it also likely to be a reference to his rank and sexuality.

Other attendees at Blunt's Tite Street suppers, which Knowles referred to as *"homosexual"* and where everyone called each other *"comrade"* included (according to Knowles) Admiral Mountbatten, Wallace Antonov Costa, Howard Dines, Bernard Floud MP, Lillian Hellman, Roger Hollis, Ray Noble, Marshall Pugh and Michael Walsh. Crabb's ex-wife has stated that his sexual behaviour was *"not normal"* which led to her leaving him.

Marshall Pugh worked for Alan Maclean at Macmillan's Press, who was Donald Maclean's brother. Pugh was also a close friend of Laurie Lee who had fought for the communists in the Spanish Civil war. Both were heavy drinkers, indeed Pugh himself died of alcoholic (and paracetamol) poisoning at the young age of 50 years in 1976.

Cdr Crabb's life-long friend and employer, Maitland Pendock was known to MI5 as a communist sympathiser.

Knowles has quoted Cdr Crabb as explaining *"One can be a patriot and a communist".*

Knowles has also stated that he was so concerned about Cdr Crabb's communist affiliations at the Last Suppers that he wrote a letter to MI5 to reveal his misgivings. A Colonel Alistair Malcolm of MI5 subsequently interviewed him on the subject.

The local civilians who frequented the Staunton Arms in Rowlands Castle near UCWE considered Crabb a *"left winger and almost communist".*

So was Cdr Crabb a communist? Had he been recruited by the KGB?

Was Admiral Mountbatten a Soviet spy?

Much speculation (with the emphasis on "speculation") concerning the unusual 100-year embargo has implicated Admiral Mountbatten.

It appears that the Lord Chancellor's option (exercised by the Secretary of State) to withhold documents relating to the royal family from the public domain may be behind the 100-year embargo. So would Admiral Mountbatten's involvement, as a second cousin once removed of Queen Elizabeth II and uncle of Prince Philip, Duke of Edinburgh, qualify for the 100-year embargo? The issue of what documents may not be disclosed to the public is covered by *"exemptions"* in Part II of the Freedom of Information Act, Sections 21 to 44. The following guidance is given:

Some exemptions apply only to a particular category or class of information, such as information held for criminal investigations or relating to correspondence with the royal family. These are called class-based exemptions.

Allegations have been made that Mountbatten himself was a spy for the Soviet KGB, the 'sixth man' along with the 'Cambridge five'.

Peter Wright wrote in his book *Spycatcher* that a defected senior KGB officer:

[Yuri] *Nossenko soon gave a priceless lead in the hunt for the British Naval spies. He claimed that the Gribinov recruitment had been obtained through homosexual blackmail, and that the agent had provided the KGB with "all NATO" secrets from a "Lord of the Navy."*

Cdr Crabb is understood to have had meetings with Mountbatten in Gibraltar during WW2. They dived together while Cdr Crabb was later working in Italy. Knowles has stated that *"on at least three occasions in 1943 in Gibraltar Commander Crabb worked for Lord Mountbatten"*. And of course, there is the alleged meeting between Cdr Crabb and Mountbatten in Cowdray Park in March 1956, just a month before his fatal dive. They were clearly on good terms with each other, and as Knowles has stated Cdr Crabb referred to Mountbatten as *"Dickie"*.

Mountbatten's involvement appears to be given further credence by the fact that he personally interviewed Lt Cdr Joe Brooks on two occasions following the Royal Navy dive for Naval Intelligence Division under the Soviet ships. This ties in with the inexplicable withholding of the details of the Royal Navy dives which were quite unspectacular and incident-free. It is quite possible that Mountbatten himself ordered the NID/Royal Navy dives following the failure of the Crabb/MI6 dive. Mountbatten was out of the country at the time, but it is almost certain he was being kept fully briefed with the shenanigans being played out in Portsmouth.

The situation is further complicated by the preponderance of homosexuality amongst the associates mentioned above. Maclean, Burgess, Blunt and Philby were all homosexuals. There are even allegations that Mountbatten was bisexual and Cdr Crabb's own sexuality was not 'normal' according to his ex-wife.

Unlike today's liberal attitudes, in the 1950s homosexuality was not only stigmatised but actually a crime. As a direct result, it was standard operating practice for the KGB to blackmail homosexuals into providing them with classified information. Admiral Mountbatten's alleged sympathy and being an agent for the Soviet Union, and being a homosexual, is given prominence in the Welhams' book *The Crabb Enigma* in the chapter *The Royal Connection*.

Unless there are any other particularly sensitive issues that have yet to be identified or suggested, then one might conclude that the outstanding issue awaiting disclosure in 2057 may, perhaps, be found somewhere in the lines above. But that could surely have no impact on the NID/RN diving operation? So why should that operation still be buried in the vaults of secrecy?

All of this speculation regrettably casts a dark shadow over the entire Cdr Crabb affair.

Sadly, the 100-year embargo can only fuel the speculation and conspiracy theories.

"Silence is a lie that screams at the light."
Shannon L Alder

The Cold War and homosexuality in perspective

It is hard to over-emphasise the overwhelming influence of the cold war on all government and military activities during the Crabbgate period.

The military threat from the Soviets was real and pressing. At the same time an equivalent and highly active, sophisticated intelligence-gathering campaign was maintained by the KGB with both long and short term objectives. Recruiting spies was one of their major roles.

This inevitably engendered a well-justified paranoia in British officialdom. Everybody fell under suspicion and there were claims of "reds under the beds" at every turn. As part of the countermeasures, the awesome authority of the Official Secrets Act was wielded mercilessly. Suspects would be visited by some gentlemen from Whitehall and whisked away.

Needless to say, everybody was on best behaviour.

This was all very well for heterosexuals, but homosexuals were forced undercover because all sex acts between men were illegal in those days – a situation which has since been remedied in the UK and much of the free world[1].

But during the cold war, it offered the Soviets a golden opportunity to blackmail and manipulate key individuals, under the devastating threat of disclosure of their homosexuality. It was an Achilles Heel in Western security. It remains a sensitive topic of discussion amongst the 'old school' to this day.

Bisexuals and homosexuals understandably therefore went to great pains to hide and disguise their true sexuality. In the military, where this secrecy was particularly difficult to sustain, the powerful loyalty within sections and between individuals led to the active protection of many such men. High rank, records of gallantry, shared wartime experiences, celebrity status and royal connections all served to enhance this protection.

Such was the case of Commander Lionel 'Buster' Crabb OBE GM.

---

1 **The legal status of homosexuality in 1956**

In 1885, the Criminal Law Amendment Act came into law. The Act was principally intended to protect girls; it included 'gross indecency', and importantly extended existing laws against 'buggery' to criminalise all sex acts between men. This remained the case until the Sexual Offences Act 1967 which decriminalised private sex acts between consenting men over the age of 21.

Military personnel could be Court Martialled, followed by a dishonourable discharge along with loss of rank and all pension rights. Civilians could be prosecuted in the Criminal Court with custodial sentences. If there was any foreign intelligence involvement, the sentences could have been anything up to capital punishment by hanging, as a traitor.

PART 5
ACKNOWLEDGMENTS

I am indebted to many individuals who have shared their experiences and information to help me produce this book. Needless to say, in view of the continued sensitivity of the subject and the incongruous continuation of the secrecy adopted by the government and associated agencies, I have been obliged to avoid attributing details to many individuals and acknowledging them by name. Nevertheless, I thank them very sincerely.

I can, however, thank Matteo Cicala for his assistance with valuable references and Mike O'Meara for a copy of his notes from his interview of Harry Cole. Peter Marshall helped enormously with his personal recollections of the Sally Port Hotel fiasco and in proof-reading the manuscript. Malcolm Barrett and Colin Turrell generously assisted with personal recollections and background on the West Sussex Constabulary and the investigation into the body parts recovered from Chichester Harbour. My thanks also go to Gianfranco Betro, Nigel Butlin, Dr Ian Calder, Matthew French, Cdr John Grattan OBE RN (Retd), Don Hale, Frances Knowles, Cdr Julian G Malec OBE RN (Retd), David Moore, Fabio Vitale, Mike and Jacqui Welham.

I am indebted to several colleagues who are sadly no longer with us, namely Lt Cdr Gordon Gutteridge OBE RN and Surgeon Vice Admiral Sir John Stuart Pepys Rawlins KBE BM BCH FTCP FFPH FRAeS.

I also gratefully acknowledge the authors and publishers of other publications on the subject whom I have quoted liberally throughout this book and the sources of the illustrations, which include The Historical Diving Society, Chichester Public Record Office, The National Archives, The Royal Navy and Cowdray House.

Appendix 1

Service Record — Commander (Sp) L K P Crabb RNVR

Temporary Sub Lieutenant (Special Branch) RNVR

KING ALFRED	07.08.41	-	21.08.41
WASP Coastal Forces Base Dover	22.08.41	-	06.11.41

Temporary Lieutenant (Special Branch) RNVR

WASP	07.11.41	-	25.11.41
PRESIDENT addl for duty			
outside Admiralty with DUBD	26.11.41	-	26.10.42
CORMORANT addl as			
BSO Gibraltar	27.10.42	-	28.12.43
CORMORANT addl			
(Special Service)	29.12.43	-	30.03.44

Temporary Acting Lieutenant-Commander (Sp) RNVR

CORMORANT addl			
(Special Service)	31.03.44	-	?
BYRSA addl for BS and RMS			
duties on staff of FOWIT	?	-	22.06.44
BYRSA addl as RMS and			
BSO Party "Jip"	23.06.44	-	11.09.44
BYRSA addl for MBDU			
No1 i/c	12.09.44	-	23.12.44
BYRSA addl (sick)	24.12.44	-	?
FABIUS addl for duty			
with NP 'C'; Taranto Dockyard	00.05.45	-	?
ST ANGELO addl	?	-	?

Temporary Lieutenant Commander (Special Branch) RNVR   27.01.45

VICTORY (not to join)	17.02.47	-	11.05.47
VERNON addl for SWD			
Refresher course	12.05.47	-	22.05.47
VICTORY (not to join)	23.05.47	-	25.05.47
STAGG addl in charge of			
'P' parties, Haifa; Middle East	26.05.47	-	14.12.47
VERNON	15.12.47	-	29.04.48

RELEASED CLASS A	30.04.48		

Lieutenant-Commander (Sp)
VERNON for RECLAIM addl   121 days training

Recalled for 18 months (but stayed 3 ½ years!); service as follows:

Lieutenant-Commander (Sp)
VERNON addl for duty with
CUCWE for clearance diving   12.10.51   -   29.06.52

Commander (Special Branch)
VERNON addl for duty with
CUCWE for clearance diving   30.06.52   -   07.04.55

RELEASED   08.04.55

PRESIDENT (RNVR) List II   08.04.55   -   date

Decorations:
George Medal   (AFO 518/44)
OBE   (AFO 7319/45)

Appendix 2

Commander Crabb's swordstick

The swordstick which became one of Commander Crabb's favourite accessories in civvy street was a gift to him from Captain N E FitzPatrick of Welton House, Gorey, Jersey.

FitzPatrick, a noted British painter, had designed it specially himself and commissioned its manufacture by José Martin in Toledo, Spain. He presented it to Commander Crabb in the summer of 1950 at the Gate House, Ennismore Mews, Kensington where they and Charles Garnet were fellow lodgers. In 1956, Captain Fitzpatrick claimed to have been a friend of Commander Crabb for 23 years.

The distinctive handle to
Commander Crabb's swordstick

Appendix 3

Harold Victor Maitland Pendock

He was born on 23 November 1899 to Charles Robert and Emily Pendock who lived at 45 Redland Road, Cotham, Bristol. Educated at Charterhouse School in Godalming. He was Christened at Brislington, St Luke, Somerset in the Church of England on 4 March 1900. He served in the army between 8 May 1918 and 3 February 1919 in the Queen's Regiment 5th Battalion Rifle Brigade leaving with the Ranks of Second Lieutenant. He was described as 5 feet 9.5 inches tall, black hair, sallow complexion, brown eyes with good physical development.

When aged 30, he married Joan Dorothea Mathews (24) 26 July 1930 at the Parish Church, in the Parish of Ewelme, Oxford and lived at 32 Clareville Street, London, SW7. Their son Simon Barry Pendock was born on 30 May 1932. But on 7 November 1938, they were divorced with Joan Pendock citing her husband's adulterous affair with Daphne Sawford at the Red Lion Hotel, Ockley, Surrey. Maitland Pendock, who did not contest the Petition, was ordered to pay £300 per annum maintenance to his ex-wife and a further £100 per annum for the maintenance of his son who was placed in the custody of his mother. Maitland Pendock was further required to pay for the educational and medical expenses of his son plus the cost of Petition, all payable in monthly instalments.

Cdr Crabb worked part-time for Pendock selling antique furniture. They had been close friends since about 1931. When Cdr Crabb had failed to return to London he had initially considered consulting a clairvoyant, Madame Theodosia.

When interviewed by Captain Sarell, Pendock said he had helped Cdr Crabb out of several *"scrapes"*. He added that Cdr Crabb was a *"very free spender, was usually heavily in debt"* and also owed his company *"a fair amount of money"*. He said that Cdr Crabb *"did not get on with women"*. With regard to Cdr Crabb's mother, he said that Cdr Crabb was not in regular contact with her and *"the usual purpose of his visits being to touch her for a loan."* He said that as far a having a steady girl friend was concerned *"it was Mrs Pat Dill, the wife of Victor Dill who was involved in a fairly recent racehorse switching case."*

MI6 also noted:

Mrs Dill has some connection with one AITKEN, believed to be a relation of Lord BEAVERBROOK, which might provide a link to the "Daily Express" should she intend to make trouble for any reason. Another member of the same set is Howard JOHNSTON of the "Daily Mirror" (the paper's Naval correspondent). All of these were in the habit of meeting at a Club near the Coliseum... [possibly Chez Marcel's drinking club at 38a St Martin's Lane where Commander Crabb had taken Mike Borrow.]

Mrs Pat Dill was the same person as Pat Rose, the name she had acquired from a previous marriage and the one she reverted to following her marriage to Victor Dill.

Pendock was already on file with MI5. They had recorded him as early as 1940 when he was in the publicity business because he was an associate of:

Claude Cockburn, the editor of "The Week" an extreme left-wing publication. PENDOCK himself was said to be a leftist and was the object of some disfavour for having spread alarmist and defeatist talk.

Captain Sarell described Pendock as *"a somewhat muddle-minded individual who may well have held advanced left-wing views in the past…"* but he did not think *"that there is any real vice left in him nowadays."* As far as Sarell could determine, Pendock knew no more than Cdr Crabb's purpose in going down to Portsmouth was to get some diving practice as an RNVR reservist. However, Lt Cdr Crawford had indicated that Pendock knew that Cdr Crabb's visit to Portsmouth was in connection with the Soviet ships.

An item in the London Gazette appears to indicate a somewhat variable course followed by Pendock's business practices:

London Gazette, 18 October, 1949

PENDOCK. Harold Victor Maitland, lately residing at 41, Bramham Gardens, London, S.W.5 [curiously close to where Cdr Crabb's fiancée had lived at No 47 in 1953] but now of no fixed address, carrying on business under the style of Hayes Marshall Interior Decorators [they operated from 28 Cork Street, London W1 between 1947 and 1950], and lately carrying on business at 69, Fleet Street, London, E.C.4, as a BUSINESS CONSULTANT, described in the Receiving Order as Harold Victor Maitland Pendock, sued as Maitland Pendock, formerly of 52, Kings Court North, Kings Road, Chelsea, S.W.3, and lately of Blayden Manor, Buckdown, in the county of Devon, but whose present address the Petitioners have been unable to ascertain but who is a domiciled Englishman, domiciled in England, and whose occupation is unknown. Court—HIGH COURT OF JUSTICE. No. of Matter—349 of 1949. Date of Order—Oct. 10, 1949. Date of Filing Petition- July 1, 1949.

Frogman Spy, by M G & J A Welham, 1990

[Maitland] owned a company called Elmbourne Ltd, with its office in Seymour Place, London … an advertising consultant, jolly, middle aged with round Pickwickian face; … sold build-it-yourself furniture … associated with Anthony Blunt, Burgess, Maclean and Philby; pp23-24.

The Welhams also mentioned that Pendock was questioned and beaten up by MI5 officers as a suspected communist sympathiser; pp74-75.

Finally, the plot thickens even more with a strange story of Pendock's ultimate demise:

Mike and Jacqui Welham – www.welhambooks.com/new_projects_2.html

After Crabb disappeared in Portsmouth, Maitland began to ask questions in high places about Crabb. He was told to drop the subject. When the body of a frogman was found and buried in 1957, he was taken and interrogated by MI5. There followed further interrogations and intimidation and in 1958, Maitland, my grandmother Helen and dad went on 'holiday' to a very remote location in Southern Ireland. It was strange because they were going to camp and the family did not do camping.

During the trip, Maitland was "irritable" and was taken to a small cottage Hospital for a check-up. Granny was told to go away and come back later that day. Returning to the Hospital to check on how Maitland was, she was informed that her husband had died. She never saw the body. There was no release form for the body; there is no evidence of an undertaker being involved and nor was there was an autopsy. None of the family actually saw the body of Maitland. There was a funeral, but granny always maintained that it was not Maitland in the coffin. At the time granny instructed the family that they were not to mention Maitland's name again.

The background to Maitland Pendock is covered in the fictionalised book *Crabb and the Grey Rabbit* by Mike and Jacqui Welham, 2015.

Appendix 4

Marshall Morrison Pugh

Born in Dundee, Scotland on 26 September 1925.

He served a Short Commission in the Parachute Regiment.

He became a freelance journalist and writer with an office at Odham's Press in London. He worked for Alan Maclean in Macmillans, Donald Maclean's brother.

He was a regular attendee at Blunt's parties.

He wrote the book Commander Crabb with the assistance of Crabb himself. The book was later adapted into a movie called The Silent Enemy which was released in 1958. He also wrote fiction.

His works included:
1958 *A Wilderness of Monkeys*
1962 BBC Home Service: *How not to write a novel*
1964 screenwriter of *Guns at Batasi*
1969 *Last Place Left*
1972 March 16 *Murmur of Mutiny*
1974 *A Dream of Treason*

On 28 November 1975 he advertised courses in Creative Writing with Laurie Lee in Chelsea.

7 July 1976 died at St Stephens Hospital, Chelsea, from accidental alcohol and paracetamol poisoning; living at 308A Kings Road, SW3.

14 July 1976 Inquest held by Coroner G Thurston.

Appendix 5

The Admiralty Underwater Countermeasures and Weapons Establishment (UCWE)

UCWE originated in the Mining Department formed in the Admiralty in 1915. In 1919 it became the Mine Design Department at HMS *Vernon*, where it remained until 1939. The Department was dispersed during the Second World War after HMS *Vernon* suffered two disasters. First on 4 August 1940 a booby-trapped mine exploded as it was being investigated killing five of the investigating teams. Second, one of several bombs that fell on HMS *Vernon* on the night of 9 March 1941 destroyed Dido Building, killing over 100 naval personnel.

The Mine Design Department moved to Leigh Park House and West Leigh in Havant. It included a "Rendering Mines Safe" (RMS) team, otherwise known as the *"Enemy mine disposal*

The staff at UCWE, C.1959. The location is the south aspect of West Leigh House. The picture was taken shortly before the establishment was relocated to Portland. *(slight overlap included at centre)*

team". They moved in to the West Leigh estate including West Leigh House itself. In 1946 it became the Admiralty Mining Establishment at Leigh Park, Havant. It undertook research into the design, location and neutralisation of mines, and into torpedoes and other underwater weapons. Several brick, timber and industrial style buildings were built in the grounds. One was called the 'Non-magnetic building' having been constructed entirely from wood and copper fastenings so that magnetic mine mechanisms could be more safely investigated there. There were several ponds two of which were square and *"quite deep"* which had been specially excavated for testing underwater devices.

Its most famous, of the many heroic staff, was undoubtedly Cdr J G D Ouvry who was responsible for first defusing a German magnetic mine. As a result, the RMS scientists were able to develop effective countermeasures. This eventually led to the neutralisation of one of Hitler's most devastating weapons that was devastating shipping traffic around the country.

The main administrative headquarters and the Mine Design Department were based in Leigh Park House while the scientific and trials departments, including the diving group, were based at West Leigh House about a mile away. The conservatory of West Leigh House became a museum of explosive devices and their components.

In 1951 it became the Admiralty Underwater Countermeasures and Weapons Establishment (UCWE). By 1953 the total staff including Naval officers, Scientific, Experimental, Assistant (Scientific) and Drawing Office, Clerical and Industrial numbered about 500. The scientific staff were divided into the following groups:

- Anti-Submarine Weapons
- Countermeasures (which Lt Cdr Crabb joined)
- Mining
- Weapon Assessment
- Trials
- Electronics
- Post-Design
- Common Services

Gordon Gutteridge was put in charge of staff requirements of a small specialist group for the development of mine investigation equipment and the relevant diving equipment *"platform"* to use it. Then to co-ordinate the effort and set up a top-of-the-line Experimental Diving Trials Team attached to UCWE, the Admiralty put Crabb in charge as Diving Officer with rank of Cdr RNVR with a 2-year contract (though he stayed in the job for four years). UCWE closed in 1959 when underwater research was moved to the Admiralty Underwater Weapons Establishment (AUWE) at Portland, Dorset. Some key personnel involved in the diving equipment development including Ray Common moved to the new Admiralty Experimental Diving Unit (AEDU) at HMS *Vernon*, Portsmouth.

Mr Winstock had a staff of about 20 which included Margaret Johnson (who worked there from spring 1951 to March 1954) and Clem Hoagan. They were involved with high speed photography of torpedoes. Cdr Crabb used to take Margaret Johnson with him on his official trips to Farnborough and Portsmouth. She said she was impressed by him but was a little scared of him. Another of his associates at UCWE was John Lintorn, who described Commander Crabb as a gentleman in every respect.

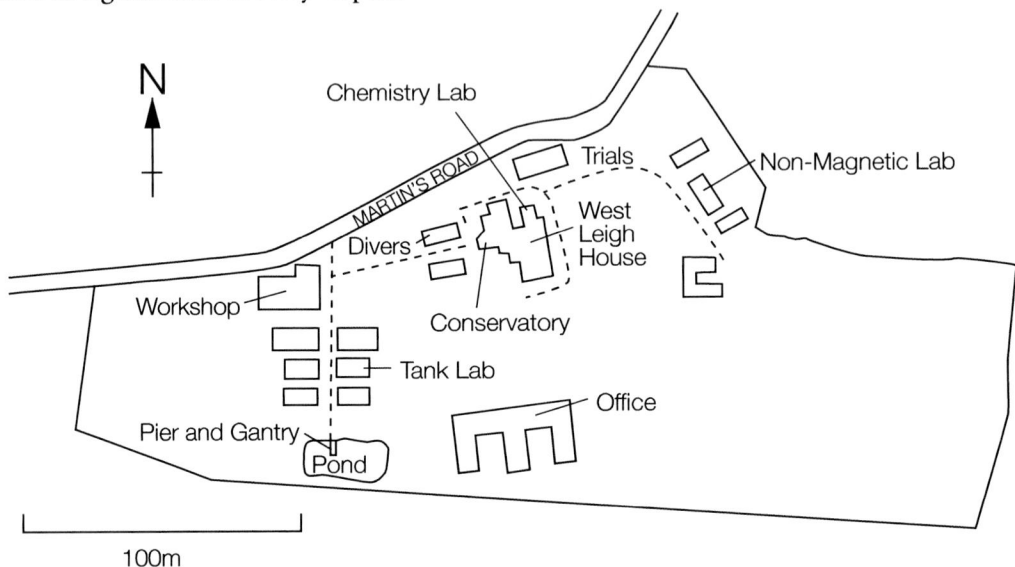

Plan of Underwater Ccountermeasures and Weapons Establishment (UCWE). The area is now a housing estate. The pond was used for trials of underwater equipment

Appendix 6

Admiralty Experimental Diving Unit (AEDU)

The Admiralty Experimental Diving Unit was formed in 1933 on the recommendation of the Admiralty Diving Committee, in order to meet the problems posed by port clearance, submarines and other naval activities which needed divers. Although staffed by naval personnel and scientists, it began its operations at the works of Siebe, Gorman and Co Ltd, the diving equipment firm. After the Second World War, it moved for a short period to Brixham, Devon, and then to HMS *Vernon* in Portsmouth in 1945 where it found a permanent home and came under the direction of the Naval Superintendent of Diving. Its premises moved around *Vernon* over the years. In 1956 it was based in a building near the "Mining Tank" (see map at Page 107).

Appendix 7

HMS *Deepwater* and Diving School

Senior Clearance Diving Officer	Lt Cdr George Albert Franklin
Instructor	Lt F J D Kelly
Instructor	Lt Taylor
Instructor	Lt K C Lewis

Appendix 8

HMS Maidstone

HMS *Maidstone* was a submarine support ship, 8,900 tons, launched in 1937. In 1956 she was the mother ship to the 2nd and 7th Submarine Flotillas based at Portland. In 1956 she was also briefly the Flagship of the Commander-in-Chief of the Home Fleet at Portsmouth. Shallow Water Diving courses were conducted on board in close association with the Diving School on HMS *Deepwater* at HMS *Vernon*. These courses were specifically in the use of oxygen rebreathing equipment. There would therefore have been a very close relationship between the head of the Deepwater Diving School (Lt Cdr Franklin) and the officer in charge of the training on board *Maidstone* (Lewis). The use of *Maidstone's* launch by Lt Cdr Franklin and Cdr Crabb for the diving operation would therefore appear logical.

HMS *Maidstone*, submarine support ship.

Appendix 9

Fort Monckton

The fort was retained by the Ministry of Defence after WW2 though virtually abandoned. It now remains the only fort in the Portsmouth area retained by MoD (Army) as opposed to the Royal Navy. Much of the original fort still exists including the bastions, sea facing casemates, guard room, one of the caponiers and the ditch. The fort retains its original drawbridge and is additionally protected by modern razor wire security fencing, CCTV cameras and high intensity lighting. The site has been heavily modified with modern offices and accommodation added on and around it. Security at the site is undertaken by an in-house civilian guard force.

The Army now refers to it as "No.1 Military Training Establishment" and it is occupied by the Ministry of Defence. Fort Monckton is now MI6's premier field operations training centre, where both basic and advanced field training is given to their personnel, as well as providing liaison training with other services including the Special Air Service (SAS) and Special Boat Service (SBS).

Appendix 10

Locations in London referred to in the text

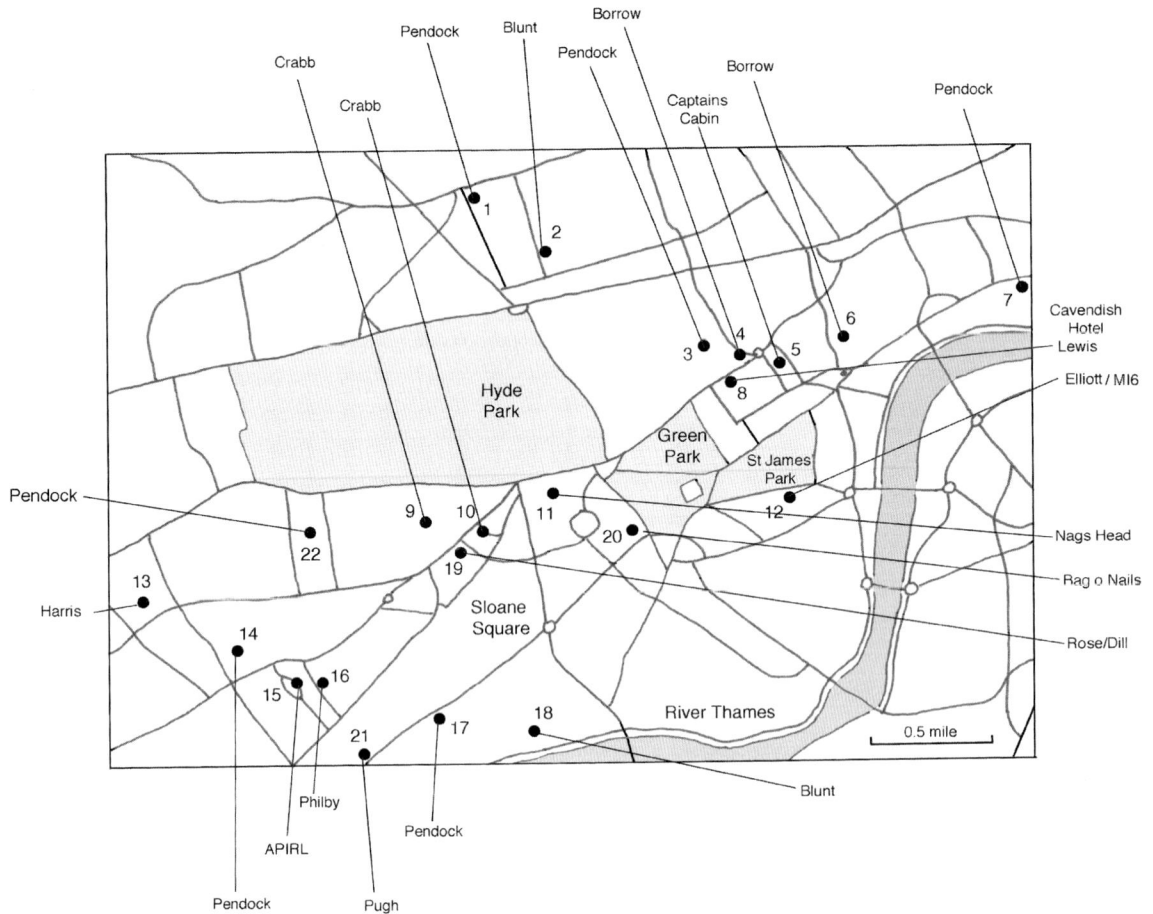

1   Pendock: Elmbourne Ltd, Expresso Furnishings, Seymour Place
2   Blunt: 20 Portman Square
3   Pendock: Hayes Marshall, 28 Cork Street
4   Borrow: P Frankenstein & Sons (Manchester) Ltd, 91 Regent Street
5   Knowles: Captains Cabin, 4-7 Norris Street
6   Borrow: Chez Marcel's, 38a St Martin's Lane
7   Pendock: Hayes Marshall, 69 Fleet Street
8   Lewis: Cavendish Hotel, 81 Jermyn St

9   Crabb: Gate House, Ennismore Mews
10 Crabb: 2a Hans Road
11 Crabb: Nag's Head, 53 Kinnerton Street
12 Elliott: MI6, 54 Broadway and Queen Anne's Gate
13 Harris: Garden Lodge Studio, Logan Place
14 Pendock: 41 Bramham Gardens
15 APIRL: 21 The Boltons
16 Philby:18 Grove Court, Drayton Gardens
17 Pendock: 52 Kings Court North, Kings Road
18 Blunt: Tite Street
19 Rose / Dill: 18 Ovington Gardens
20 Bag O'Nails: 6 Buckingham Palace Road
21 Pugh: 308A Kings Road
22 Pendock: 48 Queens Gate Terrace

Appendix 11

Red Star Article

Reproduced below is a translation of an article written by Victor Mukhrtov, Captain of the 1st Rank (retired) and published in the Soviet newspaper *Red Star* on 27 March 2008.

Some of the main points made in the article include:

- The VIPs on board the *Ordzhonikidze* included:
  - N.S. Khruschev, the First Secretary of the Central Committee of the Communist Party of the Soviet Union,
  - N.A. Bulganin, the Chairman of the Council of Ministers,
    - A.N. Tupolev, the chief aircraft designer,
    - I.V. Kurchatov, an atomic scientist, an academician, and other officials.
    - Victor Mukhrtov, Captain of the 1st Rank was the Secretary of the Communist Party organisation on the cruiser.
- He referred to the sighting of Cdr Crabb on the surface, the suspicion of spying and the concern of a mine being placed on the ship.
- He referred to Knowles' version that Cdr Crabb was a double agent and defected to Russia. Also a 'more fanciful' version that Cdr Crabb was captured by Russian frogmen and recruited by Russian intelligence to train their divers. 'Yet another version' that the ship's captain ordered the propellers to be turned which killed Cdr Crabb – except that 2-4 hours notice was required to prepare for the turning of propellers.
- He referred to a TV documentary in the 1970s explaining how a Russian frogman Eduard Koltsov discovered Cdr Crabb attaching a mine to the ship and killed him by cutting his breathing equipment and his throat and then removed the mine. He believed that Koltsov had therefore saved his life.
- He inferred that Cdr Crabb was responsible for sinking 'many ships' including the battleship *Novorossiysk* which blew up in Sebastopol in 1955.

Perhaps the most significant aspects of the article are not only the complete absence of any claim that Cdr Crabb ended up in Russia but even that such claims were fanciful. Surely, if Cdr Crabb had ended up in Russia he would have been paraded before the public to maximize the embarrassment to the UK government.

The bizarre claims that the Russians were afraid Cdr Crabb had attached a mine to their ship and the suggestion that he had been responsible for the sinking of their battleship *Novorossiysk* are typical of their propaganda designed to maintain the Russian public paranoia against the west. If they really did have Cdr Crabb, they would undoubtedly have taken the opportunity to 'arrange' a confession out of him.

Indeed, there is no evidence that Cdr Crabb ever placed a mine on any ship. He had never been employed to take any covert aggressive action. His speciality was mine clearance, i.e. removing and disabling mines.

RED STAR

Readers' post, Thursday, 'Battle under the cruiser'

by Victor Mukhrtov, Captain of the 1st Rank (retired)

In recent times in London, there has been a lot of talk about the activities of Russian intelligence services in Great Britain. However, no facts are provided. In relation to this, I would like to record the opposite – the activities of the British intelligence services. In particular, I would like to refer to an event, which I happened to witness.

In April 1956 a small group of Soviet ships including the cruiser *Ordzhonikidze* and destroyers *Smotryaschii* and *Sovershennyi* were paying a visit to England. At the time, I was the Secretary of the Communist Party organisation on the cruiser. This group of Soviet ships carried the USSR delegation to England which consisted of Party and government members – N.S. Khruschev, the First Secretary of the Central Committee of the Communist Party of the Soviet Union, N.A. Bulganin, the Chairman of the Council of Ministers, A.N. Tupolev, the chief aircraft designer, I.V. Kurchatov, an atomic scientist, an academician, and other officials.

Early in the morning of the 19th of April a watchkeeper on one of the destroyers noticed that by the side of the cruiser someone came to the surface and then submerged again. The commander of the ship was informed of this immediately, and he, in his turn, informed the cruiser. A suspicion arose that English spies were trying to carry out a secret investigation of the bottom of the ship and its propellers, because the cruiser had a very high speed – 32 knots, and excellent manoeuvrability. Sabotage, or mine installation on the bottom of the ship, was not excluded either. As soon as the cruiser reached the North Sea, she would be blown up. The loss of the ship with a government delegation on board could be explained by the cruiser exploding after contact with a wartime mine.

Safety measures were carried out; the British authorities were informed. Soon after, a corpse in a lightweight diving suit was found on one of the islands near Portsmouth, and it was identified as Lieutenant Commander Lionel Crabb, who used to be a famous diver in the past and who fought with Italian saboteur skin-divers in the Mediterranean Sea during World War Two. There was a great deal of alarm in society and in the media. A political row about the so-called Crabb affair erupted in the British government circles. Anthony Eden, the British Prime Minister, was forced to address the House of Commons and declare that the government had not been informed of the Crabb operation by the Intelligence Services and therefore could not have sanctioned it. The Labour Party which was in opposition at the time, condemned the British government for the espionage act during a friendly visit of Soviet ships, and demanded a full investigation. The article 'The Lionel Crabb affair' which was published in the newspaper *Pravda* on 11th May 1956, confirmed the fact of espionage and condemned the unfriendly act of the British government against our state.

So, what happened to Crabb himself? The official version of this was reported on 19th April 1956, when the high command of the British navy declared that Crabb '*did not return after an experimental submersion to the bottom of the sea, the purpose of which was the testing of some diving devices in Stokes Bay in the Portsmouth area'.* That is why many different versions appeared and suggestions about Crabb's fate. For example, in the article written by A. Kartsev which was published on 7th June 1991 in *Komsomolskaya Pravda*, it said that Crabb's friend and colleague Sidney Knowles, who fought alongside Crabb against the Italians, declared that Crabb was a double agent and that immediately after the war he started working for Soviet Intelligence. In the operation against *Ordzhonikidze* he used the occasion to give himself up to the Russians and move to the Soviet Union. In 2005 in the book *A Hundred Great Mysteries of the 20th Century*, in the article 'Disappearance of the Frogman', A. Rovenskii depicted a more fanciful picture. When the diver was found by the cruiser, Soviet divers chased and captured him. Then he was recruited by Russian Intelligence and he started training Soviet divers.

At the beginning of the 1970s I heard of yet another version. There was a lecturer in the House of Officers in Petropavlovsk. He gave a lecture in front of a big audience and gave a lot of interesting examples of activities of foreign intelligence services. He also spoke about what happened on the cruiser *Ordzhonikidze* in England in 1956. He claimed that when the diver was discovered, an order was given and the cruiser turned on its propellers. The saboteur was killed by the ship's propellers. After the lecture I approached the lecturer and explained to him tactfully that to turn its propellers, the cruiser needed four hours of preparation in normal circumstances, and if it was urgent, two hours. During this time, the saboteur could have swum away in the direction he needed to go in.

Only very recently a light was thrown on this event, the event which took place on 19th April 1956 in Portsmouth under the cruiser *Ordzhonikidze*. On 'Ren TV' channel, a documentary was shown. It was called 'A Revelation of a Sea Devil'. I took part in its preparation. Eduard Koltsov was the main interviewee. In his interview, Koltsov explained that at that time, when he was twenty-three years old, he was a saboteur diver. When the cruiser's sonar discovered a suspicious object under the hull of the ship, the leader of the sabotage-reconnaissance group called Koltsov and told him to go under water and act according to the circumstances. Koltsov did this. Soon afterwards he noticed a silhouette of a man in a lightweight suit. This man was planting a mine on the right-hand side of the ship, just where the battery charger room was. Being very careful, he approached the saboteur, grabbed his boots and pulled the saboteur towards him. When the saboteur's body was in line with him, he cut the breathing device with his knife, and then cut the saboteur's throat. He released the diver's corpse into the water, took the mine off the hull of the ship and took it to the corner of the pier where there were no people and there was a lot of mud and other rubbish. Eduard Koltsov was awarded the Order of the Red Star.

This is how we found out what happened in reality. As for Lionel Crabb, English archives about him are classified until 2057. Why? Apparently, the loss of many ships and maybe the loss of our battleship *Novorossiysk*, which was blown up in 1955 in Sevastopol, are on his conscience and on the conscience of the English government. In any case, during that time Crabb was a commander of the 12th sea saboteur group.

What is important for me is that on 19 April 1956 Eduard Koltsov saved my life and the lives of many others.

Appendix 12

Organigram

The following organigram is the author's interpretation of the organisational relationships between the principal groups and personnel associated with the Commander Crabb diving operation. No guarantee can be given for its accuracy.

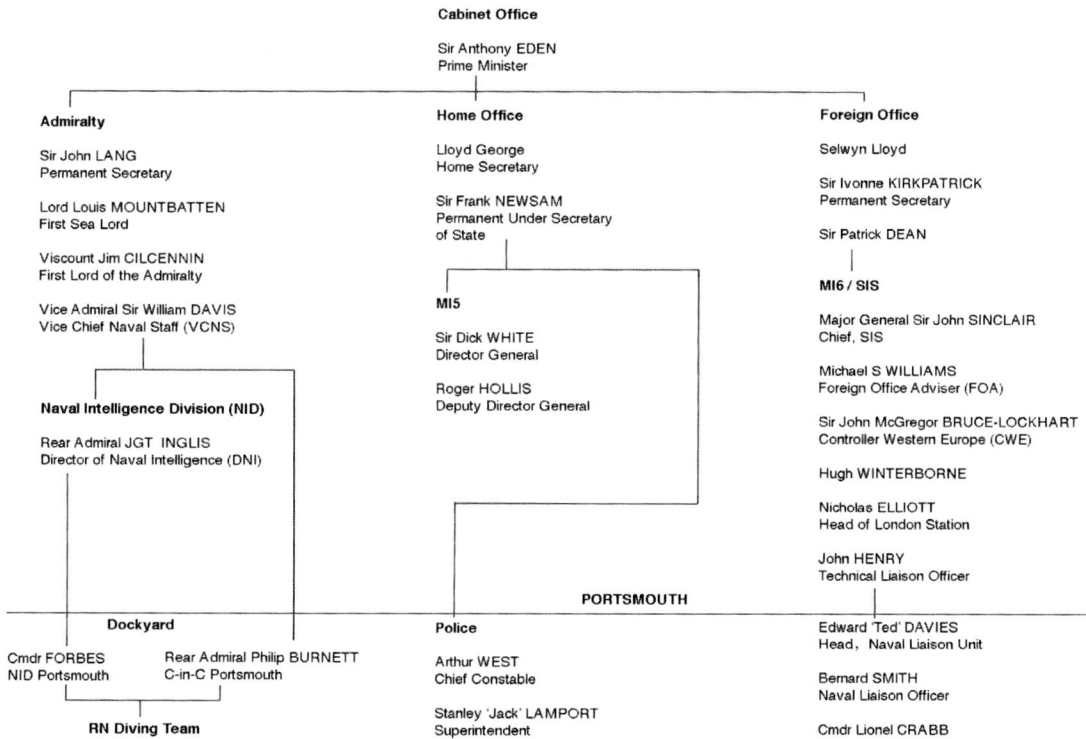

Cabinet Office

Sir Anthony EDEN
Prime Minister

Admiralty

Sir John LANG
Permanent Secretary

Lord Louis MOUNTBATTEN
First Sea Lord

Viscount Jim CILCENNIN
First Lord of the Admiralty

Vice Admiral Sir William DAVIS
Vice Chief Naval Staff (VCNS)

Naval Intelligence Division (NID)

Rear Admiral JGT INGLIS
Director of Naval Intelligence (DNI)

Home Office

Lloyd George
Home Secretary

Sir Frank NEWSAM
Permanent Under Secretary
of State

MI5

Sir Dick WHITE
Director General

Roger HOLLIS
Deputy Director General

Foreign Office

Selwyn Lloyd

Sir Ivonne KIRKPATRICK
Permanent Secretary

Sir Patrick DEAN

MI6 / SIS

Major General Sir John SINCLAIR
Chief, SIS

Michael S WILLIAMS
Foreign Office Adviser (FOA)

Sir John McGregor BRUCE-LOCKHART
Controller Western Europe (CWE)

Hugh WINTERBORNE

Nicholas ELLIOTT
Head of London Station

John HENRY
Technical Liaison Officer

PORTSMOUTH

Dockyard

Cmdr FORBES
NID Portsmouth

Rear Admiral Philip BURNETT
C-in-C Portsmouth

RN Diving Team

Police

Arthur WEST
Chief Constable

Stanley 'Jack' LAMPORT
Superintendent

Edward 'Ted' DAVIES
Head, Naval Liaison Unit

Bernard SMITH
Naval Liaison Officer

Cmdr Lionel CRABB

Appendix 13

Letter assumed to be from Lt Cdr Joe Brooks

JB/BP

<u>STRICTLY CONFIDENTIAL</u>

The Private Secretary
10 Downing Street
LONDON

27th March 1981

Dear Mr Alexander,

<u>National Security – Crabbe Incident</u>

Further to our telephone conversation this morning, you asked me to write to you.

Because of the problems that must be occupying a lot of the Prime Minister's time right now, I'm sure it would be progressive in the interests of us all, if she became fully aware of the truths of the above incident.

In brief, I was in charge of the Naval operational team who successfully surveyed the undersides of the Russian ships at the time to ensure that all was either 'safe' or 'unsafe'.

The Security Services, apart from alerting us to the need for this underwater survey operation, engaged Crabbe on a separate mission which failed disastrously. This caused political chaos from the Prime Minister downwards. An examination of this particular incident would be very useful at this stage. In my view, the problem is not just a question of bad communications.

Rest assured that I have adhered to the confidentiality of this incident. There were others apart from myself, who did the underwater work – I'm sure they too are loyal.

As a result of the interesting experiences in this particular operation, I became determined, and have succeeded in setting up a commercial company who bide by the same standards.

Yours sincerely,

Appendix 14

References consulted

National Archives
ADM 1/28941
ADM 1/28946
ADM 1/29240
ADM 1/29241
ADM 204/90
ADM 204/913
ADM 204/2382
CAB 21/3887
CAB 301/121
CAB 301/122
CAB 301/123
CAB 301/124
CAB 301/125
FO 371/122885
J 77/3841
PREM 11/2077
WO 78/5229
WO 374/53316

Imperial War Museum, Oral History recordings
8269; William Stanley Stevens
11245; Frank Edward Goldsworthy
12374; James Richard Wilson
32725; Frank Bicknell

Books (in chronological order)
Commander Crabb by Marshall Pugh; Macmillan & Co Ltd; 1956
HMS Vernon 1930 to 1955 by Cdr E D Webb RN ; The Wardroom Mess Committee
Frogman Extraordinary by J Bernard Hutton; Neville Spearman, 1960
The Fake Defector by J Bernard Hutton; Howard Baker, 1970; SBN 09 307060 8
Spy Catcher by Peter Wright ; Viking Penguin Inc; 1987; ISBN 0-670-82055-5
Frogman Spy by M G and J A Welham ; W H Allen & Co Plc, 1990; ISBN 1-85227-138-8

The Torpedomen by Rear Admiral E N Poland; 1993; ISBN 0-85937-396-7

With My Little Eye by Nicholas Elliott; 1993; ISBN 0-85955-200-4

Dive Navy by Harry Wardle ; CPW Books;2002; ISBN 0 9523162 1 8

My Silent War by H A R Philby; Random House Inc, 2002; ISBN 0-375-75983-2

Oxford Dictionary of National Biography, ISBN 978-0199562442; 2004

The Final Dive by Don Hale; Sutton Publishing, 2007; ISBN 978-0-7509-4574-5

Treachery by Chapman Pincher; Random House; 2009; ISBN 978-1-4000-6807-4

A Diver in the Dark by Sydney Knowles; Woodfield, 2009; ISBN 1-84683-082-6

The Crabb Enigma by Mike and Jacqui Welham; Matador, 2010; ISBN 978 1848763 821

Classified, Secrecy and the State in Modern Britain; Christopher Moran, 2013;
          ISBN 978-1-107-00099-5

A Spy amongst Friends by Ben Macintyre; Crown Publishers, 2014; ISBN 978-0-8041-3663-1

West Sussex Constabulary, 110 Years of History, 2008, ISBN 978-0-9557588-2-9

Papers

Covering Up Spying in the 'Buster' Crabb Affair: A Note

Michael S Goodman, in *The International History Review*, xxx. 4: December 2008, pp. 709-944;
CN ISSN 0707-5332

Newspapers

References to the *Evening News* are to the newspaper published in Portsmouth.

1948	Nov 26	*Press* and Journal	"Frogman" operates with herring fleet
1950	Jan 15	*Sunday Pictorial*	They dived into silence
	Apr 7	*Scotsman*	Search at Tobermory
	Apr 8	*Coventry Evening Telegraph*	Treasure Hunt Enters New Phase
	Apr 8	*Dundee Evening Telegraph*	Children Play at Treasure Hunting
	Apr 8	*Leicester Daily Mercury*	Treasure Hunt Delay
	Apr 8	*Shields Daily News*	Treasure Divers Entertain
	Apr 17	*Gloucester Citizen*	"D" Day in treasure ship hunt
	Apr 17	*Portsmouth Evening News*	'Treasure' diver finds cannon ball
	Apr 18	*Aberdeen Press & Journal*	Armada Cannon-ball found by Diver
1953	Apr 18	Hastings & St Leonards Observer	Naval Divers resume search
1954	Jun 23	*Evening News*	Television cameras will aid treasure seekers
	Jul 3	*The Mail*	Frogman for treasure bid
	Jul 26	*Daily Mail*	Tobermory team together again
	Aug 3	*Courier & Advertiser*, Dundee	Tobermory Treasure Hunt

	Aug 23	*Daily Mail*	Frogmen Dive
	Aug 28	*Daily Herald*	Treasure hunters reach galleon
	Sep 1	*Portsmouth Evening News*	To search the Sea for Lost Fortune
1956	Apr 5	*Evening News*	Russians' visit dispute settled
	Apr 10	*Melbourne paper*	Mountbatten visit
	Apr 11	*Evening News*	Sailings from Portsmouth
	Apr 12	*Evening News*	Russians d… Again
	Apr 13	*Hampshire Telegraph*	Soviet Leaders here Wednesday
	Apr 13	*Evening News*	Bulganin ship open to public
	Apr 14	*Evening News*	Hush-hush S… Portsmouth
	Apr 17	*Evening News*	Security Chief to visit Portsmouth
	Apr 18	*Evening News*	Naval calls are being exchanged
			Silent entry … Soviet ships
			Nelson's Column
	Apr 19	*Evening News*	Evening News staff first aboard the Soviet cruiser
			Portsmouth's State Visitors
			Hospitality warms the Russians
	Apr 20	*Hampshire Telegraph*	Russian Statesmen disembark at Portsmouth Dockyard
	Apr 21	*Evening News*	Soviet cruiser shows off her teeth
	Apr 23	*Evening News*	Portsmouth 'besieged' Soviet ship
	Apr 25	*Evening News*	Russian ships: New plan to control crowd
			Soviet Ambassador says 'Thank You'
	Apr 26	*Evening News*	… Coming to Portsmouth
	Apr 27	*Hampshire Telegraph*	Visiting Soviet Squadron leaves today
	Apr 30	*Birmingham Daily Gazette*	Navy's Pioneer Frogman Lost in Test Dive
	Apr 30	*Times*	Presumed death of pioneer 'frogman'; Cdr L K P Crabb
	Apr 30	*Daily Mail*	Frogman GM dies on secret test
	Apr 30	*Telegraph & Morning Post*	G.M. frogman missing after tests
	Apr 30	*News Chronicle*	Top frogman dies in secret test
	Apr 30	*Evening News*	Thousands welcome …
	May 1	*Evening News*	Fate of Frogman remains mystery
	May 3	*Times*	Detectives visit Portsmouth hotel
	May 3	*Daily Express*	Police probe death of G.M. frogman
	May 3	*Daily Mail*	CID act on dead frogman riddle
	May 4	*Evening News*	Frogman 'died while on service'
			Fate of frogman remains mystery
			Zealous in secret work
	May 4	*Daily Express*	Frogman riddle

May 4	*Daily Herald*	Is frogman still alive?
May 4	*Daily Mail*	MP seeks answer to Crabb's secret
		The amazing adventures of frogman Crabb
May 4	*Daily Mirror*	BBC cut voice of lost frogman
May 4	*Lancashire Evening Post*	Questions in Commons on Frogman
May 5	*Daily Express*	We saw a frogman say Russians
May 5	*Daily Herald*	Frogman's death stays secret
May 5	*Daily Mail*	Red sailor – I saw frogman
May 5	*Daily Mirror*	Yard see friends of vanished frogman
May 5	*Daily Telegraph*	Frogman may be alive says former wife
May 5	*Evening News*	Lost Frogman missed usual call
		Respected by all – even his enemies
May 5	*Times*	Russian reticence on report
		Frogman seen near cruiser
May 6	*Sunday Dispatch*	Frogman Crabb's last hours
May 7	*Daily Herald*	Who hid truth of Buster Crabb?
May 7	*Daily Mail*	Crabb's frogman friend searches
		My friend Crabb
May 7	*Daily Mirror*	Amazing theory in the case of lost frogman
May 7	*Daily Sketch*	Frogman Crabb – will there be an inquest?
		Mr Smith tells of frogman
May 8	*Aberdeen Evening Express*	Frogman death riddle
May 8	*Daily Express*	This may have been secret of frogman Crabb
May 8	*Daily Herald*	End this mystery
May 8	*Daily Mail*	I know what Crabb did
		Crabb's first mine
May 8	*Daily Mirror*	'Frogman alive' say 3 women
May 8	*Hampshire Telegraph*	No inquest on Frogman asked
May 9	*Evening News*	Commander Crabb: Premier to speak
May 9	*Daily Herald*	Admiral will not see Mrs Crabb
May 9	*Daily Mail*	Crabb report for cabinet
		His last night
		What's wrong with Crabb
May 9	*Daily Mirror*	Is this the last picture of the missing frogman
May 9	*Daily Sketch*	A wife reveals frogman secret
May 9	*Evening Express*	Crabb's death: not in public interest to give details
May 9	*News Chronicle*	Yard report on lost frogman
May 9	*Telegraph*	M.P.'s question on frogman
May 10	*Aberdeen Evening Express*	Frogman: Premier will speak in own defence
May 10	*Evening News*	Cdr Crabb: Premier prepares reply

May 10 *Evening News*	The vanished frogman
May 10 *Daily Herald*	The scandal of Buster Crabb
May 10 *Daily Mail*	Light on frogman
May 10 *Daily Mail (cont)*	Crabb censure on premier
	MPs angered by Spy attack
	Crabb gambles on enemy frogmen
May 10 *Daily Mirror*	The frogman blunder; the big cover-up
May 10 *Daily Telegraph*	Cdr Crabb "On secret service"
May 10 *Evening Standard*	Dark waters
May 10 *Newcastle Journal*	Russian divers may have fought with Crabb
May 10 *Times*	No authority for dive by Cdr Crabb
May 11 *Evening News*	Disciplinary action follows frogman mystery
	Frogman Saga
May 11 *Evening Standard*	'Shameful underwater spying' says Moscow
May 11 *Daily Express*	How did frogman Crabb die?
May 11 *Daily Mail*	Secret Crabb probe demand
	Just how secret is the Secret Service?
May 11 *Daily Mirror*	Crossman says …
May 11 *Hampshire Telegraph*	Shameful Underwater Spying - Pravda
May 11 *News Chronicle*	The cloak and dagger boys have dropped a clanger
May 11 *The Star*	Moscow: 'Crabb spied on cruiser'
May 11 *Telegraph & Morning Post*	Frogman vote tactics
May 12 *Aberdeen Evening Express*	The Crabb affair, British public outraged
May 12 *Birmingham Gazette*	Frogman: 'Sorry' we tell Russia
May 12 *Daily Sketch*	Hunt for Crabb banned
	Frogman – B and K quote Sketch
May 12 *Daily Mirror*	'Explain' says Russia
	Britain says sorry
May 12 *Daily Mail*	Crabb dived on Sverdlov too
	Britain admits it: Crabb was there
May 12 *Daily Express*	Frogman: Eden apologises
	British admiral denied diver was down
May 12 *Daily Herald*	Russians tell all about the frogman
May 12 *Manchester Guardian*	Death of British Frogman
May 12 *The Star*	Crabb: Soviet says 'Britain outraged…'
May 12 *Evening News*	Frogman – Britain tells
	Frogman: New questions
May 12 *Times*	Apology to Moscow – Diver seen from destroyer
	Case of underwater espionage

May 12	*Times*	British warships' Leningrad visit
May 13	*Sunday Express*	They attack Gaitskill
		B & K to Eden's rescue
May 13	*Sunday Times*	Frogman: 'Breach of Manners' by Soviet
May 13	*Sunday Times (cont)*	Gaitskill – No apologies to Soviet
		Diving in muddied waters
May 14	*Daily Express*	Frogman inquiry
May 14	*Times*	MP's theory on US Secret Service
May 14	*Daily Mail*	Eden may tell Crabb story
		In fairness to Crabb
May 14	*Daily Mirror*	The Frogman Blunder
May 14	*Daily Sketch*	New Crabb Shock – By red C-in-C
May 14	*Daily Express*	Eden calls frogman talks
May 14	*Daily Herald*	Eden is back for talk on Crabb
May 14	*Daily Telegraph*	Debate today on Frogman
May 14	*Evening News*	Eden may tell: Why I kept silent on Crabb
May 14	*Manchester Guardian*	Frogman affair more involved
May 14	*News Chronicle*	Will today reveal the truth about the frogman?
May 15	*Daily Herald*	Eden keeps silent on Crabb
May 15	*Daily Mirror*	The silent man in the Commons last night
May 15	*Daily Mail*	Did Crabb die on second bid?
May 15	*Daily Mail*	Not one word more
May 15	*Manchester Guardian*	"Not one word more" on the Frogman
May 15	*News Chronicle*	Eden refuses to say one more word on Crabb
May 15	*Daily Mirror*	The silent man in the Commons last night
May 15	*Daily Sketch*	Hush! I say no more!
May 15	*Daily Telegraph*	Frogman: "Not one word more"
May 16	*Times*	Voting in debate on Cdr Crabb
May 16	*Daily Mail*	Where is Crabb's swordstick?
May 16	*Daily Mirror*	The missing votes …
May 18	*Daily Mirror*	Matter of sentiment, both say
May 18	*Daily Mail*	The Crabb swordstick turns up
May 19	*Daily Mail*	Explosive
May 22	*Daily Mail*	Crabbie's stick
May 30	*Daily Mirror*	You can't ask that, MP is told
May 31	*Birmingham Daily Post*	Gifts for Soviet Nvala Officers
May 31	*Daily Mail*	Crabb award for admiral
Jun 30	*Daily Mail*	Crabb held in Moscow
Jun 15	*Daily Mirror*	Letter he sent to Paris missing
Jun 16	*Daily Mirror*	Riddle of missing letter

Jun 30	*Daily Telegraph*	Frogman 'Held in Moscow Goal'
Jun 16	*Manchester Guardian*	The mystery of Crabb's debt
Jul 14	*Daily Mail*	Buster Crabb left £1205
Jul 20	*Hampshire Telegraph*	Cdr L Crabb's £1,205 Estate
Aug 3	*Daily Mail*	Skeleton – Is it Crabb?
Aug 4	*Daily Mail*	Admiralty £100 for Mrs Crabb
Aug 16	*Times*	Wartime frogman
Aug 18	*New Statesman*	Crabb's last dive
Sep 11	*Coventry Evening Telegraph*	Skeleton on sandbank 'not Crabb'
Sep 11	*Daily Herald*	Skeleton was not Crabb
Sep 11	*Northern Whig*	Skeleton on sands may be Crabb - Rumour
Oct 27	*The Argus* (Melbourne)	Sparks in TNT didn't worry Crabb

1957	Apr 29	*Herald*	No hero to me
	Apr 20	*Lancashire Evening Post*	Buster Crabb .. Mystery frogman
	Jun 10	*Birmingham Daily Post*	Frogman's body may be Cdr Crabb
	Jun 10	*Daily Mail*	Has Crabb been found?
	Jun 10	*Evening News*	Body mystery: Cdr Crabb
	Jun 10	*Lancashire Evening Post*	Frogman riddle may be solved today
	Jun 10	*Northern Daily Mail*	Moves to solve frogman riddle
	Jun 10	*Shields Daily News*	Threefold probe on the frogman
	Jun 11	*Evening News*	Frogman: Inquest is adjourned
	Jun 11	*Daily Mail*	Crabb shirt mystery
			But was he working for the Americans?
			I won't remember Crabbie as just a body on the beach
	Jun 11	*Daily Mirror*	MI5 men will see the body
	Jun 11	*Northern Daily Mail*	Frogman's body not yet identified
	Jun 11	*Northern Whig*	Headless frogman wore Navy equipment
	Jun 12	*Birmingham Post*	Mrs Crabb Unable to Identify Frogman
	Jun 12	*Evening News*	Cdr Crabb: New expert called in
	Jun 12	*Daily Mail*	Mr Smith may break silence on Crabb
	Jun 12	*Daily Mirror*	Mrs Crabb can't say
	Jun 12	*Newcastle Journal*	Crabb's ex-wife cannot identify headless body
	Jun 13	*Evening News*	Film about Cdr Crabb
	Jun 13	*Daily Mirror*	Frogman's suit not navy issue
	Jun 13	*Daily Mail*	Crabb suit not navy's
	Jun 14	*Evening News*	Harbour mystery of frogman
	Jun 14	*Chichester & Southdown Observer*	How the body was found

	Jun 14	*Hampshire Telegraph*	Under Lieut P A White
	Jun 14	*Lancashire Evening Post*	May be able to identify frogman
	Jun 15	*Evening News*	Chichester Harbour frogman not Richmond man
	Jun 21	*Hampshire Telegraph*	Frogman: Suit identified
	Jun 26	*Evening News*	Frogman Inquest resumes today
			Requiem Mass for Commander Crabb
	Jun	*Observer*	'I am satisfied it was Commander Crabb'
			Open verdict recorded
	Jun 27	*Evening News*	Frogman was Cdr Crabb
	Jun 27	*Daily Mail*	Great Crabb riddle stays unsolved
	Jun 27	*Times*	Dead frogman Cdr Crabb
	Jun 28	*Canberra Times*	Dead frogman Crabb, Coroner concludes
	Jul 2	*Evening News*	Requiem Mass for Commander Crabb
	Jul 5	*Evening News*	Joan of Arc inscription on Cdr Crabb's coffin
	Jul 5	*Shields Daily News*	Flower anchor wreath for Crabb
	Jul 6	*Daily Mirror*	Swordstick Riddle at Frogman's Grave
1958	Mar 5	*Daily Herald*	Frogman Crabb film is nearly all fiction
	Mar 5	*Daily Mail*	Presenting Crabb – with plenty of fiction
1960	Feb 10	*Daily Mail*	Crabb works for Russians
	Feb 18	*Daily Mail*	Lloyd firm on Crabb
	Jun 10	*Daily Mail*	Crabb riddle of missing boy
	Dec 30	*Times*	Commander Crabb "Not alive in Russia"
1961	Jan 12	*Times*	Commander Crabb's disappearance
1964	Nov 8	*Dominica del Corrierre*	Crabb
1965	Mar 19	*The News*	Premier snaps out
	Mar 23	*The News*	I found frogman's head
	Mar 25	*The News*	Body in sea
1966	Apr 2	*Daily Mail*	The spy who won't lie down
	Apr 13	*Daily Mail*	Navy holds film men
	Nov 22	*Daily Mail*	Buster's room
1967	Mar 8	*Daily Mail*	'Buster' Crabb clue found
	Mar 9	*Times*	Skull yields no clue to Crabb mystery
	Mar 9	*Daily Mail*	Crabb: Teeth no clue

| | | *Times* | Diver died near Russian ships |
| | May 24 | *Daily Mail* | New Crabb clue? |

| 1968 | Apr 14 | *Tribuna Illustrata* | Crabb is alive in Russia |
| 1968 | .... | *Majorca Daily Bulletin* | Buster Crabbe is alive! |

| 1969 | Jun 23 | *Daily Mail* | New lead in Crabb mystery |

| 1973 | May 21 | *Daily Mail* | Was this Buster Crabb's capture? |

| 1974 | Sep 15 | *Sunday Mirror* | Buster Crabb is alive |

| 1975 | Feb 26 | *Daily Mail* | Mr B, the Kremlin straight man |

| 1976 | May 24 | *Daily Mail* | Protests to greet Russian warship |
| | May 29 | *Daily Mail* | Enter the Soviet Navy |

| 1987 | Jan 1 | *Times* | Veil stays on Crabb spying episode |

| 1990 | May 6 | *Sunday Telegraph* | The Buster Crabb mystery comes to the surface again |
| | May 13 | *Sunday Telegraph* | 'What happened to Crabb' plea |

| 1991 | Nov 23 | *Times* | MI6 disaster lies low beneath the covers |

| 1993 | Apr 30 | *The News* | Diver death 'Spy bungle' |

| 1995 | Mar 20 | *Daily Mail* | Crabb victim of cold, not Reds |

| 1996 | Apr 19 | .... | Still waiting for truth about Crabb |
| | Jun | *Diver* | How Buster Crabb died |

| 1999 | Dec 3 | *The News* | New light shed ... |

| 2000 | Feb 1 | *The News* | Was I the last to see ... |
| | Dec 27 | *The News* | Files stay top secret ... |

| 2005 | Jul 6 | *Daily Express* | Deep sea mystery of Crabb |
| | Oct 5 | *Diver* | Crabb was not the only diving spy |

| 2006 | Mar 26 | *Mail on Sunday* | Buster Crabb was Murdered by MI5 |

	Jun 12	*The News*	Frogman was left to die
	Oct 27	*Daily Mail*	How Navy chiefs abandoned hero frogman sent to spy on Russians
	Oct 27	*Daily Express*	The Commander Crabb cover-up
2007	Jun 22	*The News*	Buster's final moments
	Jun 26	*The News*	Crabb mystery
	Jun 27	*The News*	Crabb Mystery Continues
	Jul 4	*The News*	Was it really Crabb's body?
	Jul 5	*The News*	Headless diver mystery
	Jul 27	*The News*	Crabb mystery continues
	Sep 24	*Times*	MoD admits navy divers spied on Soviet ships
	Nov 16	*BBC News*	Russian 'Killed UK diver' in 1956
	Nov 17	*The News*	Harbour death claim a 'publicity stunt'
	Nov 17	*Daily Mail*	I murdered Buster Crabb
	Nov 17	*Daily Mirror*	Cold war spy: I slashed Buster Crabb's throat
	Nov 17	*Daily Express*	How I slit the throat of the real James Bond
	Nov 17	*The News*	I cut Buster Crabb's throat
	Nov 17	*Times*	I killed MI6 frogman
	Nov 26	*The News*	No pin-up here
2008	Mar 27	*Red Star*	Battle under the cruiser
2011	Apr 7	*The Journal*, Portsmouth	Demand for the truth
2014	May 3	*The News*	Who rewrote headstone?
2015	Jun 20	*The News*	Rare glimpse of Crabb's funeral
	Oct 23	*The News*	Secret files
	Nov 17	*The News*	Buster Crabb – What really happened?
2016	Dec 21	*The News*	The Cdr Crabb mystery

Magazines

1954	Dec	*Royal Naval Diving Magazine*	Latest News from Tobermory
1956	May 28	*LIFE magazine*	The Mystery of the Frogman's Dive for Red Secrets
1957	Apr 27	*Illustrated magazine*	One year after – we reconstruct the Crabb Mystery
1969	Nov 23	*Sunday Times Magazine*	Crabb's Last Dive

| 1996 | *London Diver* | Drop the dead dolphin |
| 2007 | *Eye Spy* | MI6 and the Crabb Affair |

INDEX